AND THE WEAK SUFFER WHAT THEY MUST?

AND THE WEAK SUFFER WHAT THEY MUST?

EUROPE'S CRISIS *and* AMERICA'S ECONOMIC FUTURE

YANIS VAROUFAKIS

NATION
BOOKS

New York

Published by Nation Books, A Member of the Perseus Books Group
116 East 16th Street, 8th Floor
New York, NY 10003

Nation Books is a co-publishing venture of the Nation Institute and the
Perseus Books Group

Books published by Nation Books are available at special discounts for bulk purchases
in the United States by corporations, institutions, and other organizations. For more
information, please contact the Special Markets Department at the Perseus Books
Group, 2300 Chestnut Street, Suite 200, Philadelphia, PA 19103, or call (800) 810-4145,
ext. 5000, or e-mail special.markets@perseusbooks.com.

Library of Congress Cataloging-in-Publication Data

Names: Varoufakis, Yanis, author.
Title: And the weak suffer what they must? : Europe's crisis and America's
    economic future / Yanis Varoufakis.
Description: New York : Nation Books, 2016. | Includes bibliographical
    references and index.
Identifiers: LCCN 2016001937 (print) | LCCN 2016003358 (ebook) | ISBN
    9781568585048 (hardback) | ISBN 9781568585055 (eISBN) | ISBN 9781568585055
    (ebook)
Subjects: LCSH: Europe--Economic conditions--21st century. | Europe--Economic
    integration. | Financial crises--Europe. | Europe--Politics and
    government--21st century. | BISAC: BUSINESS & ECONOMICS / Government &
    Business. | HISTORY / Europe / General.
Classification: LCC HC240 .V37 2016 (print) | LCC HC240 (ebook) | DDC
    330.94--dc23
LC record available at http://lccn.loc.gov/2016001937

isbn 978-1-56858-504-8 (hc)
isbn 978-1-56858-505-5 (eb)
isbn 978-1-56858-564-2 (int'l)

Editorial production by *Marra*thon Production Services. www.marrathon.net

book design by jane raese
Set in 11-point Berthold Baskerville Book

10 9 8 7 6 5 4 3 2 1

FOR MY MOTHER ELENI,

who would have savaged with the greatest elegance and compassion anyone contemplating the notion that the weak suffer what they must

CONTENTS

THE RED BLANKET

O ne of my enduring childhood memories is the crackling sound of a wireless hidden under a red blanket in the middle of our living room. Every night, at around nine I think, Mom and Dad would huddle together under it, their ears straining, bursting with anticipation.

Upon hearing the muffled jingle, followed by a German announcer's voice, my six-year-old boy's imagination would travel from our home in Athens to Central Europe, a mythical place I had not visited yet except for the tantalizing glimpses offered by an illustrated Brothers Grimm book I had in my bedroom.

My family's strange red blanket ritual began in 1967, the inaugural year of Greece's military dictatorship. Deutsche Welle, the German international radio station that my parents were listening to, became our most precious ally against the crushing power of state propaganda at home: a window looking out to faraway democratic Europe. At the end of each of its hourlong special broadcasts on Greece, my parents and I would sit around the dining table while they mulled over the latest news.

Not understanding fully what they were talking about neither bored nor upset me. For I was gripped by a sense of excitement at the strangeness of our predicament: to find out what was happening in our very own Athens, we had to travel, through the airwaves, and veiled by a red blanket, to a place called Germany.

The reason for the red blanket was a grumpy old neighbor called Gregoris. Gregoris was known for his connections with the secret police and his penchant for spying on my parents; in particular my dad, whose left-wing past made him an excellent target for an ambitious, lowly snitch. After the coup d'état of April 21, 1967, brought neofascist colonels to power, tuning in to Deutsche Welle broadcasts became one of a long list of activities punishable by anything from harassment to torture. Having noticed Gregoris snooping around inside our backyard, my parents took no risks. And so it was that the red blanket became our defense from Gregoris's prying ears.

During the summers, my parents would use up their annual leave to escape the colonels' Greece for a whole month. We would load up our black Morris and head north to Austria and southern Germany where, as my father kept saying during the interminable drive, "Democrats can breathe." Willy Brandt, the German chancellor, and, a little later, Bruno Kreisky, his Austrian counterpart, were discussed as if they were family friends who also happened to be great protagonists in isolating "our" colonels and supporting Greek democrats.

The reception of the locals we encountered while holidaying in these German-speaking lands, away from the kitsch neofascist aesthetic of the colonels' propaganda, was consistent with our conviction that we, as Greeks abroad, were bathed in genuine solidarity. And when our Morris would sadly putter back into Greece, past border crossings replete with photographs of our mad dictator and symbols of his crazy reign, the red blanket beckoned as our only refuge.

A HAND SHUNNED

Almost fifty years later, in February 2015, I made my first official visit to Berlin as Greece's finance minister. The Greek economy had collapsed beneath a mountain of debt, and Germany was its main creditor. I was there to discuss what to do about it. My first port of call was, of course, the Federal Ministry of Finance, to meet its incumbent leader, the legendary Dr. Wolfgang Schäuble.

To him, and his minions, I was a nuisance. Our left-wing government had just been elected, defeating Dr. Schäuble's and Chancellor Angela Merkel's allies in Greece, the New Democracy Party. Our electoral platform was, to say the least, an inconvenience for their Christian Democratic administration and their plans for keeping the eurozone in "order." The elevator door opened up onto a long, cold corridor at the end of which awaited the great man in his famous wheelchair. As I approached, my extended hand was refused. Instead of a handshake, he rushed me purposefully into his office.

While my relations with Dr. Schäuble warmed up in the months that followed, the shunned hand symbolized a great deal that was wrong with Europe. It was symbolic proof that in the half century separating my nights under the red blanket and that first meeting in Berlin, Europe had changed profoundly. How could my host even begin to imagine that I had arrived in his city with my head full of childhood memories in which Germany featured as my security blanket?

By 1974 the Greeks, with moral and political support from Germany, Austria, Sweden, Belgium, Holland and France, had overthrown totalitarianism. Six years after that, Greece joined the democratic union of European nations, to the delight of my parents, who could, at last, fold up the red blanket and put it away in the cupboard.

Less than a decade later, the Cold War had ended and Germany was reuniting in the hope of losing itself, in important ways, within a uniting Europe. Central to this project of embedding the new united Germany into a new united Europe was the ambitious program of a monetary union that would put the same money, the same banknotes and even the same coins (one side of which would be identical, no matter where it was issued) into every European's pocket. "Make them use the same money," an Athenian taxi driver told me once in the early 1990s, "and, before they know it, a United States of Europe will creep up on them."

By 2001 the two countries brought together beneath our family's red blanket in the bygone era of my childhood, Greece and Germany, shared the same money, along with more than a dozen other continental nations. It was an audacious project redolent with an ambition that no European of my generation could resist.

BEACON ON THE HILL

In fact, this process of European integration had begun long before I was even born, in the late 1940s under the tutelage of the United States.

It was foreshadowed by the Speech of Hope delivered by US Secretary of State James Byrnes in Stuttgart in 1946 in which he promised to the people of Germany, for the first time after their defeat, "the opportunity, if they will but seize it, to apply their great energies and abilities to the works of peace . . . the opportunity to show themselves worthy of the respect and friendship of peace-loving nations, and in time, to take an honorable place among members of the United Nations."

Soon after, Greeks and Germans, together with other Europeans, started to meet and discuss the possibility of unifying in what would later become the European Union. We were uniting despite different languages, diverse cultures, distinctive temperaments. In the process of coming together, we were discovering, with great joy, that there were fewer differences between our nations than the differences observed within our nations. And when one nation faced a challenge, as Greece had in 1967 with the military takeover, the rest came together to assist. It took half a century for Europe to heal its war wounds through solidarity and to turn into a beacon on humanity's proverbial hill, but it did.

Unifying hitherto warring nations on the basis of popular mandates founded on the promise of shared prosperity, the erection of common institutions, the tearing down of ludicrous borders that previously scarred the continent: this was always a tall order, an enchanting dream. Happily, it was now an emergent reality. The European Union could even pose as a blueprint that the rest of the world might draw courage and inspiration from so as to eradicate divisions and establish peaceful coexistence across the planet.

Suddenly the world could imagine, realistically, that diverse nations might create a common land without an authoritarian empire. We could forge bonds relying not on kin, language, ethnicity, a common enemy, but on common values and humanist principles. A commonwealth became feasible where reason, democracy, respect for human rights and a decent social safety net provide its multinational, multilingual, multicultured citizens with the canvass on which to become the women and men that their talents deserved.

"WHEN CAN I HAVE MY MONEY BACK?"

Then came Wall Street's implosion in 2008 and the ensuing global financial disaster. Nothing would be the same again.

Once the universe of Western finance outgrew planet earth, its imploding banks and the subsequent credit crunch took their toll on European nations, in particular those relying on the euro. Britain's Northern Rock was the first European bank to buckle under, Greece the first state. Thus a death embrace between insolvent banks and bankrupt states ensued throughout Europe. However, there was a great difference between Britain and countries like Greece. While Gordon Brown could rely on the Bank of England to pump out the cash needed to save the City, eurozone governments had a central bank whose charter did not allow it to do the same. Instead, the burden of saving the inane bankers fell on the weakest of citizens.

By late 2009 the Greek state's bankruptcy was threatening French and German banks with Lehman's fate. Meanwhile the Irish banks' annihilation brought down the Irish state, magnifying the woes of France's and Germany's banks. Panic-ridden politicians rushed in with gargantuan taxpayer-funded bailouts that burdened the weakest of taxpayers, as Google, Facebook and Greece's oligarchs enjoyed tax immunity. Incredibly, the bailout loans were given under conditions of income-sapping austerity that further weakened the weak taxpayers on whom the whole edifice was leaning. As nothing spreads faster than justifiable panic, Portugal, Spain, Italy and Cyprus were the next dominoes to tumble.

Lacking a credible response to the euro's inevitable crisis, Europe's governments turned against one another, pointing accusatory fingers everywhere, and falling prey to a beggar-thy-neighbor attitude last seen in Europe in the 1930s. By 2010 European solidarity had been eaten up from within, leaving nothing but a wretched shell of once solid camaraderie.

What caused the euro crisis? News media and politicians love simple stories. From 2010 onward the story doing the rounds, throughout Germany and the Protestant Northeast, went something like this:

The Greek grasshoppers did not do their homework and their debt-fueled summer ended abruptly one day. The Calvinist ants were then called upon to bail them out, together with various other grasshoppers from around Europe. Now, the ants were being told, the Greek grasshoppers did not want to pay their debt back. They wanted another bout of loose living, more fun in the sun, and another bailout so that they could finance it. They even elected a cabal of socialists and radical lefties to bite the hand that fed them. These grasshoppers had to be taught a lesson, otherwise other Europeans, made of lesser stuff than the ants, would be encouraged to adopt loose living.

It is a powerful story. A story that justifies the tough stance that many advocate against the Greeks, against the government I served in.

"When am I getting my money back?" a German junior minister asked me playfully, but with a hint of despondent aggression, on the sidelines of that first meeting with Dr. Schäuble. I bit my tongue and smiled politely.

GRASSHOPPERS EVERYWHERE

As I hope to demonstrate with this book, Aesop's fable about the grasshopper and the ant, or any narrative of this type, is terribly misleading as a description of the causes of our current crisis.

For a start, it fails to acknowledge that every nation has powerful grasshoppers, including Germany and other surplus nations. It neglects to mention that these grasshoppers, of the North and the South, have a habit of forging commanding international alliances against the interests of the good ants that work tirelessly not only in places like Germany but also in places like Greece, Ireland, Portugal.

More importantly, though, the real cause of the eurozone crisis is nothing to do with the behavior of grasshoppers or ants or any such thing. It is to do with the eurozone itself and, specifically, with the invention of the euro. Indeed, this book is about a paradox: European peoples, who had hitherto been uniting so splendidly, ended up increasingly divided by a common currency.

The paradox of a divisive common currency is a central theme of this book. To make sense of this paradox, and thus to understand the real reasons why the narrative of grasshoppers and ants, of bailouts and austerity, is so wrong, we will need first to examine the historical roots of the euro: in the postwar settlement of Europe, with the so-called Bretton Woods conference of July 1944, in which the economic structure of Europe was forged, and in the collapse of that structure with the so-called Nixon Shock in 1971. It is a story in which the United States played the critical role, and it occupies the first two chapters of this book.

EUROPE AND AMERICA:
THE BOOK IN THREE "MOMENTS"

In fact this book began life as a sequel to my previous book, *The Global Minotaur*, in which I outlined my take on the causes and nature of the 2008 global crash. Unlike *The Global Minotaur*, in which America had the lead role, this book casts Europe as the protagonist. But even though Europe is the protagonist, America provides the air our protagonist breathes, the nutrients that it feeds on, the global context in which it evolves, and also features as a potential victim of our protagonist's avoidable failures. This book turns its spotlight on three historical moments that bind together, and at once push apart, Europe's and America's fortunes.

The first occurred in 1971 when, in a bid to preserve its global economic dominance, America expelled Europe from the dollar zone (an equivalent to the eurozone that was instituted at Bretton Woods). Its influence can be felt to this day throughout Europe and, indeed, feeds back into America itself (see chapters 1 and 2).

The second moment was lengthier and came when an unhinged Europe tried repeatedly to make amends for its expulsion from the dollar zone by bundling together its many different currencies into a monetary union of sorts—first into the European Monetary System, then into its very own eurozone (see chapters 3, 4 and 5). Much of the book is devoted to showing how Europe's monetary union came about and, importantly, the manner in which its evolution was guided, often unseen, by economic decisions, past and present, made in Washington, DC.

The third moment once more began in the United States with Wall Street's implosion that set off a chain reaction that Europe's flimsy monetary union was never designed to survive (see chapters 6 and 7). The book then turns to the root causes of Europe's failure to deal with its crisis rationally and efficiently; on the ghastly effects of this failure on the peoples of Europe; and on its detrimental impact on America's efforts to recover from the never-ending crisis that the 2008 moment occasioned (see chapters 7 and 8).

In short, I intended this book as an account of Europe's crisis, of its historic connection to America's attempts to regulate global capitalism and, crucially, as a warning that the euro crisis is too important for the United States to leave to the Europeans, let alone ignore. Indeed, the euro crisis, the last chapter warns, is weighing down the United States in a manner detrimental to everyone's future.

OUR 1929

Judging by the way it sometimes repeats itself, history has a flair for tragic farce. The Cold War began not in Berlin but in fact in December 1944 in the streets of Athens (as this book will later recount). The euro crisis also started in Athens, in 2010, triggered by Greece's debt woes. Greece was, by a twist of fate, the birthplace of both the Cold War and the euro crisis. For a small nation to be the epicenter of one global disaster is bad luck. To spark off two within living memory is a tragedy.

There is another reason to look to the past as we contemplate Europe's future. Following the tumult of Europe's expulsion from the dollar zone in 1971 (which is the subject of the next chapter), European nations attempted to huddle together, like sheep in a storm. But as the solidarity of the 1970s evolved into a badly designed common currency, it turned into toxic bailouts yielding psychological fault lines along the Alps and up the Rhine. An irrepressible evil is crawling out of these fault lines (see the book's last two chapters) with the power to devastate the European project and, moreover, to destabilize the world at large. These new divisions remind us that it would be foolhardy to forget how Europe has managed, twice in the past century, to become so unhinged as to inflict stupendous damage upon itself and the world.

The moment a monetary union between different nations begins to fragment, and as the fault lines expand inexorably, only serious dialogue and a readiness to return to the drawing board can mend the fences on which peace and shared prosperity must rely. The lack of such dialogue in the 1930s led to the disintegration of that era's common currency: the gold standard. Eighty years later, it is happening all over again in a Europe that ought to know better.

Europeans have taken far too long to understand that 2008 was our version of the tragic generation's 1929. Wall Street was the epicenter on both occasions and, once finance melted, credit evaporated and paper assets went up in smoke, the common currency began to unravel. Before long the working class in one nation turned against the working classes of all other nations, looking to protectionism for succor. In 1929 protectionism took the form of devaluing one's currency vis-à-vis others. As we shall see, in 2010 it took the form of devaluing one's labor vis-à-vis others.

Unremarkably, 2008 began a depressingly similar chain reaction. It was not long before underpaid German workers hated the Greeks and underemployed Greek workers hated the Germans. With the eurozone buffeted by massive economic downturn, the whole world watched eagerly to see how this postmodern version of the 1930s would pan out. They are still watching.

DEBT AND GUILT

"A debt is a debt is a debt!" was what another high official of the Federal Republic of Germany told me during that first official visit to Berlin.

Upon hearing this, it was impossible not to be reminded of something Manolis Glezos, Greece's symbol of the resistance against the Nazis, wrote in a book in 2012 entitled *Even If It Were a Single Deutsche Mark*.[1] It carried the same message as the German official's pronouncement. Every deutsche mark of war reparations owed to Greece must be repaid. Even one deutsche mark that is repaid can help undo a gross injustice. Just as in Germany, once the euro crisis erupted and it was considered self-evident that the Greeks were insufferable debtors, so too in Greece, Germany's unpaid wartime debts may remain forever unforgiven.

The last thing I needed, as I was attempting to establish common ground with Germany's finance ministry, was this clash of moralizing narratives. Ethical issues are central to bringing peoples together. Closure must be achieved so as to heal festering wounds, as South Africa's Truth and Reconciliation Commission so vividly demonstrated. But when it comes to managing modern finance and a complicated, ill-designed monetary union, biblical economics is an insidious enemy. A debt may be a debt but an unpayable debt does not get paid unless it is sensibly restructured. Neither German teenagers in 1953—when the United States convened a conference in London to "write down" (meaning simply to reduce without payment) Germany's public debt to, among other nations, Greece—nor Greek teenagers in 2010 deserved a life of misery because of unpayable debts amassed by a previous generation.

My argument in response was that restructuring Greece's public debt was essential for creating the growth spurt necessary to help us repay our debts; otherwise Greece would have nothing with which to pay. The proposal went down like a lead balloon.

Upon hearing his statement I thought, "Yikes! Using these meetings to bring about a rapprochement will not be easy." A tale of two debts was turning into a morality play with no end. Europe is an ancient continent and our debts to each other stretch decades, centuries and millennia into the past. Counting them vindictively, and pointing moralizing fingers at each other, was precisely what we did not need in the midst of an economic crisis in which large new debt, piled upon mountains of legacy liabilities, was a mere by-product.

Capitalism, lest we forget, flourished only after debt was demoralized. Debt prisons had to be replaced by limited liability, and finance had to ride roughshod over any guilty feelings debtors were encumbered with, before "the rapid improvement of all instruments of production . . . [and] the immensely facilitated means of communication" could draw "all, even the most barbarian, nations into civilization"—to quote from none other than Karl Marx.[2]

GHOSTS OF A COMMON PAST

On the day our government was sworn in, in late January 2015, Prime Minister Alexis Tsipras laid a wreath at a memorial commemorating the execution of Greek patriots by the Nazis. The international press considered this a symbolic gesture of defiance toward Berlin and insinuated that our government was attempting to draw parallels between the Third Reich and a German eurozone imposing a new iron rule on Greece. This didn't help my job of making friends in Berlin, especially in the ultra-austere Federal Ministry of Finance.

Convinced that it was essential to emphasize that our government was not drawing any parallels between Nazi Germany and today's Federal Republic, I scripted the following text, which became part of my statement in the joint press conference with Dr. Schäuble. It was meant as an olive branch.

> As finance minister, in a government facing emergency circumstances caused by a savage debt-deflationary crisis, I feel that the German nation is the one that can understand us Greeks better than anyone else. No one understands better than the people of this land how a severely depressed economy, combined with ritual national humiliation and unending hopelessness, can hatch the serpent's egg within one's society. When I return home tonight, I shall find myself in a parliament in which the third-largest party is a Nazi one.
>
> When our prime minister laid a wreath at an iconic memorial site in Athens immediately after his swearing in, that was an act of defiance against the resurgence of Nazism. Germany can be proud of the fact that Nazism has been eradicated here. But it is one of history's cruel ironies that Nazism is rearing its ugly head in Greece, a country that put up such a fine struggle against it.
>
> We need the people of Germany to help us in the struggle against misanthropy. We need our friends in this country to remain steadfast in Europe's postwar project; that is, never again to allow a 1930s-like depression

to divide proud European nations. We shall do our duty in this regard. And I am convinced that so will our European partners.

Call it naïveté, but I confess I expected a positive response to my short speech. Instead there was a deafening silence. The next day, the German press was lambasting me for daring to mention the Nazis in the Federal Ministry of Finance while much of the Greek press were celebrating me for having called Dr. Schäuble a Nazi. Reading these divergent reactions back in Athens, I allowed myself a brief moment of despair.

Incensed by Europe's introversion and the ease with which we turned against each other, in a bid to let off some steam I decided to blame it all on another Greek: Aesop. For his simplistic fable was evidently casting a long shadow on the truth, turning one proud European nation against another. Under his influence, foes were made of partners, every European risked ending up a loser and the only winners lurking in the shadows were racists and those who never made their peace with European democracy.

This book is here to provide another narrative in the hope that it can do the opposite. It's not too late. We still have everything to lose.

AMERICA, AMERICA

During my family's "red blanket" days America was the bogeyman. The April 1967 coup had the paw marks of America's intelligence community all over it: it was undeniably aided and abetted by Washington, DC. At the same time, confusingly to us younger Greeks at the time, America was also a source of immense hope.

One hot June afternoon, a little more than a year after the colonels had cast a shadow over our lives, my mother and I were walking just outside the ancient stadium where the first modern-era Olympics had been staged in 1896. A newsboy announced, at the top of his voice, that someone called Bobby Kennedy was dead. Suddenly her eyes welled up with tears. I vividly recall her first words after regaining her composure: "He was our last chance."

America had already proven itself Europe's last chance two decades before. Europeans like to think of the European Union as a fabulous European feat. Careful, dispassionate analysis produces a different conclusion: the European Union was an American design drawing upon the New Dealers' experience of the Great Depression and its lessons for the postwar world. Bobby Kennedy was, in that sense, perhaps the last American who could keep that spirit alive in the White House. With Lyndon Baines Johnson gone from the scene, it was only a matter of time before the Nixon Shock, circa 1971, would unleash forces that unhinged Europe irreversibly.

My mother could not have, quite naturally, known any of this. For her, Bobby Kennedy represented hope that the United States would regret their support of our neofascist dictators and allow us to return to democratic rule. Unwittingly, however, she had homed in on a larger story that the following chapters attempt to tell. It is the story of how the 1971 collapse of the monetary system the New Dealers had designed back in 1944 put Europe onto the path that led, in 2010, to our current woes.

One can never know how a Bob Kennedy administration would have responded to the challenges of the late 1960s on the so-called Bretton Woods monetary system, whose eventual collapse in 1971 put Europe into a tailspin from which it has yet to recover. It is, nonetheless, possible to imagine a smoother transition to a more flexible global monetary system, compared to the abrupt discontinuity that, in 1971, forced Paris and Bonn, the then capital of West Germany, to react with a penchant for monetary integration the logical conclusion of which was our ill-conceived euro.

Hypotheticals are, of course, little more than intellectual exercises. Maybe the reason I indulged this particular hypothetical is the memory of my mother's remark. For it constituted my first insight into the importance of the United States for my impending life as a young person growing up in Europe's periphery.

AND THE
WEAK
SUFFER
WHAT
THEY
MUST?

CHAPTER 1

AND THE WEAK SUFFER WHAT THEY MUST

> My philosophy is that all foreigners are out to screw us and
> it's our job to screw them first.
> —*John Connally*[1]

It was midsummer at Camp David when Richard Nixon's treasury secretary and former governor of Texas John Connally convinced his president to unleash the infamous Nixon Shock upon Europe's unsuspecting political leaders. At the end of a crucial weekend of consultations with key advisors, President Nixon decided to make a startling announcement on live television: the global monetary system, which America had designed and had been nurturing since the end of the war, was to be dismantled in one fell swoop.[2] The calendar read Sunday, August 15, 1971.

A few hours after the president's televised address, exactly at the stroke of midnight, a military transport plane took off from Andrews Air Force Base heading for Europe. On board, Paul Volcker, Connally's under-secretary, was intent on confronting European finance ministers who were already on the verge of a nervous breakdown.[3] Meanwhile, Connally himself was preparing an address to the nation before flying to Europe to tell a gathering of uppity European prime ministers, chancellors and presidents that it was "game over." Washington was intent on pulling the plug from a global financial system that it had designed in 1944 and that it had been nurturing lovingly ever since.

While Volcker dealt with European finance ministers and bankers in London and in Paris, trying to steady their nerves, Connally was conveying, up close and personally, a blunter message to European heads of state. In effect, what he was saying was, "Gentlemen, for years you have been disparaging our stewardship of the postwar global financial system—the one we created to help you rise up from ashes of your own making. You felt at liberty to violate its spirit and its rules. You assumed we would continue, Atlas-like, to prop it up whatever the cost and despite your insults and acts of sabotage. But you were wrong! On Sunday, President Nixon severed the lifeline between our dollar and your currencies.[4] Let's see how this will work for you! My hunch is that your currencies will resemble lifeboats jettisoned from the good ship USS *Dollar,* buffeted by high seas they were never designed for, crashing into each other and, generally, failing to chart their own course."[5]

And in a sentence still resonating across Europe today, Connally summed it all up succinctly, painfully, brutally: "Gentlemen, the dollar is our currency. And from now on, it is your problem!"[6]

Europe's leaders realized immediately the gravity of their situation. They responded quickly with a sequence of knee-jerk reactions that led them from one error to the next, culminating forty years later in Europe's current circumstances.

In 2010 Europe came face to face with the consequences of these forty years of accumulated mistakes (see chapters 2, 3 and 4). The crisis of its common currency known as the euro was due to failures traceable to the events of 1971, when Europe was jettisoned from the so-called dollar zone by Nixon, Connally and Volcker.[7] The comedy of errors with which European leaders responded to their post-2010 euro crisis (see chapters 5 and 6) is also attributable to Europe's clumsy reaction to the Nixon Shock. It is this critical moment in history that will occupy this chapter.

A LONG TIME COMING

Nixon had not acceded to Connally's crude philosophy lightly. Nor was Connally's philosophy as crude as he loved to make it sound. The postwar global financial system that Nixon's midsummer announcement assigned to the dustbin of history had been creaking like a doomed hull whose inevitable sinking threatened to bring down with it America's postwar hegemony.

Lyndon B. Johnson, Nixon's immediate predecessor in the White House, and Connally's fellow Texan and political mentor, had also understood that the American-designed postwar financial system could not continue.[8] In a discussion he had in 1966 with Francis Bator, his deputy national security advisor, President Johnson was adamant that he was ready to end it, and by severing the link between the dollar and the value of gold on which that global system depended: "I will not deflate the American economy, screw up my foreign policy by gutting aid or pulling troops out, or go protectionist just so we can continue to pay out gold to the French at $35 an ounce."[9]

Distracted, however, by his Great Society programs, his intensification of the Vietnam War and his reluctance to destroy a global system that President Franklin Roosevelt's administration (the so-called New Dealers) had put together two decades earlier, Johnson allowed it to chug along.[10]

Nixon too, once in the White House, tried to delay the inevitable. Even though his squabbling team of policy makers were increasingly coming to the view that the global monetary system was broken, their warnings alone would not have sufficed to convince Nixon to unleash his shock (and John Connally) upon the befuddled Europeans.

In fact, as we shall see below, it took several aggressive moves by the French, the Germans and the British, between 1968 and the summer of 1971, to free his hand. These were foolhardy challenges to America's management of global capitalism that gave Connally and "that goddam Volcker"[11] the opportunity to impress upon the president that there was no alternative: he had to ditch the international monetary system known as Bretton Woods and he had to dump Europe along with it.

Could things have turned out differently? By 1971 everyone knew that the Bretton Woods postwar global financial system had been undermined by powerful economic forces beyond the control of either the United States or of Europe. As we shall see, Europe's error was that, instead of seeking to reform a faltering system by negotiation, its leaders overplayed a weak hand against a bold hegemon.[12] They would now have to suffer the consequences. And suffer them Europe did. In fact, Europe is still suffering them from Dublin to Athens and from Lisbon to Helsinki.

A SIMPLE IDEA FOR A STRICKEN EUROPE

The financial system that President Nixon "terminated" in 1971 was born in July 1944 in the conference rooms of Mount Washington Hotel, perched in the New Hampshire town of Bretton Woods. The pristine setting could not have been more at odds with developments forged of blood and steel in Europe and the Pacific.

D-day had preceded the Bretton Woods conference by only three weeks, its dreadful toll not yet digested by thousands of grieving, largely American, families. During the conference itself, the Red Army liberated Minsk at great human cost, the US Air Force bombarded Tokyo heavily for the first time since 1942, Sienna fell to Algerian troops under General Charles de Gaulle's command and V-1 rockets were pounding London mercilessly. On July 20, the day before the Bretton Woods Conference was successfully completed, Claus von Stauffenberg led the conspiracy to assassinate Adolph Hitler at his bunker in Rastenburg. Even though the conspirators failed, the writing was on the wall. July 1944 was, undoubtedly, the right time for the Allies to begin planning the postwar order of things.

With their heads full of the conflict back home, and considerable uncertainty about their own position in the postwar order, the delegates from the forty allied nations attending the conference hammered out an impressive financial deal in the space of three weeks. In anticipation of the guns falling silent in Europe, and before the Soviet Union had emerged as the dragon to be slain, the New Dealers in power understood that America was about to inherit the historic role of remaking global capitalism in its own image.

In the conference's opening ceremony, on July 1, 1944, President Roosevelt declared his administration's abandonment of any remnants of American isolationism. "The economic health of every country," he announced, "is a proper matter of concern to all its neighbors, near and far." Clearly, the United States, the only country that came out of the war (save perhaps for inconsequential Switzerland) with its monetary system intact, its industry booming and with a healthy trade surplus, was intent on taking a war-torn world under its wing.

One of the casualties of the European war was money. Nazi-affiliated regimes in occupied countries had printed so much of the local currencies to support the Axis's war effort that the money in Europeans' pockets was not even worth the paper it had been printed on. And even in countries that had escaped occupation, such as Britain, the costs of war and the collapse of trade had led to a combination of government indebtedness and value destruction that rendered the currency worthless, at least in the arena of international trade. In short, the greenback was the only currency left standing and capable of lubricating world trade.

Washington understood that its first task, once the German armies had been defeated, was to remonetize Europe. This was, of course, easier said than done. With Europe's gold either spent or stolen, its factories and infrastructure in ruins, hordes of refugees roaming its highways and byways, the concentration camps still reeking with the stench of humanity's unspeakable cruelty, Europe needed much more than freshly minted paper money. Something had to give value to the new notes. It was not surprising, perhaps, that the "something" the New Dealers came up with was none other than their own dollar. America was about to share its greenback with the European countries standing, at war's end, under its geopolitical umbrella.

In practice this entailed new European currencies backed by dollars at a fixed rate, meaning that a certain number of deutsche marks, of French francs, of British pounds, of even Greek drachmas, would be worth a prespecified, constant number of dollars. It was this dollar guarantee that would instantly impart global value to Europe's new money.

Would this not risk debasing the dollar? If the dollar was to be the anchor for the new European currencies, what would underpin the dollar's own value? Tapping into a long tradition of tying paper money to precious metals that no alchemist could fake, the answer was that America would guarantee a fixed exchange rate, and full convertibility, between the dollar and the gold that it held in a bunker under the New York Federal Reserve building, as well as in Fort Knox.

It was a simple idea for a simpler world. The holder of a given number of dollars ($35 was the figure finally chosen) was to be offered an unqualified claim to an ounce of gold owned by the United States, regardless of the holder's nationality or location on the planet. Equally, the holder of another amount of Europe's new money would be guaranteed a given amount of dollars, which would in turn guarantee access to America's gold. In essence, gold-backed greenbacks became the guarantors of the currencies within a new global financial system that has gone down in history, grandiosely, as the Bretton Woods system.

A DISCIPLE TO TRUMP THE MASTER

In the Bretton Woods negotiations, President Franklin D. Roosevelt was represented by Harry Dexter White, an economist who had entered public service on the coattails of Roosevelt's New Deal.[13] New Dealers like White had cut their teeth in the 1930s, following the collapse of unfettered financial markets in 1929 and the ensuing Great Depression. Their ambition was to counter deprivation and hopelessness by beefing up the federal government's existing institutions and creating new ones that would make another 1929 impossible. Bretton Woods offered White an opportunity to project the New Deal onto a global canvas. His brief for the Bretton Woods conference was nothing less than to design from scratch a stable, viable, worldwide financial system for the postwar era. At the same time, White's brief entailed staving off ambitious Europeans whom Washington was expecting to have a go at skewing the new financial system's design in their favor.

White's economics had been influenced heavily in the 1930s by the writings of Cambridge economist John Maynard Keynes. In a delicious twist of fate, the one European he had to face down at Bretton Woods was none other than John Maynard Keynes himself, dispatched to

Bretton Woods by Winston Churchill's wartime national unity government to represent Europe's last, and fading, empire.[14]

Keynes had it all planned well before he even arrived in America. He brought with him a razor-sharp perception of global capitalism's ways, a unique grasp of the economic forces that had caused the Great Depression, a splendid plan to refashion global finance and, last but not least, a poet's way with words and a novelist's talent for narrative.[15] The only person at the Bretton Woods conference who could deny him the crowning glory of putting his stamp on the new global system was his American disciple, Harry Dexter White. And this is precisely what White did.

Keynes's proposal was brimming with intellectual power. White was overflowing with the power vested in him by America's economic and military might.

As we shall see, Keynes advocated a global system that could stabilize capitalism for a fabulously long time. White's brief was to push through a system consistent with the United States' newfound strength but viable only as long as America remained the surplus nation extraordinaire.

It was surely inevitable that the two men would clash and that White would prevail, even if Keynes succeeded in persuading his adversary on every theoretical point that mattered.

And so it was that, in July 1944, with D-day fresh in the background, with American troops advancing in both Europe and the Pacific, and with the rest of the world in America's debt, Keynes returned to London a defeated man, refusing to discuss in any detail either the agreement that ultimately had been imposed by the American side or his plan that White had trashed in the Mount Washington Hotel.

Shortly afterward Keynes put his remaining energies into another negotiation with Washington's New Dealers, at a conference in Savannah, Georgia, this time in a bid to convince them to write down Britain's gargantuan wartime loans. It did not go well. During the negotiation, which Keynes described as "hell," he had his first heart attack. Soon after his return to England, at the age of sixty-two, another heart attack ended his life.

VICTORS BEHAVING BADLY, FAILING TO BE GOOD AT BEING SELFISH, AND CAUSING THE WEAK TO SUFFER MORE THAN THEY MUST

Forty years later, in 1988, while looking through Keynes's papers and books at King's College, Cambridge, I noticed a copy of Thucydides's *Peloponnesian War* in the original ancient Greek. I took it out and quickly browsed through its pages. There it was, underlined in pencil, the famous passage in which powerful Athenian generals explained to the helpless Melians why "rights" are only pertinent "between equals in power" and, for this reason, they were about "to do as they pleased with them." It was because "the strong actually do what they can and the weak suffer what they must."[16]

These words were ringing in my head during the spring of 2015 as I faced Greece's lenders and their unwavering commitment to crush our government. Keynes's head, I am certain, must also have been ringing with these words at Bretton Woods. I wonder, however, if he was tempted, as I was, to address White with a version of a line from the Melians who, in a bid to save themselves, attempted to appeal to the Athenians' self-interest:

> Then in our view (since you force us to base our arguments on self-interest, rather than on what is proper) it is useful that you should not destroy a principle that is to the general good—namely that those who find themselves in the clutches of misfortune should . . . be allowed to thrive beyond the limits set by the precise calculation of their power. And this is a principle which does not affect you less, *since your own fall would be visited by the most terrible vengeance, watched by the whole world* [emphasis added].[17]

In the case of the arrogant Athenians, these words surely resonated years later when their mortal enemies, the Spartans, scaled the walls of Athens intent on destruction. After the Great War, in 1919, Keynes had used a logic similar to the Melians' argument to warn the victorious allies that the vengeful Versailles Treaty they had imposed on defeated Germany would be a menacing boomerang that would come back to strike at the foundation of their own interests,[18] which is, of course, what happened after the Versailles Treaty engendered an economic crisis in Germany that brought Adolph Hitler to power. Perhaps the Melians' words also reflect how the surviving New Dealers felt in the mid-1960s when the Bretton Woods system that White had forced through, against Keynes's better judgment, began to unravel. By then it was, of course, too late to do much about it. Bretton Woods was at the end of its tether and the Nixon Shock simply demonstrated the ruthless efficiency with which American officials come to terms with new, unpleasant realities, in sharp contrast to their European counterparts, who will hang on to failed projects for as long as possible.

When it came, the Nixon Shock saw to it that America, unlike Athens, would continue to enjoy the trappings of uncontested hegemony—at least till 2008. That was, in essence, what John Connally had proposed to his president. Screw them before they screw us! Europe and Japan were, consequently, badly "screwed,"[19] but so was the political project of the New Dealers who had pushed aside Keynes's proposals in 1944.

Indeed, after 1965, the New Dealers and their successors lost every domestic battle they fought against the resurgent Republicans. Their abject failure to revive the spirit of the New Deal, even by democratic presidents who may have wanted to revive it (such as Jimmy Carter, Bill Clinton, Barack Obama), can arguably be traced to their dismissal of Keynes's proposals back in 1944.[20]

FAIR-WEATHER RECYCLING

Keynes's proposal was internationalist and multilateral to the core. It was historically informed (by the calamitous Wall Street crash of 1929) and theoretically buttressed by a thought obvious to everyone, except of course to most professional economists: global capitalism differs fundamentally from Robinson Crusoe's solitary economy.

What this means is that a closed, autarkic (meaning "self-sufficient") economy, like that of Robinson Crusoe in literature, or perhaps North Korea today, may be poor, solitary and undemocratic but at least it is free of problems caused by other economies, by external deficits or surpluses.[21] In contrast, all modern economies can expect to be in an economic relation with others, and in addition they can expect that these relations will almost all be asymmetrical. Think Greece in relation to Germany, Arizona in relation to neighboring California, North England and Wales in relation to the Greater London area or indeed the United States in relation to China—all cases of imbalances with impressive staying power. Imbalances, in short, are the norm, never the exception.

In 1944 Keynes conceded that, in view of Europe's frightful state, there was no alternative to a regime of fixed exchange rates relying extensively on the dollar. However, while dollarizing Europe would fix one problem, a dollar-backed fixed exchange rate system would create other misadventures down the road; misadventures that would, he predicted, cause these trade imbalances to grow with, ultimately, terrible effects first upon the deficit countries and then upon everyone else.

His logic as to why fixed exchange rates would beget instability in a world of persistent surpluses and deficits was rooted directly in the experience of the events leading to the Great Depression, which the New Dealers understood so well, and it went as follows.

Just as one person's debt is another's asset, one nation's deficit is another's surplus. In an asymmetrical world, the money that the surplus economies amass, from selling more stuff to the deficit economies than they buy from them, accumulate in their banks. But these banks are then tempted to lend much of it back to the deficit countries or regions, where interest rates are always higher because money is so much scarcer. In this way, banks help maintain some semblance of balance during the good times. If the exchange rate is likely to remain stable or even the same, banks will tend to lend more to the deficit country, unworried by the prospect of a devaluation further down the line that might make it hard for debtors in the deficit country to repay them. Bankers, in this sense, are fair-weather surplus recyclers. They profit from taking a chunk of the surplus money from the surplus nations and recycling it in the deficit nations.

But if the exchange rate is fixed, they go berserk, transferring mountains of money to the deficit regions as long as the storm clouds are absent, the skies are blue and the financial waters calm. Their "credit line" allows those in deficit to keep buying more and more stuff from the surplus economies, which thrive on a spree of exports. Import-export businesses grow fatter everywhere, incomes boom in surplus and deficit countries alike, confidence in the financial system swells, the surpluses get larger and the deficits deeper.

As long as the fair financial weather continues, fair-weather surplus recycling endures. Only it cannot endure forever. With the certainty and abruptness that a pile of sand will collapse once the critical grain is added on top of it, vendor-financed trade will always go into sudden, violent spasm. No one can predict when, but only fools doubt that it must. The equivalent of the critical grain of sand is one container full of imported goodies that goes unclaimed by an insolvent importer, or one loan that is defaulted upon by some overleveraged real estate developer. It takes one such bankruptcy in a deficit country to raise a whirlpool of panic among the surplus nations' banks.

Suddenly, confident globetrotting bankers turn into jelly. Lax lending turns to no lending at all. Importers, developers, governments and city councils in the deficit regions, who had grown dependent on the banks, are hung out to dry. House prices collapse, public works are abandoned, office buildings turn into ghostly towers, shops are boarded up, incomes disappear and governments announce austerity. In no time, bankers are left holding "nonperforming loans" the size of the Himalayas. Panic reaches its deafening crescendo and Keynes's inimitable words resonate once more: "As soon as a storm rises," bankers behave like a "fair-weather sailor" who "abandons the boats which might carry him to safety by his haste to push his neighbor off and himself in."[22]

It is the destiny of fair-weather surplus recycling to prompt a crash and occasion a complete halt to all recycling. This is what happened in 1929. It is also what has been happening since 2008 in Europe.

POLITICAL SURPLUS RECYCLING, OR BARBARISM

By contrast, when the value of a nation's money is flexible, it operates like a shock absorber soaking up the jolt caused by a banking crisis occasioned by unsustainable trade and money flows. When unsustainable banking practices caused Iceland to collapse in 2008, its currency slumped, the fish the island exports to Canada and the United States became dirt cheap, revenues picked up and, crucially, debts that were denominated in the local currency shrank (at least in terms of dollars, euros and pounds). This is why Iceland recovered so quickly after a terrible shock.

But when a deficit nation's currency is exchanged in unchanging proportions with the currency of its surplus trading partners, its international value is fixed. This sounds great if you live in such a country and possess a lot of its money. Only it is a terrible thing for the vast majority of its people who hold little of it. Once the sequence of bankruptcies has begun, incomes are destined to fall while the private and public debts to the foreign banks remain the same. The price of a fixed exchange rate is a bankrupt state in a death embrace with impecunious citizens and an insolvent private sector. A doom loop, a hideous vortex, leads the majority to debt bondage, the country to stagnation and the nation to ignominy.

John Maynard Keynes knew this too well.[23] And so did Harry Dexter White, who had lived through the desolation of the 1930s that gave him firsthand experience of what happens when the burden of adjustment falls crushingly upon the weakest of shoulders: on the debtors languishing in the deficit regions where incomes are squeezed, investment disappears, and the only thing looming increasingly larger is the black hole of debt and banking losses. White understood all this perfectly well, just as the Greeks, the Irish, the Spaniards and assorted Europeans do today.

It was because White appreciated this problem that he agreed with Keynes on one crucial point: some alternative shock-absorbing mechanism had to be introduced into the global system they were designing. One that the gold standard lacked in the 1920s and which, tragically, Europe is desperately missing today. A mechanism that can kick in the moment the bankers' fair-weather surplus recycling disappears, so as to prevent the doom loop from taking hold and plunging first the deficit countries, and then global capitalism, into another spiral of depression and barbarous conflict. What was this "mechanism" to be?

The answer was a set of political institutions that step in and recycle surpluses once fair-weather surplus recycling runs aground.

The New Dealers, whom White represented at Bretton Woods, had already tackled that problem at home. They had created federal institutions whose role was, at times of crisis, automatically to recycle surpluses to where they were most needed. Political surplus recycling, in short. The very point of the New Deal, which had preceded the Bretton Woods conference by a decade, was precisely that: Social Security, a federal deposit insurance scheme (run by the Federal Deposit Insurance Corporation [FDIC][24]) for all banks in all states, Medicare, food stamps, the military budget, etc. were institutions geared toward political surplus recycling so as to combat the Great Depression and to prevent a future one.[25]

The therapeutic impact of this political surplus-recycling mechanism can still be felt in America today. When Wall Street imploded in 2008, Nevada was one of the states where the pain was felt most intensely. As unemployment, bankruptcies and foreclosures shot up in Las Vegas and the surrounding suburbs, the state's extra cost of unemployment benefits, as well as the funds necessary for refloating Nevada's banks, were born out not by Nevadan taxpayers but by the federal government and Washington's monetary authorities, the Federal Bank ("the Fed") and the FDIC.[26]

It was not just an act of solidarity to the state of Nevada by the rest of the United States. It was rather an automated mechanism that kicked in so as to stop the Nevadan malaise from spreading further afield. Through Social Security, the FDIC's intervention, Medicare, etc., surpluses from surplus states like California, New York and Texas were automatically redirected toward Nevada's desert plains to stop the rot. Many Americans take this political surplus-recycling mechanism for granted and forget that it was first put in place under the Roosevelt administration, a few short years before the same men hosted the Bretton Woods conference.[27]

Keynes had, thus, good reason to hope that he could appeal to a New Dealer like White to augment Europe's dollarization with the creation of a political mechanism for recycling surpluses at a global scale.

For if the dollar zone were to be stretched to include Europe, and later Japan, surely political surplus recycling had to be spread out as far and as wide as the Bretton Woods jurisdiction reached.

"OUR SURPLUSES, OUR RECYCLING MECHANISM"

Keynes's blueprint for the surplus recycling that was required by the Bretton Woods system was wonderfully grandiose. It included the creation of a new world currency, a system of fixed exchange rates between this world currency and the national currencies, and a world central bank that would run the whole system.

The purpose of instituting this system would have been to maintain monetary stability everywhere, to keep both surpluses and deficits in check throughout the Western world and, at the first sign of a crisis in a troubled nation, speedily recycle surpluses into it so as to prevent contagion to the rest.

An international monetary fund would be created to play the role of the world's central bank. Like any other central bank, it would issue the world currency: the "bancor," as Keynes named it provisionally. The bancor would not be printed, just like the digital cryptocurrency bitcoin does not exist in material form today, except as numbers on some spreadsheet or digital device. But it would function as the world's currency nevertheless. Every country would have a bancor account with the International Monetary Fund (IMF) from which to draw when it bought imported goods from other countries, and into which other nations would deposit bancors when their citizens or corporations bought goods and services from it. All international trade would thus be denominated in the IMF's bancors, the global currency, with the national currencies continuing to oil the cogs of the national economies.

Crucial to this system was a fixed exchange rate between the national currencies and the bancor, and thus between all participating national currencies. The board of the IMF, on which all nations would be represented, would decide these rates centrally and by negotiation. They would then be adjusted, whenever necessary, so that countries with stubborn surpluses would see their currency buying increasingly more bancors (to make their exports more expensive and their imports cheaper), and vice versa for nations in persistent deficit.

Even more radically, Keynes's IMF, recognizing that one nation's deficit is another's surplus, would levy a tax on a nation's bancor account if its imports and exports diverged too much. The idea was to penalize both types of imbalance (excessive surpluses as well as excessive deficits; the Germanies of the world as well as the Greeces) and, in the process, to build up a war chest of bancors at the IMF so that, when some crisis hit, the deficit nations in trouble could be propped up and prevented from falling into a black hole of debt and recession that might spread throughout the Bretton Woods system.

White certainly understood the importance of political surplus recycling within the global system they were setting up. Except that Keynes's proposals sounded ludicrous to his American ears. "Is this wily Englishman," he might have asked, "seriously proposing that the Europeans should have a majority say in how our surpluses are recycled? Is he for real?"

As a good Keynesian, White agreed that Bretton Woods should do more than merely dollarize the Western world. He recognized the need for a politically administered (extramarket) surplus-recycling mechanism, which of course meant the recycling of America's surpluses to Europe.

Nevertheless, the idea that the bankrupt Europeans, who had already put the world through the wringer of two world wars in less than three decades, and still yearned for the reconstitution of their repulsive empires, would now control America's surplus was anathema to an anti-imperialist, patriotic New Dealer like White. Quite understandably, he was going to have none of it. America was the only surplus nation and America alone would decide how, when and to whom it would recycle it.

White listened respectfully while Keynes presented his grandiose scheme and then immediately rejected two of its key features. First on the chopping block was the the idea of a new, shadow, global currency (the bancor) that was to be managed by an IMF governing committee in which the United States would be one of many. The second idea White vetoed was that of taxing the surplus nations, namely the United States.

For White, the die had already been cast: Europe was to be dollarized and the dollar would be the world currency. The bancor was a great idea in a multilateral world but a joke in one where the dollar had already been crowned king and queen. Moreover, the idea that the IMF's governing committee, with the Europeans in the majority, would tax America's surpluses seemed to him too ludicrous for words. America owned its surpluses and would recycle them herself, without petitioning a group of bankrupt Europeans for their permission to do so.

DEFENSE OF THE REALM

By the end of the Bretton Woods conference, White had cherry-picked Keynes's proposal so eclectically that its multilateralist spirit had vanished. Yes, the IMF would be created, but its purpose would not be to issue a new world currency.[28] The loss of the bancor, and the official elevation of the dollar to world currency status, meant that the IMF could not function as the world's central bank. That role was now assigned de facto to America's central bank, the Fed.

Deprived of a central bank function, the IMF was to resemble the monetary council of a mini–United Nations where representatives of national governments, some of them more equal than others, constantly haggled over the exchange rates of every currency with the dollar. (As for pegging the dollar to gold at $35 per ounce, this went against Keynes's conviction that tying the new system to precious metals, gold in this case, was a dangerous throwback to a dismal past.)

This global architecture put America's central bank, the Federal Reserve Bank, in a tight spot: it was being asked to issue the world's money without having a direct say on its exchange rates with the deutsche mark, the French franc, sterling and every other European currency involved.

Europe's central banks faced a related challenge: it was the politicians who would negotiate their currencies' exchange rates (under the IMF's auspices), but the defense of these rates, primarily from speculators, would be left to the central bankers.[29] Typically, politicians loathe devaluations of their nation's currency, even if they know that a devaluation is going to be beneficial. "Devaluation" is associated in the public's mind with failure, weakness, national humiliation even. Breaking news stories dominated by graphs depicting the decline of the pound or the dollar are not good for the chancellor of the exchequer's or the treasury secretary's popularity ratings. Therefore, given a chance to delay an inevitable devaluation, politicians will take it. If they can they will force central bankers to defend an indefensible exchange rate not only at great cost to the government but also to the nation's exporters. Meanwhile speculators, who know that the devaluation will happen, seize the opportunity to profit from betting against the authorities that it will.

In other words, by vesting politicians with the power of set exchange rates it was as if the Bretton Woods system were designed to pit central bankers versus governments; a conflict that would become all too apparent once the system began to falter, toward the end of the 1960s. At times, global finance felt like a vehicle with many opinionated drivers, with some of them holding the wheel and the others taking turns on the brake and accelerator pedals.

Keynes's idea of a single, planetary central bank might have seemed utopian in 1944 but, by the early 1960s, the system actually implemented was proving even more far-fetched. The reason for this was that defending the exchange rates selected by politicians was itself not a simple technical task to be delegated to technocratic central bankers but required enthusiastic and permanent coordination between central bankers from many nations in defense of rates that they had not chosen, and with which they often had issues.

This became increasingly decisive (and decreasingly forthcoming) as the system was destabilized by trade imbalances and the resulting bank-mediated, fair-weather surplus recycling that Keynes had been so worried about. The most important of these imbalances was between Germany and France.

With every additional Volkswagen Beetle that a French family bought, unreciprocated by a German family's purchases of a Renault car or extra cases of French wine, France's trade deficit would grow. If France's trade deficit grew unremittingly, somewhere down the line the IMF board would have to decide to devalue the French franc (in relation to the deutsche mark and by extension to the dollar) in a bid to cheapen French wine in Germany, make Volkswagens dearer in France and thus redress the balance.

Even the whiff of such devaluation was enough to blow inauspicious winds into the speculators' sails, giving them the cue to take out bets that the franc would fall. What did these bets look like? Given that no sensible betting agency would give odds on currency movements, the speculators placed their bets as follows: they took out loans in Paris in French francs and used them to buy deutsche marks at the current exchange rates. Then they waited for the franc to devalue against the mark. If it did devalue, they would use their stash of marks to buy a lot more francs than they had borrowed in the first place (courtesy of the lower franc value), repay these debts in francs and keep the handsome difference.

The critical problem, though, was that unlike bets on the weather or sporting events, which do not make the predicted event more likely just because they were placed, bets that the franc would fall made it more likely that it would do so. With every franc that the speculators borrowed in Paris to buy marks, they pushed the franc's value down a little in the market for tourist currency, in informal dealings between foreign corporations and so on. Gradually, a fault line between the franc's official and unofficial values would surface. To defend the official exchange rate, the central bank of France, the Banque de France, had to use whatever marks it kept in its vaults to buy francs, hoping to defend the franc-mark rate. A game of chicken was now on. Who would blink first? The speculators? Or the Banque de France?

Without assistance and left to fight the speculators alone, the Banque de France's pile of marks and other foreign currency would eventually run out. At that juncture the French central bank could prolong the agony a little by increasing interest rates, so as to attract some foreign money into France, to be used as ammunition against the speculators. However, the higher interest rates would mean that French businesses now paid more to invest, leading to a domestic slump—not quite what the stuttering French economy needed.

Alternatively, the Banque de France could bite the bullet and ring the French finance minister with the terrible news: "We cannot defend the franc as long as our compatriots keep buying so many Volkswagens. Time to call the IMF and arrange for its devaluation against the deutsche mark and the dollar." At which point speculators would boost sales of the best French champagne, eager to celebrate in style their lucrative victory against the franc.

But there was one thing standing in the way of the speculators' route to riches and glory, and that was the central bank of Germany: the at once dreaded and esteemed Bundesbank. Were it willing to print deutsche marks (which, naturally, the Banque de France could not do) to buy francs, such an intervention would burn the speculators. The reason is simple: speculators believed that, by selling a stash of francs they had borrowed in Paris to trade for deutsche marks, they were precipitating the franc's devaluation (on the assumption that other speculators, like themselves, would be doing the same).

Indeed, a torrent of offers to sell francs would ensure that many more traders wanted to part with francs than to buy them. Just like in a farmers' market, when a bumper supply of potatoes overwhelms demand and the price of potatoes crashes, currency speculators predicted that, at the end of the day, the deutsche mark would be buying more francs than it had been earlier in the day. A 10 percent devaluation, for example, would translate into roughly a 10 percent profit for the speculators who would, postdevaluation, need only convert back into francs 90 percent of their new stock of deutsche marks so as to repay in full the French banks from which they had borrowed the pile of francs with which they entered this "game."

Here is where the Bundesbank comes in. For if the German central bank were to print extra deutsche marks, give them anonymously to selected money traders and instruct them to buy francs on its behalf, the imbalance between sellers and buyers of francs would vanish and the franc's value would not decline. This would be a catastrophe for the speculators since they would not be able to repay their loans in

Paris, and retain a profit, by converting their new pile of deutsche marks back into francs.[30]

If the Bundesbank intervened in this manner until the speculators gave up, the system would prevail despite the increasing French trade deficit in relation to Germany. That the Bundesbank had the capacity to do this, there was never any doubt, as it owned the deutsche mark printing press. The question concerned its willingness.

On the one hand, the Bundesbank had a duty—to the Bretton Woods system, to defend the realm—to see the speculators off, to hold the line. On the other hand, the Bundesbank disliked intensely printing deutsche marks in defense of exchange rates it had not chosen, and in quantities it despised, because these marks threatened later to flood back into Germany, causing domestic prices to rise and bringing back memories of the hyperinflation of the early 1920s.

Would the Bundesbank and the central banks of other surplus nations do what was necessary to support the central banks of the deficit nations, as they were meant to under the rules of the Bretton Woods system? Yes, however reluctantly, they would as long as they felt that the Bretton Woods system was sound. And the system was sound so long as America was in surplus with the rest of the world. But when the United States' surpluses withered, trust in Bretton Woods began to wane and central banks like the Bundesbank began to drag their feet when asked to defend it.

AMERICA'S DEFICIT, GERMANY'S QUALMS, FRANCE'S CONCEIT

American surpluses were everything. Unlike Europe today, where German surpluses play no stabilizing role,[31] the postwar global order depended on America's surpluses entirely, as did Europe's stability. They sustained the necessary dollar-recycling process (between the United States and Europe) and secured the future of the Bretton Woods system. As long as America sold enough "stuff" to Europeans, the dollars that America was sending to Europe (as aid, or to purchase European goods or even to fund US military bases on the continent) were steadily repatriated.

Every plane that Boeing sold to the Europeans and every John Deere excavator transported across the Atlantic soaked up greenbacks swashing around in Europe (which came to be known as euro-dollars) and brought them home. These returning dollars supported the dollar against the German, French and Italian currencies. Thus the Fed could step in and use its infinite dollar pile to buy as many francs, pounds or liras as necessary to defend their official, fixed exchange rates against the deutsche mark. American surpluses, in this sense, begat stability within Europe and afforded the Europeans good cause to think of the recycled dollars as "paper gold."

Things began to go awry, as Keynes had predicted they would, when America began consistently to spend more money on European and Japanese goods than foreigners were spending on wares made in America.[32] At that moment, when American surplus turned into deficit, the net stream of dollars reversed its flow, feeding into an ever-expanding euro-dollar lake. By the late 1960s, that stream had turned into a torrent, the euro-dollar lake grew larger than the Caspian Sea, and the Bretton Woods system came under siege.

It was now the case that the total quantity of dollars in Europe far exceeded the dollar value of America's stockpile of gold.[33] Which meant that, if the Europeans were to ask the United States to swap even a fraction of their euro-dollars for the precious metal (as Bretton Woods allowed them to), the United States would run out of gold in minutes. Convinced that the American government would prefer to dismantle Bretton Woods rather than sit idly by while its stock of gold withered, speculators predicted that, at some point, Washington would drop its commitment to selling gold at only $35 per ounce, thus allowing formally its price to rise and rise.

Nothing motivates speculators more than the prediction that they can foresee a precious commodity's rising price, especially if they think that others like them will cotton on to this expectation, thus increasing greatly the rate at which gold appreciated. Just like the speculators betting on the fall of the French franc (and the rise of the deutsche mark) financed their bets by borrowing French francs to buy deutsche marks (see above), so did the speculators betting on gold's rising dollar price borrow dollars to purchase gold, in the belief and hope that it would rise. And as they did this, the price of gold strained at its Bretton Woods leash with the ferocity of a crazed pit bull.

The speculators' plan was to amass a stock of gold, using borrowed dollars, wait until its dollar value rose above some threshold, then cash in by selling the gold for many more dollars than they had borrowed (courtesy of the rise in the dollar value of gold), repay their lenders the dollars that they had borrowed to place the bets, and keep the difference. Crucially, this "difference" would be great if their "cashing in" followed the formal collapse of Bretton Woods,[34] which is what the Nixon Shock represented. Bretton Woods and the speculators' intent were, thus, deeply incompatible. One of the two had to give.

To hold the Bretton Woods system together, the Americans had to rely on the kindness of strangers.[35] To defend the price of gold at $35 per ounce, Europe's central banks were required to join the Fed in selling gold at the official low price.[36] They were also obliged to keep printing more of their money in order to keep buying up dollars, soaking up the dollar gush flooding Europe from America. Such European solidarity with Washington was undermined not only by a widespread pessimism regarding the system's long-term chances but also by fault lines that were developing, quite naturally, between European nations whose money was on the way up (surplus countries such as Germany and the Netherlands) and those whose money was losing value (deficit countries nursing a growing deficit, such as France).

From as early as 1961, the Bundesbank began to balk at the prospect of either increasing the deutsche mark's value against the dollar at the IMF or printing as many marks as necessary to defend its current value. Revaluing the mark would penalize German exporters, whose goods would become relatively more expensive on the international market. Printing more marks smacked of inflation. Doing neither, as was the Bundesbank's preference, would damage Bretton Woods and infuriate Washington.

Meanwhile, politicians in deficit European states (like France and Italy) had reasons to be cross with America too. As their nations' currencies were squeezed by the deutsche mark, they felt the earth shifting under their feet. It was one thing for Paris, or Rome, to request a devaluation vis-à-vis the dollar. It was quite another constantly to lose ground in relation to the deutsche mark, whose value was being buoyed by Germany's trade surplus. With the Fed incapable of defending the franc or the lira, now that America was in deficit, the burden fell increasingly on the Bundesbank to prop up the franc and the lira (against its own deutsche mark) as well as the dollar (against gold and against the deutsche mark). France and Italy thus began to recognize that they were running the risk of turning, financially speaking, into German vassal states; a not too invigorating prospect, fifteen short years after the end of the Second World War.

None of this gave German policy makers much joy either. The dollar glut in Europe, and the simultaneous slide of the franc, the lira and the pound, meant that the Bundesbank had to crank up the deutsche mark printing presses ad nauseam on behalf of almost everyone else. German policy makers suddenly found themselves in a ruthless dilemma that divided them bitterly. Print marks in defense of Bretton Woods at the risk of inflation caused by a wall of deutsche marks? Or risk bringing down an international financial system which, in their eyes, was the economic foundation of Pax Americana (that kept the Soviets at bay) and of the European Union (that offered Germany perhaps its only chance to become a "normal" European state)?

At the same time that Germany was becoming reluctant to support the dollar-backed global system, President de Gaulle of France was growing angrier by the second with a global system that was diminishing French influence. Reflecting his unhappiness with Washington's stewardship of global capitalism, France's monetary authorities not only refused to sell gold in support of the dollar's gold value but, in fact, did the opposite: they followed the cue of speculators and bought gold from the US authorities, at $35 per ounce. Of course, unlike the speculators, de Gaulle's aim was to send a message of discontent to Washington, rather than to profit from buying gold cheaply and selling it at a higher dollar price.

In late 1967 de Gaulle's government attempted to harden the franc by embarking upon a harsh austerity drive. Alas, the result was a slump and rising unemployment, followed by great social unrest culminating in the world-famous May 1968 insurrection.

As students and workers poured into Parisian streets, the ever so proud President de Gaulle—the soldier who had been kept as a prisoner of war in the German town of Ingolstadt before becoming France's Second World War hero two decades later—lost control of downtown Paris and suffered the ignominy of having to flee to, of all places, Germany.

Though his army restored him to power, and he won another landslide election, a year later he resigned the presidency, despondent and amid renewed pressures on the franc. Meanwhile, Britain was feeling the pinch too. With its empire almost gone, its industry losing customers both abroad and at home, and with de Gaulle having vetoed its entry into the European Union (partly as a signal to Washington that France was unhappy and unwilling to accommodate its European lackey),[37] the United Kingdom was looking to America to stabilize its trade balance. Only America was preparing to do the opposite: to jettison the whole lot of them.

From the early 1960s America had been losing its surpluses but remained throughout the decade, understandably, unwilling to tighten its belt, crush its own economy and lose its global hegemony in order to preserve Bretton Woods.

Under the delusion that the United States could be counted on, come hell or high water, to maintain "its" global financial system, assorted European officials took liberties with Washington's nerves. The Bundesbank, struggling to retain its independence from German politicians (whom it considered susceptible to France's throttlehold), repeatedly refused to meet its commitments to help stabilize gold's dollar value and France's franc. Paris, fully dependent on the Bundesbank to defend the franc, lost no opportunity to insult the Americans verbally and symbolically, as when a French naval vessel was ordered to New Jersey packed with greenbacks to be redeemed for American gold. London too, feeling vulnerable as its empire was disappearing and de Gaulle was keeping Britain out of the European Union, also began to test America's resolve.[38] Put vulgarly, but in a manner reflecting John

Connally's and Paul Volcker's 1971 mindset, the global ship was listing and the various European rodents were testing the water. It was at that point that Connally and Volcker finally prevailed upon President Nixon to screw the foreigners.

Thus Europe was jettisoned in 1971 from the dollar zone by a United States intent on preserving its hegemony and unwilling to turn to austerity to save Bretton Woods.

EUROPE'S RESPONSE, AS we shall see over the coming chapters, was to create its own substitute, a kind of European Bretton Woods, culminating, after countless trials and tribulations, in a common currency: the euro. Disastrously, those who built up the European version of Bretton Woods were no Harry Dexter White or John Maynard Keynes. Innocent of the macroeconomic problems monetary unions throw out, they created a system that removed all shock absorbers but, at the same time, unwittingly ensured that when the shock came, as it did in 2008, it would be gigantic, causing Europe to turn in on itself.

On October 18, 2008, in the midst of our generation's version of 1929, just before boarding a plane to Washington where he was to meet President George W. Bush (for talks on how to respond to the collapsing global financial "system" that had taken Bretton Woods' place), French president Nicolas Sarkozy told journalists in his usual emphatic manner, "Europe wants it. Europe demands it. Europe will get it."

What exactly was it that "Europe demanded" and would "get," according to Monsieur Sarkozy? The answer, as provided by Manuel Barroso, the president of the European Commission at the time, was a "new global financial order."[39]

Of course, Nicolas Sarkozy did not get what he traveled to America to demand on behalf of Europe in 2008, precisely as his predecessor, President Georges Pompidou, had failed, during the later part of 1971, to convince the United States to rescind the Nixon Shock and to reconstitute Bretton Woods, albeit with fresh exchange rates.[40] Still, President Sarkozy's boisterous words confirm that, eight years after Europe's common currency (the euro) had been created, France and the European Commission were still hankering for a global system along the lines of that which Nixon, Connally and Volcker had torn down on that August day.

Europe's unhinging occurred in 1971 but is still haunting the old continent decades later, despite (in fact because of) the creation of a common currency infused with none of the lessons that the designers of Bretton Woods learned from the interwar gold standard.

John Connally would, no doubt, have chuckled at his enduring capacity to haunt European leaders. Only his enjoyment would be spoiled by an acute awareness of the clear and present danger an unhinged Europe poses to a tricky post-2008 world.

CHAPTER 2

AN INDECENT
PROPOSAL

Kurt Schmücker was not a man to give in to strong emotions. But on the morning of March 23, 1964, he could hardly trust his ears and only barely managed to contain his astonishment.

As Germany's minister of the economy,[1] Herr Schmücker was used to meeting regularly with his French counterpart, Valéry Giscard d'Estaing, President Charles de Gaulle's finance minister and a man who would, ten years later, become president of France himself. So when Giscard dropped by his Bonn office for a two-hour chat, Minister Schmücker was relaxed, anticipating another anodyne meeting, like all the previous ones—an effort to put on a show of European unity between the two erstwhile foes shouldering the burden of constructing a union at the early stages of its development: the European Economic Community (EEC), as the European Union was then known, comprising Germany, France, the Netherlands, Luxemburg, Belgium and Italy, the original six founding members and signatories of the Treaty of Rome (signed on March 25, 1957).[2]

Schmücker and Giscard normally exchanged polite views on how each saw the economic policies of the other, on how the two countries dealt with movements of money across their borders, on interest rates and trade balances, on their attitudes toward taxing business and, of course, on their joint efforts at cementing a European Union still in its infancy. Occasionally, they would also swap tales of woe on their tense relations with their own central bankers, the Bundesbank and the Banque de France. Nothing, in other words, that might have prepared Herr Schmücker for what he was about to hear. But, that morning, once the obligatory niceties had been dispensed with, Giscard came out with a shocking proposal: France and Germany should create a common currency, inviting the other four European Union members to join in when and if they were ready.

No one knows precisely what thoughts crossed Schmücker's mind at that moment, but his astonishment must have bordered on bewilderment. What on earth was the aristocratic Frenchman saying? That Germany and France ought to share the same banknotes, the same coins, the same central bank? Which one? The Bundesbank? For heaven's sake!

Outwardly, Schmücker put on a face of somber iciness, pretending not to have been taken aback. Indeed, the record shows that he responded as if he had not heard the earth-shattering proposition. Why not be more modest, he countered? Why don't we just try to stabilize our exchange rates through our central banks and on the basis of (a conservative German's strategy of last resort) "strict discipline" and "contractual rules"?[3]

Giscard was having none of it. "Why choose this system which works only as long as everybody gets along?"[4] he riposted energetically, adding that his proposal was coming from the very top—from President Charles de Gaulle himself. Flabbergasted, Schmücker tried to alert France's minister of finance to the deeper meaning of what de Gaulle was proposing: France was proposing to forfeit its national sovereignty! Was Paris serious about that? Giscard neither conceded nor repudiated Schmücker's obvious point. He bypassed it by urging quick action so that a common Franco-German currency be created forthwith, leaving it open to other European Union members to join in.

Schmücker knew that this was not an issue he had any authority to get seriously involved with. So he dutifully passed de Gaulle's proposal on to Ludwig Erhard, his chancellor.

Upon reading Schmücker's brief, Dr. Erhard smelled a rat. France could not possibly be giving up so lightheartedly its power to set taxes, to spend public funds, to set interest rates, to pursue its beloved "planification."[5] De Gaulle must have been up to something, again, thought Erhard. After all, the only reason Ludwig Erhard had risen to the highest office in Germany, a few short months earlier, was because of his role in frustrating President de Gaulle's designs.[6] This outrageous common currency proposal, thought Erhard, could only be made sense of as a continuation of those same designs.

Unwilling to enter into an official, public confrontation with France, Chancellor Erhard dutifully "misplaced" Schmücker's brief and pretended never to have received it. And so it was that a common European currency was first tabled, briefly discussed and spectacularly ignored. Nevertheless, when in 1966 he was forced out of the chancellery, among the very few papers Erhard took with him into retirement was that brief—a memento of the euro's first official appearance.[7]

A FRENCH EMBRACE TWICE SHUNNED

Giscard d'Estaing was never de Gaulle's stooge. Indeed, de Gaulle fired him from the Ministry of Finance in 1966 and Giscard had to wait for three years until a new president, Georges Pompidou, entered the Elysée Palace to reclaim the Finance Ministry—from where, in 1974, he rose to the presidency of the French Republic. Of course, back then, in 1964, Giscard strove loyally to serve de Gaulle, often against his better judgment regarding some of the former general's fixations, whether in the realm of economic policy[8] or in the French president's determination to wreck America's geopolitical dominance of Europe. However, on that occasion, on March 23, 1964, the "indecent proposal" he brought to Bonn was fully in tune with his very own thinking.

Giscard shared with de Gaulle one crucial judgment. They agreed that the hegemon was reaching for the moon. Literally and metaphorically. The Americans were starting wars in Indochina. They were announcing grand, expensive social programs at home. Their corporations bought up venerable European companies and treated them disgracefully.[9] And how did they pay for all this? By printing dollars which, once off the presses, flooded Europe's economies, forcing Europeans, particularly the French, to foot America's largesse through higher inflation. The fact that France was more susceptible than other countries to these inflationary forces also weighed heavily upon de Gaulle's and Giscard's thinking.

From Giscard's own perspective, Americans were forcing Europeans to lend them the money with which they bought up Europe and destabilized global finance. Giscard encapsulated this verdict famously in a two-word phrase: "exorbitant privilege"—an inordinate advantage enjoyed by the United States, and its currency, which America squandered. An advantage that ought to be done away with before world capitalism was destabilized for good and the opponents of the ruling bourgeoisie, especially in France, gained the upper hand.

"Exorbitant privilege" became a signifier of American financial might ever since Giscard coined it, and remains so to this day.[10] But what could be done to curb it? From Giscard's early 1964 perspective it was possible to imagine that the only way of ending America's imprudent monetary supremacy was for France and Germany, Europe's predominant nations, to get together, to forge a common currency, and thus to overcome their monetary dependence on a wayward United States. But would that not jeopardize, as Schmücker warned, France's sovereignty? Of course it would. It was a price that Giscard, a firm believer in a United States of Europe, did not mind much.

Giscard may not have minded the loss of French national sovereignty. But his boss, President de Gaulle, certainly did. Europe was important for de Gaulle, as it was for Giscard. It had to be "won." But not at any price, as far as de Gaulle was concerned. And certainly not at the price of "losing" France in the process. So why did de Gaulle send his finance minister to Berlin with a proposal that, if accepted, would dismantle Paris's levers of economic power? A common currency with Germany would rob Paris of control over France's economy. But a proposal for a common currency was not the same thing as an actual common currency.

De Gaulle was, lest we forget, a military tactician par excellence. Proposals for treaties and common currencies, just like maneuvers on the battlefield, were moves on a chessboard, packed with diversionary intent. A united Europe began to appeal to de Gaulle quite late in the piece (around 1958) and only when he started seeing it as a new vista of grandeur for France's nation-state; in sharp contrast to Germany's first two chancellors, Konrad Adenauer and Ludwig Erhard, for whom the European Union was an escape route from their nation-state.

January 1963 was a month of political fire and brimstone, with Paris at its center. On January 14 President de Gaulle gave a press conference that amounted to a declaration of hostilities against the Anglosphere. Countering Washington's express wishes, he announced that France was vetoing Britain's entry into the European Union. And as if that were not enough, in the same breath, he turned down an American offer for nuclear cooperation within a multilateral force.

Eight days later, on January 22, the German chancellor, Konrad Adenauer, went to Paris. In the splendor of the Elysée Palace, amid considerable pomp and ceremony, Adenauer and de Gaulle put their signature on the Elysée Treaty; a treaty that was presented to the world as the cornerstone of French-German rapprochement, testimony to the permanent cessation of hostilities between Europe's predominant nations, and the beginning of a "beautiful friendship." Washington was incensed. George Ball, under-secretary in the State Department, later wrote: "I can hardly overestimate the shock produced in Washington by this action or the speculation that followed, particularly in the intelligence community."[11]

Washington's ire had nothing to do with opposition to France and Germany burying the hatchet, getting closer and reinforcing European unity. The US government fretted that de Gaulle was up to something; something aimed at America's military dominance over Western Europe as well as its financial control of the capitalist global order. More precisely, they were concerned that de Gaulle was attempting to lure Adenauer into a strategic alliance with a twofold aim: at the level of international finance, to undermine the dollar-centered Bretton Woods system while, at the level of geopolitics, to bypass NATO in offering Moscow a nonaggression pact, cutting the United States out of the deal.

De Gaulle's strongest hand was his grand vision of a Europe spanning "from the Atlantic to the Urals." It appealed to a plurality of Europeans keen to remove the nuclear threat that hovered over their continent (especially after the Cuban Missile Crisis of the previous October) and hopeful of raising the Iron Curtain, which dissected it so brutally. For Germans in particular a Europe from the "Atlantic to the Urals" packed added significance, as it hinted at Germany's reunification. Washington was convinced that de Gaulle was ensnaring Adenauer into an alliance that would end America's predominance in Europe. These fears were heightened by the fact that the German chancellor was a Catholic Anglophobe with a long history of seeking unity with France.[12]

A day before the Elysée Treaty was signed, an American diplomat[13] enlisted the only member of Adenauer's cabinet who had the power and interest to oppose Adenauer's drift into de Gaulle's embrace: Ludwig Erhard. Adenauer's respected finance minister, Erhard had overseen Germany's Wirtschaftswunder, the economic miracle that had transformed Germany from 1949 to that day. The German industrial phenomenon, which Erhard was credited with, had relied on investment-led, ultrarapid growth, aided by American policies of giving Germany massive debt relief,[14] encouraging Wall Street and US multinationals to invest in the Federal Republic and making possible (through the Bretton Woods system) stable prices and copious markets for German exports.

Erhard did not act rashly. He bided his time before coming firmly down on the side of Washington and against Adenauer's plan to join forces with de Gaulle. When Adenauer convened the federal cabinet in Bonn on January 25 to discuss the Elysée Treaty, Erhard kept quiet. Four days later, however, Erhard gave a forceful speech critical of French foreign policy, taking the unprecedented step of "predicting" that the Elysée Treaty would never be implemented.

In the following cabinet meeting, in Bonn, on January 30, Erhard went wild, speaking against "de Gaulle's French dictatorship,"[15] even comparing the French president with Hitler. In an article published in *Die Zeit* on February 5, Erhard warned his compatriots that Germany "cannot run with the hare and hunt with the hounds," signaling clearly his allegiance to Washington and throwing down the gauntlet at Adenauer for having become too close to de Gaulle for comfort. On that same day, President Kennedy signaled that Germany had a clear "choice between working with the French or working for us."[16] Erhard led the opposition to Adenauer, shifting the German cabinet's choice America's way.

By April 1963, Erhard's decisive intervention had diminished Adenauer's position within the ruling Christian Democrats. Erhard had emerged as the party's sole candidate for replacing the aging chancellor. On May 16, after a great deal of backroom dealing, Erhard and his allies succeeded in passing through the federal parliament an amendment to the Elysée Treaty, in the form of a preamble, that ended de Gaulle's dream of a Franco-German alliance in opposition to America.[17] Meanwhile, secure in the thought that de Gaulle had been "seen off," the US State Department recalibrated its European strategy, avoiding further confrontations with de Gaulle and focusing instead on cultivating stronger ties with Bonn. In October 1963, Ludwig Erhard moved to the chancellery, bequeathing the economics ministry to Kurt Schmücker.

THE SECOND EMBRACE

Having his embrace shunned so spectacularly, it was quite remarkable that President de Gaulle bore no grudges against Germany's new chancellor. Even being compared with Hitler washed over him like water off a duck's back. When Erhard was made chancellor, he made a point of visiting Paris immediately to reaffirm the "great new friendship between the two nations"[18] and their leaders. President de Gaulle welcomed him with open arms, as he would a long-lost friend. And six months later, he dispatched his finance minister, the charming Valéry Giscard d'Estaing, to Bonn to astound Herr Schmücker with his proposal for an instant Franco-German monetary union.

Was de Gaulle just not getting it that Germany was averse to another of his asphyxiating embraces? Whatever else was going on in the general's mind, one thing was for sure: he was under no illusion. The notion that de Gaulle expected Erhard to agree to a Franco-German common currency is as absurd as the alternative notion, namely that de Gaulle wanted such a currency. The shared money proposal had two tactical features that attracted France's strategizing president: the element of surprise, and a capacity (even if the proposal were ignored or rejected) to rope Germany into a relationship with France sufficiently close to afford de Gaulle more degrees of freedom in his opposition to the United States.

The element of surprise was, undoubtedly, there. Erhard and Schmücker had every reason to expect that, after Adenauer's departure, de Gaulle would have left them alone. A common currency proposal was the last thing they anticipated. As Schmücker told Giscard, nothing in Paris's demeanor signaled a willingness to forfeit national sovereignty or even to defer important decisions on France's economy to supranational institutions. He was right. France, and in particular de Gaulle, was guarding her economic levers jealously and had no interest in letting go of them. For well over a decade[19] de Gaulle had stood alone among conservative European politicians in dogged opposition to the new French-German economic relationship that America's New Dealers were keen to turn into the emergent European Union's backbone.[20]

Unlike many of his enchanted compatriots, who took great pride in the European integration project and waxed lyrical about it as a great achievement of the European spirit, de Gaulle had recognized the European Union project as an "American design" that privileged German industry in order to cement American dominance globally. The common European market and the process of European integration was, in his eyes, part of an American global plan that de Gaulle deemed ill founded, unsustainable and, therefore, detrimental to both France and Europe.[21]

Eventually, by 1958, de Gaulle had softened his opposition to the European Union, after repeated American pledges in the 1950s that France would remain Europe's administrative center. But he only embraced it so long as, in his own words to a visiting journalist, the European Union would resemble "a horse and carriage: Germany [being] the horse and France . . . the coachman."[22]

Alas, by 1963 it was clear that the horse was developing a mind of its own and the coachman was losing his grip. France's accelerating trade deficit with Germany meant that Paris would be forced into a perpetual Sophie's choice. Regularly go cap in hand to the IMF for permission to devalue the franc, admitting to permanent national weakness. Or rely forever on the Bundesbank to print deutsche marks with which to buy francs, conceding to an unending dependency upon the old enemy. Either way, France's aspirations for political and diplomatic domination of the European Union were unraveling.

It was a nightmare for de Gaulle but also for the French establishment, which saw in the general a fearless champion of their interests and ambition, domestically as well as across Europe. De Gaulle's brashness sometimes clashed with polite society's sense of decorum but, when it came to addressing German politicians, American officials and Anglo-Saxon financiers, the French elite liked their president's inherent suspiciousness, his readiness to speak out, as well as his commitment to hard money—to a stable, noninflationary currency that would revive France's image, bolster its banking sector and, importantly, weaken the recalcitrant French trade unions.[23]

De Gaulle was always cagey about an ever closer union with Germany. He saw unity across the Rhine as a fine sentiment fraught with danger, whatever its merits for France. Even after 1958, when he embraced the idea of a European Union erected along the Franco-German axis, de Gaulle remained guarded about it. When Henry Kissinger once asked him how France would prevent German dominance of the European Union, the French president replied, *"Par la guerre!"*[24] France's war hero was not joking. Indeed, his indecent proposal for a common currency with Germany, which Giscard conveyed to a gobsmacked Schmücker, was a form of war by other means. De Gaulle used the common currency proposal like a troubled boxer employs a strategic embrace: as a ploy to catch his breath before launching into an uppercut.

Chancellor Erhard knew this. At the first glance of de Gaulle's common currency proposal he recognized it as a ploy to smother his country, neuter the Bundesbank, enhance France's standing at the expense of Germany's and drive a wedge between Germany and Washington.[25] He could see that, whatever his response, he was on the losing side. If he accepted de Gaulle's offer, he ran the risk of surrendering the Bundesbank to Paris or, at the very least, incurring the Bundesbank's undying wrath. If he dithered for a while, de Gaulle would have bought precious time (as the speculators would cease betting against the franc until the dust settled) and Erhard would have looked indecisive. If he rejected the offer outright and publically, his own European unionist credentials would have suffered and de Gaulle's would have strengthened.

Erhard had undermined Adenauer and risked everything to help his country wriggle out of de Gaulle's first embrace. He was not going to submit to this second one. Unwilling publically to push back against de Gaulle's clasp for a second time in a year, and fearful that any public response to the common currency proposal would damage his government, the German chancellor pretended never to have received Schmücker's note.

And so it was that, in early March 1964, the idea of the euro lit up Europe's skies ever so briefly and unseen by most Europeans. It was only when Europe was jettisoned in toto from the dollar zone[26] that it resurfaced.

WAR BY OTHER MEANS

Unperturbed by Bonn's silent rebuff, de Gaulle decided to go it alone. On January 4, 1965, he called a news conference. With superb lyricism he countered his compatriots' fear of national decline with an open attack on America's "exorbitant privilege," aiming to restore the glory of France by demonstrating it was the only Western power capable of, and willing to, stand up to the hegemon. With his slings and arrows trained on the dollar, and America's alleged failure properly to manage global finance, de Gaulle called for a new global currency.

And what would he replace the dollar with? His mischievous answer was to call for the restoration of gold to its rightful throne:[27] "We . . . consider it necessary that the system of international exchanges be re-established . . . on an indisputable monetary base which bears the mark of no country in particular. What base? *Eh! Oui.* Gold, which does not change its nature . . . which has no nationality, which is held eternally and universally as the inalterable fiduciary value par excellence."[28]

Behind the evocative rhetoric, the French president was only talking gold up, and the dollar down, because he felt, quite astutely, that a fraying Bretton Woods was no longer consistent with his ambition for a France that dominated Europe.[29]

It is tempting to dismiss de Gaulle's "interventions" as the whims of a man embittered by his wartime struggle to get the British and the Americans to recognize a defeated France, and himself personally, as one of the Allies that beat Germany into submission. De Gaulle never forgave the Americans for having denied France a place at the victors' table in the closing stages of the Second World War, especially in the Yalta meetings between Franklin D. Roosevelt, Winston Churchill and Joseph Stalin. But to imagine that this was the reason for his 1965 attack on the dollar, and America's Bretton Woods, is to underestimate de Gaulle's legitimate intellectual concerns regarding the propensity of superpowers to grow arrogant and eventually destabilize themselves.[30]

De Gaulle's objections to America's postwar global design went back at least to 1946. To September 6, 1946, to be precise, when James F. Byrnes, the US secretary of state, traveled to Stuttgart to deliver his Speech of Hope—a significant restatement of America's policy on Germany. Until then, the Allies were united in their commitment to convert "Germany into a country primarily agricultural and pastoral in character."[31]

Byrnes's speech was the first postwar sign the German people were given of an end to a revanchist deindustrialization drive that, by the end of the decade, had destroyed 706 industrial plants. Byrnes's words heralded a major policy reversal with the phrase that "the German people [should] not . . . be denied to use . . . savings as they might be able to accumulate by hard work and frugal living to build up their industries for peaceful purposes."[32]

Of course, one person's hope is another's nightmare. De Gaulle, for one, was exasperated. For he knew that, in the context of a financial system pegged on the dollar, a reindustrialized net-export-producing Germany would render France financially dependent on the Anglosphere, on America, even on Britain—heavens forbid!

General de Gaulle was the embodiment of the French army's obsession with Prussian military and industrial prowess. He feared and admired German resolve and efficiency in equal measure. In the 1930s he had opposed the building of the defensive Maginot Line, accusing

France's Ministry of Defense of trying to fight the Great War all over again. De Gaulle's vision of the oncoming Second World War was precisely how the Nazis' High Command was planning it: highly mobile, based on tank columns moving rapidly and liberated from snail-like infantry divisions, who were to follow later in trucks and lorries. When the war broke out, de Gaulle's tank units were the only ones to have covered themselves in some glory, while the Maginot Line's static defenses proved a national embarrassment.

De Gaulle's disgust at his country's failure was replete with respect for how German tactics and industry combined to humiliate France, occupy as much of it as Berlin wanted, create a vassal Nazi state with the town of Vichy as its capital and start another French civil war (pitting Vichy supporters and collaborators versus the Resistance and its spirit) that lasted, at the discursive level, well into the 1980s.

It is the mark of ancient societies that contemporary tribulations reinvent old fears. De Gaulle was born and bred in a cloud of national disgrace. Twenty-eight years before his birth, in 1862, Prussia's chancellor, Otto von Bismarck, had delivered his Blood and Iron Speech, where he presciently declared that Prussia would settle the "great questions of the day" not "through speeches and majority decisions . . . but by iron and blood." The idea of a reindustrializing Germany, cranking up its steel output in the 1950s, could never appeal to a man whose life, from a tender young age, had been shaped by images of German iron liberally spilling French blood.

Even worse, de Gaulle was burdened by the capacity of the French to spill their own blood while German smelters and Bessemer converters were spewing out high-quality steel. In 1871, as Bismarck was proclaiming German unification and crowning his Prussian king emperor of the German empire, France's government army was entering the French capital to commence a pitiless battle against revolutionaries of the Paris Commune, killing tens of thousands in the process. For de Gaulle, the first part of the twentieth century was nothing more than a recapitulation of that sorry contrast: French impotence juxtaposed against German industrial success that made France dependent on the Anglo-Saxons.

Fierce French resistance to the reversal Secretary Byrnes had fore-shadowed with his 1946 Speech of Hope slowed down the process of rehabilitating Germany. However, once Washington had decided, for its own reasons, that Germany was to play a crucial role within America's plan for the postwar world, it was only a matter of time before Germany was, indeed, rehabilitated and its industrial base not only spared but bolstered as well. A speech on March 18, 1947, by Herbert Hoover, President Roosevelt's predecessor, flagged America's new policy on Europe. "There is an illusion," Hoover said, "that the New Germany . . . can be reduced to a pastoral state. It cannot be done unless we exterminate or remove 25 million people out of it."[33]

It was then that General de Gaulle, and the majority of France's policy makers, understood they had a new clash on their hands requiring a fresh strategy to contain the New Germany. The strategy he chose was odd, though not illogical: an asphyxiating embrace with which France would attempt to stifle its revived neighbor. The Elysée Treaty, in January 1963, and Giscard's indecent proposal, in March 1964, were early manifestations of that strategy. Many more were to follow.

AMERICA'S GLOBAL PLAN[34]

It was not for humanitarian motives that Washington decided to spare Germany a return to a bucolic past.[35] Nor was America's change of heart caused exclusively by the gathering clouds of the Cold War and the all too real imperative to contain the Soviet Union. While the geopolitical incentive was clear and present, New Dealers like James Byrnes, James Forrestal,[36] George Marshall[37] and Dean Acheson[38] had another excellent reason for allowing Germany to retake its place among the industrialized nations.

The Bretton Woods system, already set out in 1944,[39] posited the dollar as the sole lynchpin holding together the edifice of global trade and finance. If, for any reason, the American economy were to go into a slump, the dollar might function like a superconductor for recessionary waves that would immediately travel unimpeded to the far corners of global capitalism. Even small American recessions could pick up speed and ferocity reaching Europe, Japan and the rest of Asia, where they might cause a great deal more damage than in Chicago or Ohio. Shock absorbers were urgently needed to prevent this.

In a global system of fixed exchange rates, shock absorbers require strong regional currencies, issued by potent central banks, to act as secondary pillars in support of the system's main pillar: the dollar. There was need for, at least, one such pillar in Europe and another one in Asia. Of course strong regional currencies cannot be anointed by Congress. Heavy industry powerhouses must underpin them. But here is the tricky part. Industrial powerhouses produce more manufacturing goods than their domestic economies can absorb—think China today. To keep going, "powerhouse" economies need markets; a surrounding hinterland that will be in permanent deficit with them so that they can remain in surplus.[40]

The first question, though, was which would these powerhouse economies be in Europe and in Asia, buttressing America's own economy and its dollar?

In Europe the United Kingdom was an early candidate. Only, like most early frontrunners, Britain went by the wayside. Its elites were determined to retain their grip on an empire that, in Washington's eyes, was both repugnant and unsustainable. Its returning soldiers, having shed their blood for king and country, were determined not to return to prewar pitiful wages and abject living conditions. This was why Winston Churchill, the nation's wartime tower of strength, was swept away in a 1945 electoral landslide that ushered in a radical-sounding (especially in American ears) Labour government.

A year later a fiscal crisis ended the sterling's convertibility and further tarnished Britain's candidacy as the European pillar of America's global plan. These developments gave Washington second thoughts that were multiplied manifold by the British establishment's delusion that it had won the war, and thus deserved to dictate terms in peacetime.

Looking at the Far East, the American administration saw that the only nation capable of playing the necessary shock-absorbing role there, and developing a suitable currency, was Japan: a mighty industrial power whose factories were largely unharmed (except perhaps in Hiroshima and Nagasaki), whose workforce was highly skilled and impressively disciplined, whose constitution the United States had had the opportunity to script and, last but certainly not least, a country ruled by America's armed forces. Once their gaze turned back toward Europe, the puzzle dissolved: West Germany was the obvious equivalent and, indeed, a splendid candidate for the role of the global plan's European shock-absorbing pillar—certainly not Britain!

Why not France? For three excellent reasons. First, German industry was far more advanced than France's. In 1945, despite the hammering it received from the Allies in the final stages of the war, German factories produced more than twice as much output as France's. Secondly, the defeated Germans, fearing a pastoral future, would breathe a sigh of relief if the United States were to patronize their economy, invest in it and, generally, take it under their wing. In contrast, General de Gaulle, and the vast majority of the French, would be incensed by any hint of similar intervention, let alone a takeover. Thirdly, just as in the case of Japan, America wrote the constitution of the Federal Republic of Germany and even created the Bundesbank from scratch. The fact that American armed forces controlled West Germany's land, sea and airspace did not harm the notion either.

The second question now remained: who would provide the hinterland to be in deficit to Germany's and Japan's powerhouse economies?

DE GAULLE'S INSIGHT

To take their plan further, from conception to implementation, Washington needed to overcome de Gaulle in particular and French opposition generally. General de Gaulle could see all this evolving into a global system in which France would be reduced to a third-rate power, bringing back painful memories of his nation's wartime humiliation. His opposition to this prospect hit the shoals of a postwar Central European conservative consensus that was enthusiastic about Europe's dollarization. On January 20, 1946, high inflation and a broad

dissatisfaction with de Gaulle's austere conservatism caused his removal as leader of France's provisional government. The interesting
question is, Why did de Gaulle not attempt a comeback soon after?
Why did he volunteer to go into the wilderness and stay there until
1958?[41]

De Gaulle could sense that the French elites were not keen to share
his deeply felt misgivings about America's global plan, and thus to risk
losing the plush perks that America was offering them for going along
with it. He strove to warn them against the idea of a global dollar standard in which the deutsche mark would be the greenback's supportive currency within Europe. He could see that, to play this role, the
deutsche mark required a German heavy industry that, in turn, necessitated neighboring nations in perpetual trade deficit to Germany.
Only thus could the missing demand for German industrial exports
be generated. Could his people not see this? They could. Except that
Washington played a smart game, making French officials and bankers an offer they could not refuse: the opportunity to administer the
emerging united Europe under the aegis of Pax Americana.

France's comparative advantage has always been the quality of its
administrators. Every year the *grandes écoles* produce a steady stream of
men, and more recently some women, of remarkable erudition, with
a predilection for public service, superior numeracy and a capacity
to run multinational bureaucracies efficiently and with panache. This
was the lasting legacy, the gift to the French nation, of Napoleon Bona-
parte. Additionally, French banks were far more sophisticated than
Germany's. Cognizant of this, the New Dealers offered the French
establishment a powerful incentive to acquiesce to Germany's reindustrialization: at the price of accepting German industrial might, and the
inevitable power of the deutsche mark, French administrators would
run a unified Central Europe (from Paris and from Brussels) while
French banks would handle the flow of capital and German profits
both within and without this European Union.

De Gaulle was perhaps one of very few establishment figures in
France who refused to be lured by this tempting offer. Figures like
Jean Monnet (one of the fathers of the European Union), Jacques Rueff

(an influential economist) and Robert Marjolin (who was to lead the Marshall Plan administration that evolved into today's OECD) understood that de Gaulle would have none of it. Unlike them, he suspected that, despite Washington's promises, France would languish if America's global plan were implemented.

The fact of the matter was, and this is where de Gaulle was right, that a reindustrialized, export-oriented Germany would always procure a weak French franc within a global monetary system of fixed exchange rates relying on the dollar. France would then depend on Washington's support to keep its currency at a par with Germany's money. But such transatlantic support for France could only be provided if America continued to generate surpluses. De Gaulle's premonition was that the United States would squander its surpluses and, at that point, Paris would become dependent on the kindness of the Bundesbank. Which is exactly as things panned out.

THE GREEK TRIGGER

There was one other crucial factor that lay behind the United States' commitment to Germany: the Cold War. What most people forget is that my tiny nation had been the harbinger of this larger drama too.

The first clash between East and West occurred in the streets of Athens in the aftermath of the Nazis' April 1944 withdrawal, and it involved right-wingers supported by Britain and left-wing partisans supported by the USSR. These clashes reached a crescendo in December 1944, culminating later in Greece's sordid 1946–1949 civil war that left every Greek family I know indelibly marked.

It was the prelude for an East-West confrontation that furnished the US Treasury and State Departments with the opportunity, and congressional clout, to implement an audacious experiment in Europe: the bringing together of France and Germany into a European union that was part and parcel of a global economic design.

The reversal of the plan to demolish Germany's heavy industry was facilitated by these increasing tensions, which first erupted in Athens. American diplomat George Kennan's so-called Long Telegram from Moscow, warning of the Soviets' expansionist ambitions, imbued Washington with the urgency to contain the USSR and coincided with the full escalation of Greece's civil war. Byrnes's Speech of Hope, fore-shadowing Germany's steady rehabilitation, came after the Greeks had been plunged into the despair of a hideous fratricidal conflict that was the original proxy confrontation between the emerging Cold War superpowers.[42]

The Truman Doctrine, announced by President Truman on March 12, 1947, focused on winning Greece for the West[43] but constituted, more importantly, the president's unofficial declaration of the Cold War.[44] It shaped America's Europe. From that moment onward, and beginning with Greece, the United States would make the contain-ment of Soviet influence its top priority. At the very sound of Truman's proclamation, Paris shuddered.

French leaders, with de Gaulle first and foremost, understood that the new American emphasis on Soviet containment translated into a German industrial revival. Germany's reindustrialization happened only because the United States chose to make it happen. Equally, the European Union was formed because Washington understood that a strong deutsche mark needed a successful German heavy industry, which needed neighboring markets for its wares, which necessitated an American-brokered deal with Paris. A deal that the French establish-ment reluctantly accepted but which pushed General de Gaulle out of politics for more than a decade.

SOME YEARS LATER, in 1953, Hermann Josef Abs, a Nazi-era director of Deutsche Bank,[45] led a German government delegation to London. The occasion was a conference convened by the Americans to reach the so-called London Debt Agreement. In essence, the United States leaned on Britain, France, Greece, Italy, Spain, Sweden, Yugoslavia, Norway, Switzerland and many other countries to write off the great-est part of Germany's prewar debt to them. The British government protested, arguing that Germany had both the capacity and the moral duty to pay. Washington vetoed London and, to lead by example, in-stantly wrote off new loans that it had forwarded to Bonn after 1945.

Thus nations and private creditors owed money by the German state and by German corporations were leaned upon, by Washington, to write off more than 70 percent of the money they were due.[46]

Debt relief is essential for any person, company or nation that has fallen into the unforgiving clasp of insolvency. Without it, individuals languish in debt prison and nations wither until either their inhabitants migrate or rise up against the creditors and their quislings.

If capitalism grew from strength to strength in the nineteenth century it is because debt prisons were replaced by limited liability. If General Motors is alive and kicking today, it is because in 2009 President Obama's administration wrote off 90 percent of its debt. If Germany rose up in the 1950s to become an economic superpower, it did so because the United States strong-armed other Europeans to give it substantial debt relief.

Europe's fallen nation, Germany, thus emerged from its ashes while Greece—the first country to have pushed back the Axis's military encroachments[47]—was having a disastrous postwar: first it burned in the flames of its 1944–1949 civil war and then, after that sorry episode ended in 1949, was almost emptied of its people, who took the long road of economic emigration. During the early 1950s, the Greeks were migrating to the United States, Canada, Australia, Belgium and, ironically, to Germany, as highly productive Gastarbeiters (guest workers); and the Greek government was bowing to pressure to write off substantial sums owed it by Germany. Meanwhile, while their postwar fate was nowhere near as tragic as Greece's, France and Britain, supposedly the war's victors, braced themselves for interesting economic times ahead.

Ironically, if Greece today remains in a deep depression, it is because (since 2010) Germany has been refusing point-blank to grant Athens debt relief and no one, including the United States, is willing or able to strong-arm Berlin to do for Greece that which America did for Germany in 1953. The result is not just a predictable economic depression but also the rise of the Golden Dawn Nazis.

In my first official visit to Berlin, on February 5, 2015, I invoked the specter of our Greek Nazis, and the debt-fueled depression that propelled them into parliament as Greece's third-largest party (recall the preface). The combination of annoyance and rejection with which my plea was met confirmed my, and the rest of Europe's, worst fears: the German establishment had either lost all memory of America's act of mercy toward it or believed that the German state deserved, immediately after the end of a terrible war that it had started, special treatment that other European states do not.

DOLLARIZED CARTEL

To establish the European pillar of its global plan, Washington had to make a significant concession. The European economic union that it coveted as the deutsche mark's hinterland would have to be built around a Central European cartel of heavy industry enjoying a degree of market power that the New Dealers were allergic to. But they had no other option. The only two unifying European movements they could draw support from, and work with, were the internationalist Marxist Left and a time-honored conservative Central European tradition associated with catchwords such as "Mitteleuropa" or "Paneuropa." There was no contest.

At its most wholesome, Mitteleuropa evoked a multinational, multicultural intellectual ideal for a united Central Europe that a nonchauvinistic section of its conservative elites were rather fond of. However, Mitteleuropa was also the title of an influential book by Friedrich Naumann, authored in the midst of the Great War,[48] which advocated Central European economic and political integration, run along the lines of German principles and with the "minor" states placed under German rule.

A great deal more liberally minded than Mitteleuropa, Paneuropa was the brainchild of Count Coudenhove-Kalergi, an Austrian-Japanese liberal intellectual who ran a lifelong campaign to bring about a Paneuropean political and economic union.[49] Despite their differences, Mitteleuropa and Paneuropa were aimed at protecting Europe's "center" from the geopolitical and economic encroachments of Russia from the East and of the Anglosphere from the West. They also shared a view that European unity would have to be overlaid on top of Central Europe's existing national institutions and, indeed, on top of prevailing corporate power structures.

A European union, consistent with the Mitteleuropa and Paneuropa visions, would have to operate by limiting competition between corporations, between nations, and between capital and labor. In short, Central Europe would resemble one gigantic corporation structured hierarchically and governed by technocrats whose job would be to depoliticize everything and minimize all conflicts.

Needless to say, the Mitteleuropa-Paneuropa vision enthused German industrialists. Walter Rathenau, chairman of AEG (the Allgemeine Elektricitäts-Gessellschaft) and later Germany's foreign minister, went as far as to suggest that a Central European economic union would be "civilization's greatest conquest."[50] The idea appealed greatly not only to corporations like AEG, Krups, Siemens, etc., but also to the Roman Catholic Church and to politicians like Robert Schuman, another one of the European Union's fathers, who was born in Germany and ended up French, courtesy of a shifting border.

In September 1947, as the New Dealers were contemplating the form of the European union consistent with their global plan, Count Coudenhove-Kalergi was giving a speech at the European Parliamentary Union Conference that he had convened in a bid to bring together Central European parliamentarians. The theme of his talk was the urgent need to bring forth a united Europe by building a large Central European market with a stable currency. What he neglected to say was that this "market" would, by necessity, be dominated by several large corporations at liberty to coordinate their prices so as to avert any real competition among themselves, from upstarts and, importantly, from the Anglosphere.

These were the people, men like the good Count Coudenhove-Kalergi, Robert Schuman and Jean Monnet, that the Americans had to do business with. The process of building Mitteleuropa-Paneuropa, once it began, was inexorable. In January 1946, at the behest of the US Mission to France, the Planning Commission (Commissariat général du Plan) was established in Paris. A few months after the Truman Doctrine was made public, George Marshall, Truman's secretary of state, addressed a Harvard audience with a speech that marked the beginning of the Marshall Plan: a massive aid package, amounting to more than 2 percent of US national income, that kicked off Europe's dollarization.[51]

Within weeks, the Commissariat général du Plan was distributing one-third of all Marshall aid to Europe, setting growth targets across Europe and employing no fewer than three thousand employees in Paris to do so. On April 3, 1948, President Truman established the Economic Cooperation Administration, and thirteen days later the United States and its European allies created the Organization for European Economic Co-operation (OEEC), with a remit to work out where to channel the funding, under what conditions and to which purpose. In 1961 the OEEC changed its name to what we know to-day as the OECD: the Organization for Economic Cooperation and Development.

While France's elites were being placated with plush administrative roles and oodles of money to fill them, the real game was being played in the realm of heavy industry. In 1950 the European Union was officially born in the form of a German-dominated cartel of coal and steel, run of course by a cross-border French-dominated administration located in Brussels. Its name? The European Steel and Coal Community. It was a remarkable departure from American principles of governance which, since President Theodore Roosevelt, included a healthy dose of cartel busting. However, America's global plan could not fly in Europe unless it made its peace with the Mitteleuropa-Paneuropa ideology that was intimately associated with Central Europe's cartels.

Making their peace with Central European corporatism, American policy makers had to swallow not only the idea of building the New Europe on a cartel of big business but also the unsavory political agenda that went with it. Corporatists like Robert Schuman and Jean Monnet were bent on constructing the Brussels-based bureaucracy as a democracy-free zone. Count Coudenhove-Kalergi put it succinctly in one of his speeches when he declared his ambition that Europe "supersedes democracy" and that democracy be replaced by a "social aristocracy of the spirit."[52] As it always happens when a technocracy harboring a deep, Platonic contempt for democracy attains inordinate power, we end up with an antisocial, dispirited, mindless autocracy.

Europeans recognize this in today's Brussels-based bureaucracy. Every survey of public opinion finds large majorities who have no trust in the European Union's institutions. While it is true that citizens around the world (e.g., Britain, the United States, India) are highly critical of their state's institutions, the discontent toward Brussels is qualitatively different. Take Britain, for instance. The British state evolved as a set of institutions whose function was to regulate the struggle between different social groups and classes. The tussle between the king and the barons gave rise to the Magna Carta: a deal between them the essence of which was to limit the king's powers. After the merchant class acquired economic power disproportionate to its social and political rank, the state evolved further to accommodate their interests with those of the aristocracy, especially after the 1688 Glorious Revolution. The industrial revolution brought new social strata into the mix (industrialists, trade unions, local communities made up of former peasants), thus extending the franchise and refining the state's apparatus.

Meanwhile, on the other side of the Atlantic a similar process was spawning the American constitution.

The US government, along with its bureaucracy, also emerged at a time of intense conflict between vested interests and social classes. Slave-owning landowners, mainly in the South, clashed with East Coast traders and manufacturers in Illinois, Boston and Wisconsin. The Louisiana Purchase triggered a variety of new tussles among multiple interest groups. A brutal civil war proved impossible to avert and facilitated America's consolidation. Later on, the rise of the labor unions and the military-industrial complex signaled fresh rivalries. To bring the nation together, and to homogenize its institutions so as to deal with the political, social and financial crises that these tensions threw up, Congress had to play a central equilibrating role. Indeed, no authority in the United States can defy Congress or ignore it. Whatever demerits American democracy may feature, there can be no doubt that the democratic process is essential in keeping the union together.

In contrast, the European Union's institutions did not evolve in response to similar social conflicts. National parliaments and institutions did all the heavy lifting in terms of ameliorating social conflicts while the Brussels bureaucracy was devised for the purposes of managing the affairs of an industrial cartel made up of Central European heavy industry. Lacking a demos, a "we the people" to keep them in awe, and indeed to legitimize their activities, Brussels bureaucrats both disdained democracy and were shielded from its checks and balances. While the cartel they administered was doing well under the auspices of the American-designed global financial system, the European Union's institutions enjoyed widespread acceptance. However, unlike America's Congress-centric system, the European Union lacked the democratic process that was necessary to fall back on in times of trouble.

From the viewpoint of its official ideology, the European Union sounded very similar to the United States, even to liberal Britain. Free market liberalism seemed to be the order of the day and a single market free of state patronage its objective. And yet, it is quite remarkable that the European Union began life as a cartel of coal and steel producers who, openly and legally, controlled prices and output by means of a multinational bureaucracy vested with legal and political powers superseding national parliaments and democratic processes. The equivalent in the United States would have been a Washington bureaucracy, operating without a Senate or a House of Representatives to keep the bureaucrats in check, but able to overrule state governments on almost anything, and bent on fixing prices to levels higher than the market would have selected. It only takes mentioning this to an American to make her or his blood curdle.

Indeed, the inaugural task of the Brussels bureaucracy was to forge a cartel of steel and coal products, fixing their price but also removing all restrictions in the movement and trading of steel and coal among the cartel's member states. Curiously perhaps, this made perfect sense: what would be the point of a cross-border cartel if its products were stopped at the borders, taxed and generally impeded by national government officials?

The next step was obvious too: once tariffs on coal and steel were removed, it made sense to remove all tariffs. Except that the French farmers, who always exerted exceptional influence in the French political system, did not like the idea of untrammeled competition from imported milk, cheese and wine. So to co-opt French farmers, a so-called common agricultural policy was established. Its purpose? To secure the farmers' consent to a European free trade zone by handing over to them a chunk of the cartel's monopoly profits.

By the end of the 1950s, a fully fledged European Union (then known as the European Economic Community, which was the "evolution" of the European Steel and Coal Community[53]) had sprung out of the multinational heavy industry cartel and its political incarnation in Brussels. Dollarized by the United States, it soon began to create large surpluses that funded postwar Central European prosperity in the stable world environment provided by a Bretton Woods system, which was itself constantly stabilized by a United States ready and willing to recycle to Europe a large chunk of America's surpluses. A golden age dawned brimming with high growth, nonexistent unemployment and low inflation and spawning, little by little, the dream of Europe as the realm of shared prosperity. It was an American triumph that Europe's elites were determined to portray as their own.

TUMULT ACROSS THE RHINE

Europe's golden age began to frazzle as soon as America's surpluses withered. The rise of German and Japanese manufacturing exports, which the United States had variously supported, led its two protégés, Germany and Japan, to build up their own surpluses. And since one economy's surplus is another's deficit, German and Japanese surpluses came at the expense of a United States more concerned with the continued stabilization of the world economy than with the preservation of its own surpluses. So even when it was becoming obvious that America was turning from a creditor to a debtor nation, from an economy that enjoyed a trade surplus to one nursing an increasing trade deficit, Washington officials knew that tightening their nation's belt (i.e., reducing government expenditure, increasing taxes and printing fewer dollars) in order to rein in the emerging deficits would destabilize a global order reliant on American largesse. And so the Fed, America's central bank, continued to produce as many dollars as necessary for the purpose of preventing a sharp recession throughout global capitalism. As a result, the US government and private sector got deeper into the red, becoming net debtors toward Europe and Japan. But as long as America maintained its monopoly over the world's single currency, the dollar, exploiting what Giscard had referred to as its "exorbitant privilege," there was still some life left in the Bretton Woods system.

Meanwhile, America's Europe began to turn in on itself. President de Gaulle's twin attempts, in 1963 and then again in 1964, to lure Germany into an asphyxiating embrace were a mere reflection of his anxiety at the sight of an American global plan fraying at the edges and threatening France's political predominance within the European Union.

When Chancellor Erhard snubbed his proposal for an immediate currency union, de Gaulle responded by upping the ante against the United States and Bretton Woods. Convinced that America had more power than was good for it (but less than it often realized), a few months after his provocative January 1965 press conference, where he had called for a return to the gold standard, the French president ordered the removal of 25,900 bars of gold, weighing more than 350 tons, from the basement under the New York Federal Reserve and their immediate transportation to Paris.[54] No one can deny that, when it comes to semiology, the French are unbeatable.

The news led several European companies, and various European central banks, to demand from the American authorities gold in exchange for their stockpiled euro-dollars. As we saw in the last chapter, speculators sniffing blood joined in; they borrowed oodles of dollars to buy gold and, thus, the unofficial price of gold rose to more than $70 per ounce, when America was still legally bound to sell gold at only $35 an ounce. To add injury to insult, de Gaulle also pulled France's military forces from NATO, demanding the removal at once of all NATO facilities from French soil.[55]

Meanwhile, in Germany, a parallel drama was unfolding. The Bundesbank's reluctance to support Bretton Woods was coming to a crescendo at a time when it was proving of the essence. Supporting Bretton Woods meant, in practice, that the Bundesbank printed more and more deutsche marks with which to soak up the dollars and francs that speculators were borrowing from commercial banks awash with dollars and francs in order to buy deutsche marks (betting, as was their wont, on a rise of the German currency). As long as the Bundesbank did this, the speculators were kept at bay. The moment, however, the Bundesbank slowed down its deutsche mark printing presses, the dollar's and franc's official (Bretton Woods) values would become untenable. At such moments of Bundesbank reluctance, either the politicians needed to get together at the IMF's Washington offices to agree to a politically poisonous revaluation of the exchange rates[56] or the whole system would perish. It would not be far-fetched to say that, by the mid-1960s, the future of America's postwar design depended on the Bundesbank's readiness to print.

Irritable German central bankers saw in Chancellor Ludwig Erhard a loathsome figure. They considered him Washington's man, a politician who cared more about helping America stabilize Bretton Woods (and fending off de Gaulle's overtures) than the Bundesbank's crusade to keep the lid on German prices, which they feared would escalate if they were forced to print more money. Harboring long memories and packing sharp knives, they had never forgiven Erhard for having (while finance minister, in 1961) overruled their objections to an American request that the deutsche mark be revalued.[57]

So what did these Bundesbank men do? In a move more reminiscent of a banana republic than a European democracy, Germany's central bank engineered a sharp recession to oust the government. How did the Bundesbank do that? Simple. It curtailed the capacity of commercial banks to issue business and household loans. This cap on liquidity sufficed to reduce economic activity, tighten up the labour market and cause a short recession that the electorate blamed on Erhard's government. And how do we know this? We know because the Bundesbank's president, Karl Blessing, admitted to it years later.

Without a smidgeon of regret he said that "we had to use brute force to put things in order."[58] By "order," Herr Blessing meant the accession to the chancellery of Georg Kiesinger, another former member of the Nazi party, who led a grand Right-Left coalition government that granted the Bundesbank, courtesy of the new administration's weakness, a great deal more freedom to drag its feet in defense of the Bretton Woods system.

In the three-year period that followed the Bundesbank's "putsch," a dual monarchy arose. Christian Democrats (the Right) and Social Democrats (the Left) ruled together[59] as part of a national unity effort to overcome a recession that their central bank had caused in its bid to oust Erhard and usher them in. To this effect, they came up with the so-called Stability and Growth Pact, a blueprint for recovery that was based on a simple logic: wage restraint (to keep German inflation lower than France's, Britain's and America's) and a push to export more. Within a year, the Stability and Growth Pact had borne fruit. Germany recovered, as German exports flooded France, Britain and the United States, at the expense of everyone else, further destabilizing the Bretton Woods system.[60]

Meanwhile, west of the Rhine, France was at boiling point. De Gaulle knew that his grip over organized labor was minuscule compared to that of the German elites who had incorporated trade unions not only into government (courtesy of the Social Democrats' participation in it) but also in the boardrooms where unionists took their seats next to company directors, delivering "wage restraint" in return for power. De Gaulle imagined that by adopting hard money, either the gold or the deutsche mark "standard" would bolster the French state and weaken the leftist riffraff. However, as Germany had refused his overtures and the return to the gold standard was just rhetoric, de Gaulle was stuck in a morass of uncontrolled inflation and rising discontent. In a last stand against the tide, he ordered Giscard d'Estaing to tighten the monetary reins in a bid to make the franc stronger,[61] more deutsche mark–like.

The result was the worst of both worlds: employment in France shrunk, prices continued to rise, the French-German trade balance went deeper into the red and speculators kept borrowing francs to buy deutsche marks in anticipation of one more Waterloo for the franc. As we've seen, in May 1968 French students led an uprising that was to mark a generation and cause de Gaulle the greatest embarrassment possible, as the French strongman had to flee Paris and seek refuge in Germany. Even though, with his army's support, he managed to hold on to the presidency, a year later he resigned, passing the baton on to his deputy, Georges Pompidou.

In one of President Pompidou's first interviews, when asked to comment on France's economic weakness relative to Germany, his disturbing answer was, "The Germans have their Deutsche Mark and we have our bombinette," meaning their nuclear capability.[62] Clearly, the French establishment had bowed to a German financial dominance that was, to them, as inescapable as it was abominable, hoping that France's nuclear weapons would counteract its economic inferiority.

A few months later, in September 1969, Germany was to have a general election. Speculators sensed that the next government would have to revalue the deutsche mark in order to restore a modicum of balance in European trade. So they borrowed from anyone who would lend them dollars, francs, liras or even gold to buy marks. A wall of money invaded Germany, threatening the inflation-phobic nation with rising prices. The Right-Left administration shut down the stock exchange and the financial system for four days, hoping to stem the tide.

The election result was mixed. While the Christian Democrats won most votes, Willy Brandt's Social Democrats increased their vote more than any other party and would go on to stake a claim to government in alliance with the small Free Democratic Party. While this deal was being hammered out, the caretaker Kiesinger government had to figure out what to do with the money markets. The Social Democrats in the cabinet surprised everyone by suggesting that the government should bite the bullet and revalue the mark handsomely; this was the equivalent of a British Labour Party leader today advocating more austerity than what the Tories want or an American Democrat advocating for a reduction in Social Security deeper than the Tea Party's proposals. Social democrats were, indeed, known for their reluctance to harm the export industries on which their largest constituency (i.e., the industrial working class) relied. And yet, on this occasion, they proposed a large devaluation of the German currency.

Kiesinger balked, worried that German industrialists, and assorted exporters, would rise up against him.

During the standoff, the vice president of the Bundesbank, Otmar Emminger, came up with an intriguing compromise: "Do nothing. Just relieve us, silently, from the obligation to defend the dollar's value!" Exhausted, the politicians gave the Bundesbank the go-ahead: Bretton Woods would be set aside, even if only temporarily, the Bundesbank would be allowed to give the deutsche mark printing presses a rest, while the deutsche mark would float into uncharted waters.[63]

WHEN THE MARKETS opened, the mark began to rise while the Bundesbank, in gross violation of its Bretton Woods obligations, sat on its hands. For a whole month, until the new Brandt administration was in place, the Bundesbank allowed the German currency to rise in relation to the dollar but intervened to restrain its rise in relation to the franc, so as to sustain German exports into France. Paris was furious while Washington remained nonchalant. Giscard d'Estaing sent fiery missives to Bonn and to Frankfurt, blaming the Germans for tearing up the postwar monetary order and jeopardizing the European Union.

Washington's initial hesitancy to scold Bonn resulted from a certain relief occasioned by the temporary lull in the pressure to defend the dollar: as the mark rose, stemming the flow of dollars into Germany and limiting American purchases of Mercedes-Benz automobiles, the Fed could relax a little. Soon, however, the Nixon administration came to see the mark's unilateral flotation as an aggressive act. Even though Bonn was eager to explain that the float was temporary and that the deutsche mark would only be allowed to crawl for a while until it was locked back (at a higher value) into its proper Bretton Woods station, it was clear that putting the genie back into the bottle would be very hard indeed.

BRITAIN AND FRANCE were on their knees. The mark's rise was not fast enough to rebalance their trade with Germany. Volkswagens and Siemens washing machines were now dearer in London and in Lyon but not sufficiently so to make a significant dent in Germany's trade surplus. However, the impressive rise in the deutsche mark, and the realization that authorities had not intervened to stop its free-floating ascent for the first time since the 1940s, led rich people with money to spare to predict that the deutsche mark would rise further. Seeking to take advantage of this new trend, they sent their cash to Germany, causing an exodus of money from Paris and London to Frankfurt.

Faced with an increasingly impossible situation, Giscard d'Estaing remembered his 1964 trip to Bonn and issued fresh calls for a common currency, only this time (freed from General de Gaulle) he wanted it to include other European nations in the deliberations. Bonn repeated its sensible argument that a common currency would have to be preceded by political integration that France would not fathom.

Indeed, this pattern was to repeat itself again and again in the 1970s, the 1980s, the 1990s, indeed to this day: Paris would call for a monetary union and the German government would agree on condition of a political union that would allow it to control French government expenditure. Even after the monetary union was implemented, and especially once the euro began to feel the heat of its crisis, the same disagreement carried on. I have firsthand experience, circa 2015, of heated arguments between French and German top officials along precisely these lines. Indeed, it is clear to me, as a result of these encounters, that the euro crisis is being kept on the boil because Paris and Berlin cannot agree on this fundamental issue (for more on this, see chapter 4), and as part of Berlin's strategy to get Paris to accept supervision of its national budget.

RETURNING FOR NOW to March 1971, the world of finance woke up one morning to unbelievable news: the Federal Republic of Germany was holding more foreign reserves, in dollars, yen, etc. than the US government did. Merely two and a half decades after Secretary

Byrnes's Speech of Hope, which marked America's decision to allow Germany to bounce back, Germany had overtaken its much larger and richer benefactor, the US government, in the amount of foreign money, including dollars, it possessed.

The news startled the world, elevated German economic power to mythical status and played a psychological role in speeding up capital's flight into Germany. The expectation that America would have to give up on its pledge to redeem one ounce of its gold for a pitiful $35 grew even stronger, convincing speculators that gold's dollar price was about to explode. Dollars were swapped for gold in droves. And when traders could not find enough gold to buy, convinced that the dollar was doomed, they even started swapping their dollars for francs and pounds. Paris and London found themselves with a new stash of dollars, even though they were continuing to lose ground to Germany.

On May 9, 1971, Chancellor Brandt attempted to steady President Pompidou's nerves with a handwritten letter restating his unwavering personal commitment to "the establishment of [European] economic and monetary union." Pompidou was not convinced.[64] At the same time that Brandt was reassuring him, Pompidou had it on good authority that the Bundesbank was preparing to refloat the mark, as it had done in 1969. The consequences of this would be terribly destabilizing for both France and Britain. As the summer was approaching, Paris asked of the Americans that its newfound dollar stash be swapped for gold. Washington was livid. So, when on August 11, 1971, London joined in, requesting that $3 billion of its own euro-dollar stash be swapped for American gold, Paul Volcker told John Connally, who immediately agreed, that it was time to persuade President Nixon to throw the book at the Europeans. On August 15, the Europeans heard the news: it was game over.[65]

A CLOSE FRIEND of mine once told me that, upon informing her father she was getting married, he responded by asking, "Against whom?"—exactly in the spirit of de Gaulle's 1964 monetary marriage proposal to the Federal Republic of Germany. Lacking the economic might to subdue German industry and the Bundesbank in a straight tussle, France was to offer its hand in monetary matrimony instead.

France always envisaged a monetary union against, rather than with, Germany. That this was not just one of de Gaulle's fixations has been confirmed repeatedly since then. Possibly the best example occurred on September 18, 1992, soon after France and a reunited Germany had agreed to create a common currency: the euro. French conservative daily *Le Figaro* had this to say on its front page: "In the 1920s it was said that Germany would pay reparations. Now Germany is paying. The Maastricht Treaty[66] is a Versailles Treaty without war!"[67]

German officials knew it in 1964, as they knew it in 1992: for the French elites, a common currency with Germany was an attempt to neuter Germany, indeed to conquer the Bundesbank without firing a single shot. German decision makers, especially Bundesbank officials, would never allow themselves to forget that.

But why did Germany eventually agree to a monetary union knowing full well that it was part of a French strategy aimed against it? Conventional wisdom has it that Chancellor Helmut Kohl bowed to French demands for monetary union as the price for German reunification.

Though this was not an insignificant consideration, the answer lies elsewhere: it lies in the naked truth that Germany's export-led economy could never afford its own genuinely free-floating currency. The reason is simple: if the deutsche mark's international value were to be determined freely in boisterous money markets, Germany's surpluses would create demand for Germany's money and that would push up its value until German goods became so expensive abroad that German surpluses would disappear. The ambition to remain a surplus nation could not be served by a free-floating deutsche mark.

While the mark was embedded in America's global plan, and its value was fixed within the Bretton Woods international monetary system, German leaders and officials could behave like the managers of a beautiful workshop. Of Europe's gleaming factory. They could, in such a world, concentrate solely on making sturdy cars and impressive gadgets, letting America mind global capitalism. Exactly as the United States had planned things in the late 1940s.

Alas, once the United States jettisoned Bretton Woods, and Europe along with it, German leaders could no longer treat the global environment like they treated the weather; that is, as a natural system impervious to their actions and beliefs. They had to concede that the international economic environment was no longer divinely ordered and independent of what they decided. They had, in other words, to do something to shape that international environment in ways consistent with Germany's continued economic success.

Reluctant to think globally or to try to shape the world in their image, German officials took the minimalist position: they surmised that a European Bretton Woods might suffice as a substitute to the American original. And if such a European monetary system could be made to work in the interests of German industry, the common currency that Paris was going on and on about might, eventually, become acceptable to them. But only after they had crushed France's ambitions to remain in the coachman's seat while German industry did all the pulling.[68]

CHAPTER 3

TROUBLED PILGRIMS

On a dull autumnal afternoon, two men in suits exuding immense authority entered Aachen's Cathedral. They were there to pay their respects to the remains of Charlemagne, the ninth century Frankish king who had briefly reunited the Roman Empire and whose spirit encapsulated, at least for traditionalist Central Europeans, the longing for a borderless Christian European realm: Mitteleuropa or Paneuropa, as they variably called it.

Standing above the Christian warrior's grave, and next to his ancient throne, the two men sought to quell their considerable trepidation caused by what they had just done: commit their two countries, France and Germany, to bundle their money together. Earlier that day, on the morning of September 15, 1978, they had signed a bilateral agreement to create the so-called European Monetary System (EMS)—the euro's precursor.[1]

"Perhaps while we were discussing monetary affairs," said one of the two pilgrims to an Italian journalist that same afternoon, "the spirit of Charlemagne brooded over us."[2] His name? Valéry Giscard d'Estaing, the finance minister President de Gaulle had dispatched to Bonn in March 1964 to startle the German government with a proposal for immediate currency union, and who was now the proud occupant of the Elysée Palace, France's twentieth president. The second pilgrim appealing to Charlemagne's ghost for its approval of the monetary union with France was German chancellor Helmut Schmidt, a social democrat with a commitment to a United States of Europe as strong as Giscard's.[3]

Acerbic Eurosceptics, especially those of an Anglo-Saxon persuasion,[4] dismiss Giscard's and Schmidt's visit to Charlemagne's resting place as another example of Euro kitsch; as a piece of Central

European soap opera intended to win over the support of traditionalist French and German voters. Anyone who has watched a Eurovision song contest will recognize familiar elements of cheesiness in the notion that the president of France and the chancellor of Germany felt the need to visit the tomb of an ancient king to get his blessing for their attempt at a monetary union. While subsequent statements that Charlemagne's spirit instilled in them the idea of a European central bank[5] stretch credulity beyond breaking point, there is no doubt that the two men had good cause to be very, very worried. Lesser fear has been known to drive significant men to quainter pilgrimages.

Giscard was haunted by the memory of France's late exit from a previous catastrophic experiment with monetary union: the midwar gold standard. Unlike Britain, which had unshackled herself in 1931 from the asphyxiating stranglehold of a fragmenting gold standard, and unlike the United States, which followed Britain in early 1933, France had held on to the bitter end—until 1936. The result was that its economy was crushed by recession,[6] its politics became chaotic as a result and the whole nation so weakened that it could not resist the invasion of Nazi Germany,[7] suffering ignominious defeat. Of course, monetary union with Germany was Giscard's own idea, which he had unsuccessfully taken to Bonn in 1964. Still, as a thoughtful man, Giscard must have been painfully aware that the most vengeful of gods grant us our sincerest of wishes. Would France do better in this fresh monetary union than it had done between the wars? Had he just agreed to an institution that might lose France without winning a united Europe spanning Charlemagne's imperium? I would not be surprised if Giscard did indeed say a little prayer that afternoon appealing to Charlemagne's spirit.

Helmut Schmidt was also a seriously worried man. The memory of what had happened to Chancellor Ludwig Erhard in 1966 weighed heavily upon him. For if the Bundesbank felt justified to engineer a recession to oust a chancellor, during the relative calm of the mid-1960s, for the heinous crime of having disagreed with it once on the deutsche mark's exchange rate to the dollar,[8] Schmidt had good reason to shiver at the thought of how the Bundesbank would react if it were to get a whiff of what he had been up to with Giscard since the previous April. Indeed, Schmidt had kept both the Bundesbank and his own cabinet in the dark about their European monetary system plan, lest it be scuttled. It would not be surprising if, standing above Charlemagne's grave, Schmidt said a little prayer too, along the lines of, "Please, Charlemagne, let the Bundesbank not pounce on me, thinking that I am turning its authority over German money into a dowry for the French."

A SERPENT SLITHERS IN A WORLD UNHINGED

Terrible earthquakes drive snakes out in the open, causing them to slither in a daze until the tectonic plates have settled again. The Nixon Shock had been such an earthquake. It caused burgeoning fault lines to appear in Europe out of which, almost immediately, there emerged a noteworthy serpent. The so-called snake was Europe's initial reaction to the collapse of the Bretton Woods system.

As the dollar began to plummet, and the deutsche mark soared, Europe's currencies were destined to be torn apart. Some managed to keep up with the mark; others followed the dollar's plunge enthusiastically. If nothing were done to glue them back together soon, German exporters would be up in arms. Their cars and washing machines were turning prohibitively expensive in Britain, in Italy and in France where a different discontent was taking root: anger at rising prices and falling living standards.

Prior to 1971, Europe had been lulled into a false sense of American-managed stability. European nations had become used to postwar money underpinned by the greenback and varying only very slightly in value from one European country to another. The institutions of the European Union were also calibrated to function under the assumption that all European currencies moved gradually together, like boats rising or falling as the economic tide comes in and goes out, only very occasionally rocked by some wayward surge.

So, when in 1971 Europe was jettisoned from the "dollar zone," and exchange rates between European currencies bopped up and down crazily, some of them falling as violently as others were rising, the European Union had real trouble managing the heavy industry cartel as well as the common agricultural policy that were its core. Without stable steel, coal and agricultural prices across France, Germany, Belgium, the Netherlands, France and Italy, cartel-like price fixing was impossible. And without that Central European cartel, the European Union would lose its raison d'être, descending into price wars that would undo the established distribution of political power, soon to be followed by the disbanding of Brussels bureaucracies, open antagonism between European capitals and unregulated social tumult in a continent that was struggling to put behind it a tumultuous past.

It was in response to this that Europe's so-called snake in a tunnel would be born. The idea behind it was to simulate the fixed exchange rates of Bretton Woods within Europe. While Europe could do nothing to convince Washington to rehinge its currencies to the dollar, its leaders began to imagine that European currencies could be glued together, pegged on the continent's dominant deutsche mark. So it was that in 1972 European Union countries, including Britain, Ireland, Denmark and Norway,[9] agreed to restrict the fluctuations of the exchange rates between their currencies around extremely tight constraints.[10] To describe this quasi-fixed exchange rate system, the unfortunate metaphor of a snake in a tunnel was employed, to convey the idea that each exchange rate (between, say, the franc and the deutsche mark) would be allowed to slither up and down within a very confined space.

Europe's snake wriggled along happily in its tunnel for a few months. Its main body was the surplus economies centered on Germany, its tail comprising deficit nations like France, Italy, Britain and Ireland. Alas, when the dollar price of oil exploded in 1973, the snake's tail fell off like a lizard's tail in times of trouble.

The reason the snake could not hold on to its tail was the same as the cause behind Bretton Woods' demise: in the absence of some Leviathan recycling surpluses to parts of the system that nursed debilitating deficits, nations in deficit could not sustain a fixed exchange rate with the rest, especially in times of crisis. To remain within Europe's monetary snake, a country nursing a trade deficit, France for example, faced the immediate task of attracting foreign money to finance its net imports. Foreign money is attracted by high interest rates and deterred by the prospect that the state will not be able to pay its bills or repay its creditors. In other words, to stay in the snake, Paris would have to make borrowing dearer and, at once, reduce public spending. But dearer money would reduce investment by French business, which would, in turn, depress employment and private incomes. And if, on top of that, government spending were also reduced to steady foreign investors' nerves, overall spending (private plus public) would diminish. But what does overall spending equal? National income of course. In short, for France, as for Britain, Italy and Ireland, to have stayed in the snake, they would have had to crush their economies.[11]

Leaving the snake was not much fun either. It meant devaluing the currency, in relation to the deutsche mark, pushing up not only the price of Volkswagens in the deficit countries but also the prices of imported machinery that made Britain's National Health Service function, Alstom nuclear reactors run, Fiat cars accelerate and the trains arrive on time. Led by rising import prices, including oil, the specter of generalized inflation threatened to infuriate organized labor and farmers, a combined oeuvre the French establishment has lived in terror of since the 1780s.

Given the rotten choice between pulverizing one's economy and invoking social conflicts caused by inflation, most governments—certainly Washington—would have opted for the lesser evil of inflation than what would result from leaving the snake. That was certainly Britain's position. However, across the English Channel in France another priority occupied the establishment's collective will: saving what was, for the elites at any rate, a fabulously lucrative Central European cartel and its large multinational bureaucracy in Brussels.

Of course, no economic imperative partial to the interests of a relatively small elite can automatically prevail over the interests of a large majority. To do so, there needs to be a dominant ideology that permits the elites to co-opt the rest, to present their own vested interests on the broader canvas of some General Will. The European Ideal was, and remains, such an ideology. The image of Charlemagne is, in this context, not as kitsch and insignificant as it may seem to those residing outside Central Europe.

The European ideal, undoubtedly powerful and worthy in its own terms, offered politicians in Paris and Rome a glittering ideological veil with which to disguise an underlying determination to do whatever it took not to cut themselves off the gravy train of power and funding that the cartel's political-administrative arm offered. Even if it meant a sharp, painful recession for their domestic economy, the national politicians of countries intertwined inextricably with the cartel could usually be counted upon to keep their nations permanently attached to it.

Which begs the question, Why was it that, in the event, the French, the Belgian, the Dutch, the Italian elites abandoned Europe's first monetary union experiment, the snake, relatively quickly? Was it the economic cost it was imposing upon their populations, especially on laborers with no unearned income? Judging by the tenacity with which they held on to more recent reincarnations of the snake,[12] this is a most unlikely explanation.

An more convincing explanation has to do with the snake's failure to offer worthy job prospects to the ambitious graduates of France's grandes écoles and other alumni of various European nurseries bringing up the next generation of Brussels-based bureaucrats. The snake came with no new institutions dedicated to it; there were no buildings with its logo, no army of bureaucrats whose livelihood and perks relied on it, no impressive titles for functionaries whose life's work would be to sing the serpent's praises. In short, the snake was unloved by the elites and thus doomed from the start. Within a year of its birth, it had lost its tail and what was left of it was next to useless for Germany, a living humiliation for France and an embarrassing nuisance for Brussels's technocrats.

The European Monetary System that Giscard and Schmidt brought into being in 1978 to replace the deceased snake did more than invoke Charlemagne's spirit in Europe's monetary universe: it came complete with new jobs and opportunities for Brussels's bureaucracy. Unlike the snake, which had generated no new institutional "innovations," the EMS required central management from Brussels bureaucrats who would run it in conjunction with bureaucrats in the great capitals of Europe—a mouth-watering prospect for elites seeking a greater vista on which to unleash their powers.

A PECULIARLY DECENT PROPOSAL

Five months before the Aachen pilgrimage,[13] Helmut Schmidt had met with Roy Jenkins, then president of the European Commission and a former Labour Party government minister. In that meeting, Schmidt confided to Jenkins that, if the French Left were to lose the following month's parliamentary elections, as the German social democrat hoped they would, he would propose "a major step towards monetary union; to mobilize and put all our currency reserves in a common pool . . . to form a monetary bloc."[14]

The difference between such a monetary bloc and the bygone snake could not be more pronounced. A monetary mechanism or bloc, like the proposed EMS, would need to have new rules and a bureaucracy to impose it. Just like Bretton Woods was built upon the IMF, and to a lesser extent the World Bank, so the EMS would require a bureaucracy that pooled the foreign exchanges of the participating central banks together, coordinated their deployment and, hopefully, stabilized the exchange rates. Supranational bureaucrats were clearly necessary, with the power to make these decisions outside the confines of national governments. Brussels all of a sudden got a whiff of a new source of power: power over the member states' foreign exchange reserves and interest rates.

This was, in fact, a major shift in the German chancellor's attitude. Only a few months before he had said "yes to monetary union but not if it meant German inflation going to 8 percent." What did Schmidt mean by this condition regarding German inflation? The chancellor was, sensibly, alluding to Germany's fear of a repeat performance of the Bretton Woods final years when, to stabilize the franc, the Bundesbank had to keep printing deutsche marks; an unavoidable response to the tendency of the French franc to devalue, courtesy of Germany's trade surplus in relation to France.[15]

The only way the franc's deutsche mark value could be kept constant was, indeed, for the Bundesbank to keep doing the one thing it detested: to incessantly buy francs using freshly minted deutsche marks. Were these marks to remain stashed in the vaults of the French central bank, or anywhere for that matter, the Bundesbank would not have minded much. Only these creaseless German banknotes did not stay under lock and key but were steadily repatriated into Germany, as the French used them to buy more Volkswagens and speculators converted their francs into marks convinced that, at some point, the Bundesbank would let the franc slide, netting them a substantial windfall. And why would the Bundesbank let the franc slide? Because the repatriated deutsche marks were increasing the quantity of money circulating in Germany, pushing prices up and causing inflation in a nation that despised rising prices with all its heart; a nation that trusted the Bundesbank to prevent this from happening.

Schmidt's fear that a monetary bloc, a fixed exchange rate regime between France and Germany, would lead to increasing German prices and Bundesbank apprehension was conventional wisdom in Bonn and in Frankfurt. Pegging the franc on the mark could easily return the Bundesbank and the federal government to the situation they so loathed back in the 1960s: having to print German banknotes to prop up the French currency, with Paris constantly pressuring Germany to print more while at the same time chastising Bonn for not being a good European citizen.

Nonetheless, true to his word, when the French Right, Giscard's ruling coalition, unexpectedly won that election on April 2, 1978, Schmidt met Giscard in Rambouillet and told him of his change of heart. Giscard's face lit up and, together, they plotted the next steps that led them, a few months later, to paying Charlemagne's tomb a visit, after first signing the Franco-German EMS accord. Which begs several questions:

What caused Helmut Schmidt to make Giscard the peculiarly generous proposal he had mentioned in passing to Roy Jenkins? Were there new grounds for adopting Giscard's 1964 idea, the very one Chancellor Erhard had unceremoniously rejected? Was there a reason that the proposal was conditional on a defeat of the French Left? And where did he find the courage to go behind the Bundesbank's back and risk invoking its fury?

Chancellor Schmidt was a committed Europeanist, without a doubt. This explains why he wanted monetary, economic and political union, though not necessarily in that order. But it does not explain his sudden change of heart, his setting aside of inflation jitters and his apparently careless disregard of a potentially vengeful Bundesbank. To understand his generous offer to the French president one needs to recall that Schmidt was, in addition to being Europeanist, also a committed Atlanticist.

While talking to the French and arguing with the British, Schmidt's eyes were trained on the other side of the Atlantic, tuned in to the ways that the postwar hegemon, who had shaped postwar Europe, was deploying its extensive means to achieve its undiminished hegemonic ends. Schmidt set aside his reluctance to risk German inflation, and to upset the Bundesbank, because of a historic development that he thought made the creation of the European Monetary System timely: the birth of a new type and a new era of American financial predominance that would establish itself in the 1980s and beyond.

THAT "GODDAMN" VOLCKER, AGAIN

The year was 1960. Postwar American monetary supremacy, in the form of the Bretton Woods system, was rock solid. One morning, a young Chase Manhattan banker was startled when an aide stormed into his office with terrible news: "Gold rose to forty dollars!" In a world made in America's image, where gold was supposedly fixed ad infinitum at $35 an ounce, the news struck Paul Volcker, the young banker of our story, as apocalyptic. On that day, Volcker got it: the Bretton Woods system was on its way out. Would American postwar hegemony perish with it? Not necessarily, he surmised.

As the 1960s were running out of puff, youngsters all over the world were rebelling against the uneasy affluence Bretton Woods had brought and reveling with every sign of its faltering. The Paris 1968 rebellion, Woodstock even, were political and cultural echoes of a global system in trouble. By then, Volcker had already risen through the ranks of successive Democratic and Republican administrations to become instrumental in the dismantling of the Bretton Woods system.[16]

The 1971 announcement of the Nixon Shock may be remembered in John Connally's Texan accent but it was "probably that goddamn Volcker," as President Nixon once referred to Paul, whose intellectual and technical work underpinned it. Volcker's concern and purpose? To ensure that the demise of the Bretton Woods system, made inescapable by America's slide from surplus to deficit nation status, should bestow more power upon the United States of America, not less.

A few short weeks after Giscard and Schmidt had made a pilgrimage to Charlemagne's tomb, having signed the Franco-German European Monetary System agreement, Volcker gave a momentous speech to students and staff at the University of Warwick.[17] It was November 9, 1978, seven years after the Nixon Shock, and Volcker addressed his audience in his capacity as president of the New York Federal Reserve. Ten months later, President Carter was to appoint him chairman of the Federal Reserve system, giving him an opportunity to put into practice what he preached in Warwick.

Volcker's Warwick speech[18] is relatively unknown but it must surely go down as probably the most significant ever in central banking history.[19] "It is tempting to look at the market as an impartial arbiter," Volcker said adopting a phrase so banal that even first-year economics students might have yawned at it. Of course the sting was in the word "tempting," as Volcker is not a man often tempted by blandness. His next sentence was crafted to prove this, packing a degree of brute honesty that central bankers are not known for: "But balancing the requirements of a stable international system against the desirability of retaining freedom of action for national policy, a number of countries, including the US, opted for the latter."

And as if such unbridled veracity were insufficient, Volcker added a phrase equivalent to undermining all the assumptions on which Western Europe and Japan had erected their postwar economic miracles:

"[A] controlled disintegration in the world economy is a legitimate objective for the 1980s."

It was a fitting epitaph for the Bretton Woods system and the clearest exposition of the second postwar phase that was dawning and which Volcker had been busily working toward. But why would a "disintegration in the world economy," even if "controlled," help the United States in the 1980s?

Volcker had been trying to answer the questions he had asked himself in 1960, when out of the blue the price of gold shot up to $40. How could America retain its hegemony once it went into deficit in relation to Japan, Germany and, later, China? If the United States had no surpluses to recycle, how could it dominate global capitalism? It took Volcker some time to develop a fully fledged answer. By 1978 he was ready to present it to his Warwick audience, just before moving from the powerful New York Federal Reserve to the almighty Fed.

The essence of his Warwick University lecture was, if America cannot recycle its surplus, having slipped into a deficit position back in the mid-1960s, it must now recycle other people's surpluses! But how, one may reasonably ask, can a deficit nation recycle other nations' surpluses? Surely those with the money, the surplus owners, have the power to do as they please with it, paying next to no attention to the musings of those in deficit. Usually, but not always, thought Volcker.

The trick for America to gain the power to recycle other countries' surpluses in the 1980s, Volcker believed, was to persuade foreign capitalists to voluntarily send their capital to Wall Street. Tricky but not impossible. The trick was to hit two usually contradictory targets at once: on the one hand, push American interest rates through the roof while on the other, ensuring that Wall Street offered a more lucrative market for investors than its equivalents in London, Frankfurt, Tokyo, Paris or anywhere else.

High interest rates are wonderful for those living on unearned income, the so-called rentiers,[20] but not so good for manufacturers who see their investment costs skyrocket and the purchasing power of their customers plummet. For this reason, combining high returns to financial capital (requiring high interest rates) with high profit rates for

American businesses (requiring low interest rates) was never going to be easy, and Volcker knew this. It was a combination that could only come about if another way of providing that profit could be found. And one way to do that would be to reduce wages. On the one hand, the Fed would push interest rates through the roof while, at once, the federal government would turn a blind eye, indeed promote, policies that crushed the real wage prospects of American workers.

For the first time in American history, including the Great Depression,[21] American blue-collar workers were to face an age of declining real wages. That secular decline, in a global economy buffeted by the "controlled disintegration" Volcker unashamedly spoke of, was the price poorer Americans were to pay so that the United States could maintain world dominance despite being a deficit nation. Soon, the fate of America's working class was to infect the circumstances of weak citizens in Britain, in France and, by the 1990s, even in Germany. As for Africa and Latin America, the weak there suffered losses that only the great novelists can begin to recount.

Once ensconced as chairman of the Federal Reserve, Volcker lost little time in putting his plan into action. Dollar interest rates topped 20 percent, American inflation was defeated, the Third World went bankrupt, Africa's sputtering industrialization ended, Soviet satellites that had borrowed heavily from the West in greenbacks (such as Yugoslavia, Poland and Romania) failed and workers everywhere were forced into a race-to-the-bottom, having to choose between undercutting the wages of workers living elsewhere and unemployment.

Disintegration was in the air and the majority of people in a majority of countries eventually acquiesced to the notion that labor was overvalued and overprotected, manufacturing was overrated, while finance was undervalued and in need of "unshackling." Everything became increasingly reducible to its financial value. Manufacturers of note, like General Motors in America and Cadbury's chocolate makers in Britain, were reduced to their stock exchange value, losing their place in the public conscience as venerable institutions. Engineers lost out to young, brash MBA graduates who, despite their striking inexperience, rose up to lead giants like Ford and General Electric.

Workers were financialized too, as they were forced to take increasing risks in the housing market and with their pensions. The new mantra that "there is no alternative," TINA in short, had been born, soon to be given an ideological wrap by Margaret Thatcher in Britain and Ronald Reagan in the United States. Financially stressed citizens, made so by their lack of access to capital goods and unearned income, were facing an onslaught they had not experienced since the 1930s; an onslaught that New Deal and Great Society programs in the United States and the social contract implicit in the European Union's cartelized economy had, supposedly, made impossible in the postwar era.

In continental Europe, a borderless cartelized economy comprising different currency jurisdictions faced special challenges. Volcker's "disintegration" inserted the thin edge of a large wedge into its flesh. With every interest rate rise, every jolt of divergence in the value of the currencies of surplus and deficit European nations, the Europe that America had built up in the late 1940s was torn apart. Central European politicians, like Schmidt and Giscard, held on to the hope that their European Monetary System could act as the cement that kept their postwar realities together. History was to prove them badly mistaken.

NOT BY CHOICE

History has no time for the democratic process. It simply surges ahead like a steamroller bent on flattening our collective preferences. Occasionally this is a good thing. If Europeans living under feudalism had been asked to choose the coming of the industrial revolution over their feudal bonds, they would have almost certainly declined. The collapse of Bretton Woods was not such a development. Even Paul Volcker, who had played a major role in its demise, would have preferred it to survive. And he would have been right.

Bretton Woods was meant as a balanced system of international trade and financial flows. America pursued the Cold War on behalf of a Western world that it both dominated and equilibrated. The New Deal that stabilized 1930s America, albeit imperfectly, was internationalized after the war, extending its righteous reach to the four corners of the so-called Western hemisphere.

The fact that inequality between and within nations shrank during Bretton Woods was a design feature.[22] As a result, in the 1950s and 1960s the poor, as the phrase goes, never had it so good, courtesy of a Leviathan keenly aware that its self-interest was best served by an enlightened equilibration of world capitalism—involving controls on finance, limits to all sorts of profiteering and the active redistribution of incomes to the have-nots.

Central to that global plan, of which Bretton Woods was the monetary component, was America's surplus position: the fact that the United States exited the war exporting a great deal more manufactures and agricultural products than it imported. To stabilize its global dominion it used its trade surplus judiciously, politically and hegemonically; fully aware of the profound difference between hegemony and authoritarianism. In that world, bankers like Paul Volcker were kept in a box.

During the 1950s and 1960s, American bankers were indeed forced to labor within strict confines set by the New Deal institutions. Their salaries were substantial but no more than six or at most seven times that of their building's janitor, compared to today's obscene factors of three hundred and beyond. They paid taxes at rates today's bankers would laugh at, and with no recourse to an archipelago of tax havens. Interest rates were fixed, at close to 5 percent, and opportunities for gambling with depositors' money were severely circumscribed by draconian restrictions harking back to Franklin Delano Roosevelt's administration.

Bretton Woods had kept Paul Volcker and his fellow bankers on a tight leash forged in the workshops of the Great Depression and designed to prevent another bout of 1920s-style "financialization"[23] (in which the trade in financial products outweighs all others, such that more profit is made from loans and debt than from capital) from wrecking capitalism again. It would be a grave error, however, to imagine that Volcker worked toward demolishing Bretton Woods because of these restrictions on his "liberty" to profit. Unfettered banking was not his thing. Indeed, Volcker was himself a New Dealer who cut his teeth defending, upholding and attempting to stabilize the Bretton Woods system. It was only when he was convinced that Bretton Woods' global balancing act was doomed by forces beyond America's control that his pragmatism kicked in.

Instead of going into the bunker to defend a system crumbling all over them, as Europeans habitually do, Volcker and many others of his ilk did what they knew best: they tried to overtake events, to lead them, to forge the next global financial system out of the debris of the one they blew up once they had realized that it was pointless trying to save it. Volcker symbolizes the self-confident American policy maker whose greatest fault is an unquestioning conviction that what is good for the United States is good for the world; a weakness compensated for with an astonishing capacity to look into the future and distinguish between that which is desirable from that which is feasible.

If Volcker had had a choice, he would have opted to repair and re-tain Bretton Woods, despite the restrictions it placed upon his banking activities. Why? Because he understood that true and sustainable he-gemony requires a rejection of the Athenian generals' logic in Thucy-dides's *Peloponnesian War*.[24] The New Dealers may have seemed unbear-ably arrogant in the eyes of Europeans like President de Gaulle but, nonetheless, they recognized a simple truth: that if "the weak suffer what they must," their very capacity, let alone willingness, to repro-duce the power of the strong declines precipitously.

CONDORCET'S LITTLE SECRET

Do the weak really reproduce the power of the mighty? Don't the strong do what they can, with no help from the weak for whom solace comes from a moralistic glorification of their misery?

In 1794, as the French Revolution was preparing to give its place to a new despotism, the French thinker Marquis de Condorcet (1795) alluded brilliantly to "the secret that real power lies not with the op-pressors but with the oppressed."[25] It was a point the New Dealers were painfully aware of but which European elites have still to grasp.

The power to accumulate trade surpluses, to amass a large part of the jointly produced wealth, to set the agenda; these are not forms of might that can be maintained for long on the basis of brute force or authoritarianism. Crushing those in deficit, when they cannot meet their obligations, is bound to destroy the surplus position of their stronger partners. Putting defaulters into debt prison guarantees that their debts will never get paid. Moreover, only when the weak have decent reasons to defend the system that reproduces their subservience does the empire of the powerful stand a chance to survive.

Volcker, like all New Dealers, harbored a deep appreciation of power's capacity to undermine itself, both at the level of a national economy and, even more so, internationally. He had seen in his youth how unbridled financialization led to the wholesale liquidation of capital and how unfettered international relations brought on the indiscriminate liquidation of millions of people in battlefields, in concentration camps, in the dustbowls of the Great Depression.

It is unlikely that Volcker had ever read Thucydides's account of the Melian representatives' speech, or indeed Marquis de Condorcet's insight. However, he was of a generation for whom the weak could be trampled upon only at the peril of the mighty. And yet by 1978 he had surmised that America's postwar attempt to create a system that protected the economically challenged citizens and nations was dead in the water.

To salvage the American way of life, and its global dominion, the world economy had to be "disintegrated" in a "controlled" fashion. And monetary policy, over which Paul Volcker was about to acquire decisive authority, was to be his weapon of mass disintegration.

VOLCKER'S GAUNTLET PICKED UP

Volcker felt a duty to raise interest rates to levels hitherto unknown in leading capitalist economies. The standard interpretation is that he was firing a silver bullet at the inflation bogeyman: by raising interest rates substantially he would encourage Americans to save. Since higher savings can only be achieved by cutting down on spending, consumers would reduce their demand for goods and services, thus causing a slowdown in price inflation. But this is a very small part of the story. Volcker's reasons were much deeper.

The postwar system that restrained admirably the exercise of financial power by the strong upon the weak, people and nations alike, was kaput. And it was so because America had lost its surplus—that great stabilizing instrument that had kept the postwar world order together.

When John Connally crudely explained to President Nixon, relying on Volcker's underlying analysis, that "all foreigners are out to screw us and it's our job to screw them first,"[26] what he meant was that the Bretton Woods balancing act was becoming imbalanced by the surpluses of countries like Germany and Japan.

Impervious to the global responsibility that comes with large trade surpluses, these foreigners were trying, childishly, to take advantage of the United States' commitment to global balance, the result being a complete collapse of the postwar equilibrium. Like immature children that know not what is good for them, European governments and Japan, sporting increasing surpluses, were taking advantage of America's difficulty in maintaining order with detrimental results for everyone. They had to be put in their place.

And put in their place they were, not once, not twice but three times. Once in 1971 when European currencies were jettisoned from the dollar zone, an event that today's journalists might have called "Eurexit." A second time with the oil crises of 1973 and 1979, which limited the cost advantage of European and Japanese industry vis-à-vis America's. And last, but not least, Volcker's interest rate hikes between 1979 and 1982 that hit Europe and Japan far, far more than they hit America's more tenacious economy, their effect being a stupendous collapse in economic activity as the cost of *not* sending one's capital to Wall Street skyrocketed.

Volcker's 1978 Warwick speech had given the Europeans ample warning. He effectively threw down the gauntlet to Bonn, Paris, London and Tokyo. Between the lines he was foreshadowing the second phase of America's postwar global dominance. In 1971, Volcker implicitly told his audience, America dismantled the monetary system whose integrity Europeans had foolishly undermined. Its next move would be to bring about a highly imbalanced global system that the United States controlled fully because, rather than in spite, of America's twin deficits (its trade deficit and its federal government budget deficit).

The price for that new system, which would extend America's dominance, was high: weak people and fragile countries were, once more, left to their own devices, suffering not what was globally optimal but that which they "must" in a world economy unrestrained by New Deal–like rules and institutions. Politics would become toxic, social solidarity would weaken, international relations would turn nastier, abject poverty would multiply in Latin America and Africa. Nonetheless, the United States was bound to emerge as a net beneficiary of this painful "disintegration," a thought that consoled Volcker for his hand in deconstructing the universalized version of the New Deal that had shaped him as a young man keen to devote his life to pubic service.[27]

The dawn of this new, less confident era was what made 1978 such a significant year, motivating Chancellor Schmidt to rethink the idea of the Franco-German monetary union initially proposed by Valéry Giscard d'Estaing in 1964. The new American global design, founded on a Washington-led "controlled disintegration" of international trade and banking, suddenly added appeal to the idea of an institutionalized, monetarily united Mitteleuropa.

Charlemagne's spirit was to get a postmodern spin as Chancellor Schmidt, with President Giscard in tow, was picking up Volcker's gauntlet.

A TRIUMPH OF OPTIMISM?

The European Monetary System was being born as Volcker readied his "controlled disintegration." The German chancellor diagnosed that, in Volcker's brave new financial world, the EMS might deliver more than just lucrative jobs for Central Europe's elite boys in fancy new Brussels directorates. Under the circumstances of America's new role, it was just possible that the EMS might work, proving more than another triumph of hope over experience.

Chancellor Schmidt knew that the Americans were about to put the global economy through the rapids of financialization, using US interest rates as the lever. Since Erhard's time, Bonn was always more tuned to Washington's ways, at least compared to self-satisfied Elysée officials for whom America was to be more scorned than second-guessed. While Giscard's team were besotted with the goings on in Brussels and absorbed with Germany's attitude to their plans, German officials were busily working out the likely impact of a monetary bloc that had to thrive within Volcker's new design.

The snake, they knew, failed for two reasons, each of which was perfectly capable of spelling its early demise. One reason was the lack of common institutions to pursue a common monetary policy. The EMS would have those, in the form of brand new Brussels "committees." The second, potentially more important, reason was the same that doomed Bretton Woods in the late 1960s: the absence of a mechanism for supporting the fixed exchange rates via recycling surpluses; that is, taking superprofits from the countries that produced (or least received) them and redirecting them to the deficit regions or nations.

The Bretton Woods system had had the institutions necessary to coordinate interest rates and the central banks' interventions in money markets. But this did not help alleviate the tensions between the Bundesbank and the German federal government after America had lost its capacity to regulate trade and financial flows through exporting its own surplus. Why would the EMS, even if it possessed the "right" institutions, succeed in the late 1970s and early 1980s where Bretton Woods had failed in the late 1960s?

Here is a thought that gave Chancellor Schmidt hope: if Volcker's global design could occasion a constant torrent of German capital gushing perpetually into Wall Street, maybe a monetary union with France could be made to work. "This time things might be different," was the optimistic prospect that explains, at least partly, Schmidt's change of heart. Was this optimism sensible prescience or pie-in-the-sky wishful thinking?

The 1980s, 1990s, even the noughties, confirmed that there was some sense in the optimism behind the EMS. Volcker's "disintegration," effected initially through sizeable interest rate increases, enabled the United States to accomplish a feat unique in history: to enhance the power of its empire by increasing its trade and budget deficits! Only American policy makers could have fathomed this. German bureaucrats would self-flagellate if their minds ever permitted such a thought to slip in. Faced with burgeoning twin deficits, they would immediately hit the fiscal and monetary brakes.

America's top policy makers decided to do the opposite: to boost the nation's deficits. "But who would pay for them?" the Calvinist might have asked. "The rest of the world!" Paul Volcker would retort. "How?" "By means of a permanent transfer of capital that rushed ceaselessly across the two great oceans to finance America's twin deficits" was the answer America's policy makers gave in practice, even if never in so many words.

While German officials would rather die than emulate America's designer profligacy, Helmut Schmidt's team could see an opening for a European Bretton Woods, an EMS, within this new phase of American deficit-driven dominance. The ever-expanding US deficits would operate like a giant vacuum cleaner, absorbing Germany's surplus goods and surplus capital. Under these conditions, there was a possibility that the French franc could be harmlessly pegged to the deutsche mark.[28]

As in the late 1960s, the Bundesbank would have to print deutsche marks to buy francs to stop the French currency's decline. But unlike in the late 1960s, German inflation was less of a threat with Volcker on the loose. The American vacuum cleaner, powered by Volcker's high interest rates, could now be counted upon to suck the fresh deutsche marks in, preventing them from making their way immediately from France back into Germany. The Federal Republic could thus, for a second time since Byrnes's 1946 Speech of Hope, look to America for assistance in cementing its position, and reputation, as Europe's powerhouse.

Chancellor Schmidt, in acceding to President Giscard d'Estaing's monetary union plans, could look forward to the benefits of stabilizing the European Union along the Franco-German axis, bolstering the Central European industrial cartel, and maintaining a constant demand for German industrial goods from France and the other Latin countries attached to it. And all that without the earlier worries of German inflation that enraged the Bundesbank.

That the Bundesbank's anger was not, in the end, averted, confirmed that Schmidt had good cause to be worried as he was putting his signature on the EMS agreement. Still, it was not totally wrong to anticipate that this time things might be different. Powered by America's deficits, the world's leading surplus economies, Germany, Japan and, later, China, kept churning out the goods that America absorbed. Almost 70 percent of European profits were being transferred back to the United States, in the form of capital flows to Wall Street. And what did Wall Street do with them? It financed the rise of financialization; a process which the French and German banks joined in enthusiastically.

The bankers' emancipation from their New Deal fetters was both a symptom and a prerequisite for the new phase of American dominance. Who else but the bankers could facilitate the vast capital transfers, the perpetual tsunami of capital, necessary to satiate American deficits that had to keep growing in order to maintain the illusion of what Ben Bernanke, one of Volcker's successors, named the Great Moderation? Fair-weather recycling, writ large, had taken over globally from the planned, political recycling that was the essence of the Bretton Woods system. Though this was never going to end well, it had the capacity to put the global economy on a spending spree that lasted three decades before crashing down in 2008.[29]

French and German banks participated joyfully in all this and, through their frenzied lending, underpinned Europe's attempt at monetary union—first the EMS, later the single currency. It was only in 2008 that Europe was to come face to face with the tremendous damage its bankers had done to the project of monetary union. Two years later, by 2010, the euro crisis was in full flight and Europe in disarray.

A TIMELESS BEAST

Once upon a time, as a famous Greek myth has it, the reign of King Minos secured peace, enabled trade to crisscross the high seas in bountiful ships and spread prosperity's benevolent reach to all corners of the known world. Alas, a terrible secret was buried deep inside the foundations of the good king's palace.

For inside the mazelike palace basement, known as the Labyrinth, there lived a creature as fierce as it was wretched. The product of the queen's incest with a sacred bull, the creature's intense loneliness was comparable only to the fear it inspired far and wide. The Minotaur, for this was the tragic beast's name, had a voracious appetite that only human flesh could satiate. And satiated the fiend had to be or the king's reign would be cut short by the gods' wrath.

Every now and then, a ship loaded with youngsters sailed from far away Athens, a city that Minos had subdued in battle. Bound for Crete, the ship delivered its human tribute to be devoured by the Minotaur. It was a gruesome but essential ritual for preserving the era's peace and for reproducing its prosperity.

The specter of the Minotaur, confined for millennia to mythology, emerged again to haunt Europe as Paul Volcker delivered his University of Warwick speech. Unwittingly, Volcker was presenting a narrative that bore a striking resemblance to the Cretan myth; both were accounts of how a terrible secret was to underpin a seemingly stable world order.[30]

More specifically, in both narratives, equilibrium and trade-based prosperity were built on tributes flowing from the periphery (Athens in mythological times, Europe and Asia in Volcker's version) into the seat of power (Crete and Wall Street respectively). These tributes kept feeding the story's menacing aberration, the Minotaur in one case, America's trade deficit in the other. It was as if Volcker was outlining the birth of a new, a global, Minotaur, its Labyrinth located deep in the guts of America's economy, taking the form of a US trade deficit devouring the rest of the world's net exports and keeping their industries humming nicely.

What to shrewd commentators looked like some "Great Moderation" was the most immoderate, least stable equilibrium the world economy had experienced. The common secret no one dared discuss openly was that the new global order depended on the constant inflation of America's twin deficits. In other words, the Great Moderation was riding on the thin walls of a constantly expanding gargantuan bubble.

The more US deficits grew the greater the Global Minotaur's appetite for Europe's and Asia's capital. Its truly global significance was due to its role in recycling financial capital (profits, savings, surplus money) through the international circuits that Wall Street had established. It kept the gleaming German factories busy. It gobbled up everything produced in Japan and, later, in China. And, to complete the circle, the foreign (and often the American) owners of these distant factories sent their profits, their cash, to Wall Street—a form of modern tribute to the Global Minotaur.

What do bankers do when such a tsunami of capital comes their way daily? When billions of dollars, net, run through their fingers every morning of each week? They find ways to make it breed on their behalf. Throughout the 1980s, the 1990s and all the way to 2008, Wall Street took in the daily influx of foreign capital and, on its back, built mountains of derivative trades which, in time, acquired the properties of private money.

Financialization, as we now call this process, was the critical by-product of maintaining, and enhancing, US dominance on the back of increasing trade imbalances and in the interest of financing America's ever-expanding twin deficits. It began as froth on top of the stream of profits flowing from Germany and Japan to Wall Street, once Volcker's "controlled disintegration" of the world economy was taking effect. But soon the froth took over, usurping the underlying stream of actual values, turning finance into the driver and industry into its servant.

Just like its mythological predecessor, our Global Minotaur kept the world economy going. Until, that is, in 2008 when the pyramids of private money built upon the Minotaur's feeding frenzy caved in under their own impossible weight. Europe's monetary system, born in 1978, was to suffer a terminal blow. America was to feel its impact too, but it was Europe's weakest link, Greece, that was flattened.

ATHENS PILGRIMAGE

The Greek dictatorship collapsed in the summer of 1974, at the end of my first year in high school. As our military regime melted away, the presidential airplane of Valéry Giscard d'Estaing was to carry a Greek politician, and personal friend of the French president, to Athens to take over the reins of government. Five years later, in 1979, and a year after the signing of the Franco-German European Monetary System agreement, the same airplane carried Giscard to Athens.

During the preceding night and day, the Greek authorities proved their capacity for brutal efficiency by completing at breakneck pace the multilane thoroughfare connecting the old airport to the center of Athens. It was a gesture for the French president's benefit toward Greece's modernizing intentions, for Giscard was visiting the Greek capital in order to sign the treaty by which a year later, in 1980, Greece would become of full member of the European Union.

Here is how Giscard was to relate to France's leading daily newspaper the reasons behind his pilgrimage to Athens in 1979, which marked Greece's entry into the European Union:

> Our partners were extremely reluctant. The country [Greece] was disorganized, its democracy had not yet solidified and it lacked a common border with any member-state. I took the decision emphasizing that we had to do this [induct Greece into the European Union] in order to reinforce democracy. And since at the time I held the rotating Presidency of the European Common Market, I signed the act by which Greece was admitted into the community on 28th May 1979 in Athens. The logic of my decision was purely political. It was imperative that Greece was supported after shedding dictatorship. But it also had symbolic importance. My education, the education of my generation, was based on the idea of democracy, of politics, all ideas that came from that country. To us, Greece is synonymous with civilization. In this sense, the idea that it would remain outside the gates of Europe was unbearable.[31]

Thirty-six years later, less than a month after I had become Greece's finance minister, Giscard was to give an interview to another French newspaper[32] to argue that, while "Greece belongs to the European Union," it should leave its monetary union—the single currency that was the "natural" conclusion of his, and Schmidt's, 1978 EMS treaty. Just as Volcker, Connally and Nixon began to think of Eurexit as the solution to the dollar zone's troubles, so today some of the pioneers of the eurozone are toying with "Grexit" as the common currency's fix.[33]

Clearly something had gone terribly wrong.

Irrespective of whether Giscard was right to bring Greece into the European Union in May 1979, or to advocate "Grexit" in February 2015, a splendid irony was unfolding: the monetary union he and Schmidt inaugurated in September 1978 first asphyxiated our government during the Spring of 2015 and, then, on July 12, 2015, with the Euro-Summit "Agreement" on Greece, unthinkingly crushed Greece's democracy; the very same democracy that Giscard had worked so hard to protect by bringing Greece into the European Union.

THE 1980s AND early 1990s were not kind to Europe's monetary system, as the next chapter confirms. The decade kicked off with a major global recession (1979–1982) that complicated the task of keeping Europe's currencies pegged to each other. And by the time some stability had returned, causing Europe to attempt to tighten its monetary union, a fresh recession in the early 1990s devastated it.

After almost two decades of trying and failing to fix their exchange rates, to create a European Bretton Woods following the Nixon Shock, a stark choice was foisted on Europe's leaders: Abandon monetary union altogether. Or go all out, turning a system of many currencies with quasi-fixed exchange rates into a single currency: the euro.

At that juncture, between 1991 and 1993 to be precise, it was Giscard's and Schmidt's direct successors, President François Mitterrand of France and Chancellor Helmut Kohl of Germany, who were the driving force behind the euro project. Mitterrand's former finance minister, Jacques Delors, by then an all-powerful president of the European Commission, warned Mitterrand that a proper monetary union required more than "rules" and Brussels-based committees. At the very least, it required some common public debt (as Alexander Hamilton, the first secretary of the treasury, argued at the founding of the United States) and a common investment policy (as the New Dealers knew well).

Mitterrand's reaction circa 1993 was typically nuanced: yes, he acknowledged, we need both some common debt and a union-wide investment program. But this required a degree of political union that he and Helmut Kohl did not have the power to impose on France's and Germany's powerful elites.

Mitterrand's solution, such as it was, was to put, intentionally, the cart before the horses and to wait for a large bump in the road to convince Europe's backseat drivers that the configuration needed changing. European currencies would be glued together first. And when the next global financial crisis came along, it would persuade France's and Germany's powerbrokers to merge their political systems into some sort of federation.

Mitterrand appreciated that a single currency without common debt, or an aggregate investment policy that took surpluses from the surplus countries to invest into the deficit ones, was asking for trouble. At least that is what he conceded to Jacques Delors in private.[34] He realized that a sharp financial crisis would find the euro wanting. But he also believed deep in his bones that, when that next global crisis came, his and Kohl's successors would have no alternative but to acquiesce to the political union necessary to salvage it. If they did not, the euro would shrivel and die.

Heartbreakingly, Mitterrand's and Kohl's successors came up particularly short when the mother of all financial crises hit in 2008, putting the euro into a tailspin eighteen months later. During the spring of 2015, I was privileged (if that is the word) enough to sit in long meetings with them, or to listen in during teleconferences that went on until the wee hours of the morning. I can unequivocally testify: Mitterrand would be spinning in his grave witnessing how his, and Kohl's, heirs and successors failed to rise to the occasion once the euro crisis hit. They had plenty of opportunities to help build the missing political union, as Mitterrand had hoped. And they missed every single one of them (see chapter 5). The question is why. Why did Europe fail to consolidate in response to its long, post-2008 crisis? The United States came out of every financial crisis (from the early nineteenth century onward) stronger and more united. Why not Europe?

It is common for Europeans to bemoan the lack of quality leadership and to long for leaders of decades past. "If only we had a Mitterrand, a Giscard, a Kohl or a Schmidt in government" is today a standard lament in Europe's bars, taxis and even parliaments, the implication being that, if we did, Europe would be uniting now as America did after 1929 under the stewardship of Franklin D. Roosevelt. But things are not that simple. First, Europe's union is nothing like America's, for reasons outlined in the previous chapter: it was founded as an administration for an industrial cartel, rather than as a political mechanism by which to balance competing interests in a democracy.[35] Second, there are reasons why political leadership is not what it used to be across the world.

This is not, of course, due to some deterioration of the current generation's leadership gene. Rather, the depoliticization of political life, itself aided and abetted by Europe's technocratic monetary union, has turned naturally gifted political animals away from politics. The more that crucial political decisions are turned over to unelected second-rate technocrats, the fewer gifted men and women enter politics. Would the young Mitterrand, I wonder, have entered politics in a Europe where questions of interest rates, taxation and social welfare policy were deferred to faceless bureaucrats?

Inadvertently, Mitterrand and Kohl contributed to a technocracy revolving around a monetary union that eradicated the type of political leadership necessary to step in during a crisis and complete their creation. Adding a political amalgam to the monetary union that Schmidt and Giscard began, and which they took so much further, requires leaders that their monetary union weeded out.

It is not, therefore, a simple case of heirs and successors proving lesser than the task bestowed upon them by the pioneers. It is, instead, a case of pioneers who put into place monetary institutions which, at once, needed future politicians to complete them, while at the same time ensuring that this caliber of politician would be driven out of politics. The stuff of tragedy had been weaved into Europe's monetary union from the outset.

There is a sense in which the euro's pioneers, from Giscard and Schmidt to Mitterrand and Kohl, should be excused. The European

Union began as a cartel of Central Europe's heavy industries whose excellent by-product was the impossibility of waging another European war, once the instruments necessary for its orchestration had been Europeanized. Why should they not imagine that political union would follow from the Europeanization of money?

Could Mitterrand know that monetary union would have the opposite effect to that which he anticipated? That it would make political union harder, rather than a natural development of a single currency? That it might even crush democracy sequentially, beginning with weak links like Greece before doing immense damage to France's and Germany's democracies?

The answer is, I submit, that not only could Mitterrand and Kohl have known but that they should have known.

> It is a dangerous error to believe that monetary and economic union can precede a political union or that it will act (in the words of the Werner report[36]) "as a leaven for the evolvement of a political union which in the long run it will in any case be unable to do without."

These words were penned by Cambridge economist Nicholas Kaldor not in 2015 or 1993 but in 1971, at a time when the good professor could see the Nixon Shock coming and Europe itching to respond by putting the cart before the horse.[37] Kaldor had seen enough evidence that the Europeans were about to commit a "dangerous error." A clash between France and Germany was already developing even at that early stage and Kaldor's sensitive antennae picked it up.

The 1970 Werner Report, which Kaldor read and referred to, explicitly talked of the need to "coordinate national spending and taxation" as a prerequisite to a workable monetary union. This reference was put in the Werner Report by the German representatives, with help from their Italian and Dutch colleagues but against the express wishes of the French. France, reflecting de Gaulle's vision of using Europe as a means of enhancing (rather than diminishing) the French nation-state, opposed this federalist dimension.

Paris wanted to have its cake (a Europeanized deutsche mark) and eat it too (retain national sovereignty over budgetary matters). When the European Commission backed Paris, as it usually did in the pre-euro days, Germany's enthusiasm for the whole idea crumbled. It was only eight years later, in 1978, that Chancellor Schmidt, influenced by America's new "game," would revive the idea.

Kaldor took a quick look at this emerging opposition along the Franco-German axis and, well before Giscard and Schmidt had risen to the top, issued a clarion warning: "[If] the creation of a monetary union and Community control over national budgets generates pressures which lead to a breakdown of the whole system, it will prevent the development of a political union, not promote it."[38]

Rather than take heed of such wise counsel, official Europe chose to bob merrily across a sea of self-satisfying myths. Denial of basic economic laws had become its foundation stone and hubris its response to reality's protestations. Nemesis, as Greek tragedians might have warned, was biding her time, waiting for her moment in history.

CHAPTER 4

TROJAN HORSE

L ondon, November 1990. After weeks of a bitter struggle to fend off a pack of toffee-nosed cabinet ministers hell-bent on toppling her, Margaret Thatcher made her last stand in a now famous cabinet meeting at 10 Downing Street. The issue that had allowed Conservative Party grandees to unite against their prime minister was Europe's monetary union. She wanted none of it. They were keen to hook Britain's sterling to the European Monetary System.

Soon after the cabinet meeting began it was clear that her eleven-year reign was over. One after the other even her hitherto loyal ministers abandoned ship with all the cowardice that one expects of politicians sensing that their bread will be better buttered, and their seats made safer, by a new leader. It has been said that the Iron Lady shed a single tear, a sign of the humanity over whose existence many had expressed doubt.

On that same evening, she made her last appearance in the House of Commons at Prime Minister's Question Time. It was a memorable performance. Pressing into service her impressive command over Parliament, Thatcher was never going to miss one last opportunity to avenge herself before her colleagues by demonstrating that none of them would ever dominate the opposition the way she could. Her earlier tear was a cataract of rhetoric, peppered with humor, leveling her opponents.

The leader of the opposition, Neil Kinnock, must still regret that he chose Europe's monetary union as a topic on which to score points against the outgoing premiere. "Will the prime minister tell us," asked one of Kinnock's deputies, in misguided expectation that Thatcher would be discomfited by the subject, "if she will continue her personal fight against a single currency and an independent [European] central bank?" Before she could answer, another opposition deputy mischievously interjected, "She should be the governor!"

"What a good idea!" Thatcher replied after a great deal of merriment had filled the House. And then went on playfully to say, "I had not thought of it. But if I were, there would be no European central bank accountable to no one, least of all to national parliaments. Because *under that kind of central bank there will be no democracy,* [and the central bank will be] taking powers away from every single parliament and be able to have a single currency and a monetary policy and an interest rate policy that takes away from us all political power" (emphasis added).[1]

It was perhaps the first and last time a prime minister of a major European nation would hit the nail on the head regarding the nature of Europe's monetary union. The notion that money can be administered apolitically, by technical means alone, is dangerous folly of the grandest magnitude. The fantasy of apolitical money was what rendered the gold standard in the interwar period such a primitive system whose inevitable demise spawned fascist and Nazi thugs with effects that we all know and lament.

The gold standard was, indeed, underpinned by the idea of depoliticizing money by linking its quantity to the quantity of gold—a metal that politicians could not conjure up from thin air since it was provided exogenously by nature. Today, the same fantasy of apolitical money can be found not just in the construction of a European central bank that is answerable to no parliament (as Thatcher pointed out so astutely) but also in newfangled digital currencies, like Bitcoin, whose selling point is the lack of political authority over them. Margaret Thatcher's precious point was that controlling interest rates and the supply of money is a quintessentially political activity which, if taken out of the purview of a democratically elected parliament, would occasion a steady descent into authoritarianism.

Her final phrase on the matter resonated in my mind during the five months I served as Greece's finance minister. Every time I looked across the aisle in Greece's parliament to see the thugs of the Golden Dawn sneering at me, and with every Eurogroup[2] meeting, in which

Mario Draghi, the European Central Bank's president, would set the parameters within which we politicians had to labor, with no recourse to any parliament or to any process that might be thought of as democratic, Thatcher's words rang true: "A single currency is about the politics of Europe."[3]

Occasionally I return to the off-color clip of Thatcher's final parliamentary performance as prime minister to extract some bitter joy. "I am enjoying this! I am enjoying this!" Thatcher concluded happily before sitting down, satisfied that her executioners were reminded of their mediocrity.

Having spent my formative years joining every demonstration I could find against Mrs. Thatcher and her government's policies, my personal appreciation of her prescient critique of the euro's built-in democratic deficit is particularly delightful. Politics, I now understand, is at its best when it enlightens us via an opponent's insight. In meetings I addressed in London in September 2015 to celebrate Jeremy Corbyn's elevation to the leadership of the Labour Party, I dared mention this appreciation of Margaret Thatcher's critique of apolitical money. To my great satisfaction, the crowd seemed to welcome my tribute to a politician who, for us left-wingers, symbolized everything that we had stood against.

THATCHER'S ERROR

That the monetary union was a political project was never in dispute. Its pioneers openly and proudly wore their political agenda on their sleeve. President Giscard and Chancellor Schmidt alluded in 1978 to the creation of a Central European realm that Charlemagne's spirit would approve of. In the late 1980s and early 1990s, French president François Mitterrand imagined the single currency as a prelude to federation. The euro was always, in Thatcher's words, "about the politics of Europe."

The question was, what kind of politics? The kind that promotes the idea of common prosperity within a democratic Europe? Or the other kind that divides Europeans and turns their democracies into empty shirts hanging out to dry on an unaccountable central bank's clothesline?

Alas, that was a question never seriously put. The political dimension of monetary union was confined to sermons on how it was part of Europe's historical duty toward "ever closer union." Any concerns that a shared currency might, perhaps inadvertently, cause ruptures in Europe's social economy were dismissed instantly as the mutterings of dangerous, deluded populists unfit for admittance to polite society. Indeed, on the run-up to the euro's establishment, the slightest doubt about the solidity of the new currency's architecture was routinely used as evidence that the doubter was un-European, nationalist, populist, a charlatan perhaps. It was not too different a treatment to the one reserved in the United States for critics of the Pentagon's plans prior to the invasion of Iraq or Afghanistan.

While establishment politicians dared not offer nuanced views on monetary union, bureaucrats did occasionally call a spade a spade. In 1991, a year after Thatcher's performance in the House, German economist and politician Wilhelm Nölling, who was a member of the Bundesbank's governing council, confirmed her assessment: "We should be under no illusion that the present controversy over the new European Monetary Order is about power, influence and the pursuit of national interests."[4]

It is bewildering that Europe had been lulled into the illusion that criticism of its monetary union was driven, necessarily, by nationalism and, conversely, that championing the common currency was reserved for those who had shunned their national interest in favor of Europe's. Nölling's point was, correctly, that its French and German champions saw monetary union as a means of gaining power and pursuing what they perceived to be in their national interest, often against the interests of their European partners. War by other means—as President de Gaulle considered his own plan for monetary union with Germany back in 1964.[5]

Ideally, Europe's institutions should have harmonized the national interests of its members into a common European will. But to assume that monetary union would automatically achieve this harmony, as long as Europe's money was bundled together, was a flight of dangerous fancy. That monetary union is good for Europe's economy and consistent with European democracy ought to be a theorem. Europe, however, decided to treat it as an axiom.

Margaret Thatcher's objections, which incidentally coincided with those of Europe's radical Left, were twofold. Monetary union would produce an economic disaster. And it would undermine parliaments together with their hard-won democratic rights. In an interview she gave a few months after her removal, she prognosticated that "this single currency, like all fixed exchange rate regimes, will crack in the end. It will not result in harmonious developments."

Large-scale crisis is inevitable when control over different nations' money is deferred to technocrats unchecked by a parliamentary process to keep them in awe or to back them up when necessary. Once the inevitable crisis hits, national interests resurface with a vengeance. Considerable naïveté is required to agree with Mitterrand that political union would somehow subdue the rise of nationalist bigotry.

Thatcher was, in short, echoing Nick Kaldor's prophetic point (recounted at the end of the previous chapter) that monetary union will impede, rather than enable, the formation of a democratic political union across Europe. The moment control over the money of separate political jurisdictions is depoliticized, decision making over things that matter is removed from parliaments, parliaments lose their raison d'être, democratic legitimacy wanes and, when the inescapable economic crisis hits, authoritarian, highly political solutions appear as the only alternative. Thatcher's beloved TINA ("there is no alternative") emerges then in its most horrendous form—one that even Thatcher feared.

There is, however, one crucial matter on which Thatcher was in error. Referring to the single currency, in that House of Commons debate, she claimed that it constituted "European federation by the back door." It is true that some of her foes on the other side of the British channel had that intent. President Mitterrand, Thatcher's charming antagonist, did indeed intend the euro as a Trojan horse with which to smuggle through Europe's defenses a federation that Europeans would have, otherwise, rejected, unready and unwilling to transfer political authority from their national parliament to some federal institution in Brussels.

Thatcher's mistake was to assume that Mitterrand's scheme would succeed. She failed to recognize, as Mitterrand had also failed, that it was not in the European Union's DNA to carve a federation out of its monetary union's troubles. The monetary Trojan horse would deliver no federation. As I explain below, it was not in the nature of the beast (that is, of the euro and its bureaucratic minders) to spawn a federation. Only inefficient, sweeping authoritarianism could emerge from its wooden underbelly.

NOT IN ITS NATURE

If the custodians of Europe's monetary union were crypto-federalists, as Thatcher had feared and Mitterrand had hoped, why is a European federation further away today than it has ever been? François Mitterrand, and probably German chancellor Helmut Kohl too, knew that the common currency would spearhead unsustainable flows of money, from the surplus to the deficit countries. They could see that a large-scale crisis was inevitable. But they hoped that the crisis would create the political momentum toward a federal Europe. It did no such thing.

The euro crisis that hit hard in 2010, beginning with Greece, was the perfect opportunity for politicians and bureaucrats desirous of federation to make their move. As banks were going under, taking down with them the governments that had to bail them out (such as in Ireland and Spain), and while other banks were being bankrupted by the insolvent states in which they were domiciled (such as in Greece and Portugal), the creation of proper federal-like institutions would have been the perfect medicine.[6]

Instead, European officials are, even today, doing everything in their collective power to avoid moves toward federation. At the cost of unnecessarily inflaming the crisis, a series of ramshackle simulacra of federal institutions were created, always taking care to ensure that they looked federal when in essence they were anything but.[7] A confederacy of incompetence thus rose up from the clamor of stressed social economies in disconfirmation of Thatcher's anxiety.

Were the crypto-federalists that Mrs. Thatcher saw everywhere in 1990 gone or silenced by 2010? Or were they never dominant in the first place? I have already taken sides on this question, arguing in previous chapters that the European Union's genes were geared from the outset, from 1950, toward the depoliticization of political decisions. Europe's elites wanted a megabureaucracy in cahoots with large, oligopolistic business without the "vagaries" of federal democratic politics. In this vein, a "Europe of states" was set up in intentional opposition to a "Europe of citizens."

Brussels was built along the lines of "we the governments" to preclude the ideal of "we the people." This megabureaucracy was invented to serve a cartel of large business seeking common rules and industry standards in perfect freedom from any parliament with real power over its actions. It is no accident that the European Parliament, once instituted to give the European Union a semblance of democratic accountability, lacked the capacity to legislate.[8]

The great hope among European democrats was that, be that as it may, democracy would slip inconspicuously into the European Union exactly as it had into the institutions of nation-states such as Britain and France. Nation-states of this sort began as the instruments of the powerful but, despite that, if Britain, the United States, Germany could turn into liberal democracies, why could not the same fate transform Brussels?

English Euroscepticism retorts that authentic parliamentary democracy is built on a bedrock of common bonds and evolving conventions that only a nation can generate. If so, a multinational Europe will never evolve into a democratic realm. In this skeptical reading, "European" is a geographic and possibly cultural signifier that cannot act as the cement of European democracy because it will always be trumped by the underlying French, Italian, German or Greek identities.

But this view is either logically incoherent or grossly offensive to, say, the Scots. For if true, it must mean that the United Kingdom either lacks democratic legitimacy or that the Scots and the English are no longer bona fide nations. Think about it for a moment. If the Scots are indeed a nation, the view that a single parliament must correspond to a single nation leads to the sole conclusion that the London-based House of Commons is unrepresentative of the Scottish nation and merely helps project England's illegitimate authority north of Hadrian's Wall.[9] The only alternative consistent with the one-nation-one-sovereignty perspective is that the Scots are no longer a nation, in their own right, but have been subsumed into a British nation. But if so, the English do not constitute a nation either, the two separate identities (English and Scottish) having merged some time ago into an overarching British identity capable of buttressing a British parliamentary democracy.

In this sense, one-nation conservatives, whether they are British Tories or Madrid-based opponents of Catalonia's independence from Spain, better make their minds up. If a joint European identity and a sense of supranational belonging is impossible, the European Union ought to be disbanded and, at the same time, Scots and Catalans should also agitate for Scotland's and Catalonia's independence from London and Madrid. On the other hand, if a supranational, European identity is possible, and capable of generating a European sovereign people, then a democratic European Union is possible.

Most Europeans (including this writer) side with the second view, convinced that the European Union's troubles cannot be due to the impossibility of forging an overarching European identity that does not usurp their separate national identities. They are simply bamboozled as to how the European Union can evolve from bureaucratic institutions in the service of an economic cartel to a European democracy serving a sovereign European people.

The nineteenth century is brimming with examples of how commodification, the triumph of capital accumulation over feudal authority and the concomitant removal of internal borders, put into the blender of identity creation a variety of regional characters to construct new national identities. German unification, effected by Prussia's iron hand, is an excellent example. The notion that economic union would, one day, spawn a European identity, a "we the people of

Europe," was neither far-fetched nor unwholesome. Indeed, the path of institutional consolidation that had begun in the 1950s might well have gone that way. Student exchange programs are the best example of a Brussels-guided process cultivating the promise of instilling a European identity among Europe's young.

The European Union's prospect of evolving into a democratic federation built on the shoulders of an advancing European identity was damaged badly by our monetary union and its discontents, rather than by the impossibility of an evolved European identity. The unification of Europe's money amplified both the power of the bureaucrats over elected officials and the force of any future economic crisis. One fed incessantly into the other, with the prospect of democratizing the European Union the ultimate victim.

Monetary union, as both Margaret Thatcher and François Mitterrand had predicted, generated a large-scale crisis. What neither of those astute politicians had seen coming was that the crisis, in turn, empowered the bureaucrats to increase the authority[10] with which they fended off all democratic pressure to reduce their power.

In a never-ending cycle of mutual reinforcement, monetary union, economic crisis and the democratic deficit were to coalesce. No federation can spring out of such a toxic brew. And none, therefore, did.

FRANKFURT'S LONG SHADOW

The German central bank, the Bundesbank, could see the purpose of lessening exchange rate fluctuations, even fixing them. What it detested was the idea that politicians would be doing the fixing, even if they were German.

When Helmut Schmidt announced his and Giscard's intention to create the European Monetary System (EMS), the Bundesbank went into overdrive to place limits on the EMS, on politicians and, of course, on Brussels bureaucrats. It also began a campaign to overturn Schmidt's promise to Giscard of a bailout fund, to be called the European Monetary Fund, whose purpose would be to lend to member-states that were temporarily unable to stay glued to the deutsche mark.

The value of German money would be determined by the Frankfurt-based Bundesbank, its governing council insisted. Period. The burden of any adjustment to the value of other currencies, to keep the EMS going, should fall on the weaker currencies, not on the deutsche mark. Put simply, the Bundesbank demanded control of the mark's exchange rate with the dollar and the yen; Europe's stragglers, especially France, would have to do what they could to keep up. Its demand was tantamount to a declaration that it would never push the deutsche mark's value up to help Paris.

If the French franc was falling behind its EMS minimum value, the French had to suffer more recession, courtesy of significantly higher interest rates, to push the franc up to where the EMS treaty said it should be. Frankfurt refused, point-blank, to lower its interest rates to give the franc a helping hand. It is for this reason that the unlikeable Norman Tebbit, Margaret Thatcher's favorite cabinet minister, liked to refer to the Exchange Rate Mechanism (ERM: the part of the EMS that was meant to keep exchange rates stable) as the Eternal Recession Mechanism.

Chancellor Schmidt tried his best to placate the Bundesbank in 1978. At some point, driven to exasperation, he resorted to blackmail, telling its president that further recalcitrance from Frankfurt would force him to legislate a curtailment of the Bundesbank's coveted autonomy. His successor, Chancellor Helmut Kohl, would have to repeat this threat fifteen years later, in 1993, to get Germany's central bank to play ball in the formation of the euro. It would be a gross understatement to say that the relationship between Germany's federal politicians and their central bank counterparts was an uneasy one.

Unexpectedly, at least from Frankfurt's perspective, the EMS, and the ERM embedded in it, worked well at first. The reason? Volcker's design was functioning in a manner that Chancellor Schmidt had shrewdly anticipated. Shopping malls across the United States flooded with imported German, Japanese and, later, Chinese goods while Wall Street was awash with money gushing in from the rest of the world. American blue-collar workers fell off the escalator that had kept them for more than a century on a path of increasing real income but could now rely on readily available credit instead and on the hope that their mortgaged home would appreciate magnificently in price. From Helmut Schmidt's perspective, the American economy had begun to operate like a vacuum cleaner, sucking into the United States Germany's surplus money, thus preventing inflationary pressures from building up in the Federal Republic.

The dollar's appreciation, following Volcker's exorbitant interest rates, was a godsend for the Bundesbank, improving its attitude to the EMS. As the deutsche mark's value declined in relation to the greenback, it slipped even in relation to the Italian lira or the Spanish peseta, currencies traditionally more responsive to the dollar. Basking in the warmth of the midrange of its target value vis-à-vis its Latin counterparts, the deutsche mark experienced between 1978 and 1980 two or three years of comfort in the bosom of Europe's fledgling monetary union.

The downside of Volcker's disintegration was not far off the horizon, though.[11] By 1980 it was causing a global slowdown. France's prime minister, Raymond Barre, took his task of sticking to the EMS-ERM project seriously, determined to trade jobs and economic activity in France for a stable franc value.[12] So, while French unemployment was rising, he adopted what we now know as austerity (i.e., cuts in benefits, increases in sales tax, reductions in public investment), thus sacrificing many more jobs on the altar of keeping the franc's deutsche mark value within the agreed limits. A year later, in 1981, Barre's fiscal parsimony cost Giscard the presidency and brought socialist François Mitterrand into the Elysée.

On the other side of the Rhine, Chancellor Schmidt was fretting. Worried that he would have the same fate, he went in the opposite direction. Keen to boost employment, he allowed Germany's federal budget to go into deficit. Even though employment held on, as planned, the Bundesbank's deficit phobia determined that Schmidt's chancellery days were numbered. With inflation picking up, and the German trade balance going unprecedentedly into the red, the Bundesbank responded violently. When prices rise fast and net imports balloon, there is only one short-term remedy that deficit-phobes appreciate: an increase in the cost of domestic money (i.e., of the interest rate) that douses local demand, puts a lid on both prices and imports and, meanwhile, pushes the domestic economy into recession.

Helmut Schlesinger, the Bundesbank's vice president, convinced the board to out-Volcker Volcker and push short-term interest rates up to an astounding 30 percent. Schmidt's coalition partner, the Free Democratic Party (FDP), demanded austerity and so the combination of extraordinary interest rates by the central banks and spending cuts by the federal government ensured that, by 1982, German unemployment had doubled.

At that point the German federal government's tail shed its main body: the small FDP abandoned Schmidt and his Social Democrats, going into coalition with Helmut Kohl's Christian Democrats instead. Alongside Schmidt's government, Schmidt's pledge to the French to add a European Monetary Fund to the EMS bit the dust. Any chance that Europe's Bretton Woods might resemble America's original design had perished.

By 1982 Volcker had unwittingly caused the replacement of the Giscard-Schmidt pair in Europe with another pivotal Franco-German pairing: François Mitterrand and Helmut Kohl. As America began to play in earnest its role of Minotaur on the world stage, the couple who instituted monetary union in 1978 passed the baton on graciously to another pair who, in 1994, would found the European Central Bank and christen its new offspring: the euro.

Never too far behind this long string of concessions, deals and shenanigans, and against the backdrop of momentous world events (like the Cold War's end), the Bundesbank was always there, guiding, enabling and actively undermining the Franco-German axis around which the European Union rotated.

ASPIRATIONAL RIFFRAFF

The Franco-German axis is the European Union. While no one will ever admit to this, in truth other member-states—such as Italy, Spain, the Netherlands, and even more so in the case of states that later defected from Soviet influence to join in—merely add liturgical sanctification to whatever the German and French leaders decide.

This is because the influence of its Franco-German origin and center has never waned, even as the union's borders expanded, giving rise to an ever-growing European periphery. Following Giscard's pilgrimage to Athens in 1979, which brought Greece into the fold in 1980, the European Union expanded from ten to twenty-eight member-states, and counting. After incorporating former right-wing dictatorships (Greece, Spain and Portugal), the melting of the Iron Curtain opened up an expansive hinterland that was steadily assimilated, including three former Soviet republics.

With Germany and France busily struggling to keep the flame of monetary union alive, the new member-states eagerly jettisoned their monetary independence and threw their lot in with whatever emerged from the Franco-German monetary laboratory. Paradoxically, monetary union was reinforced by the aspirations of those least capable of surviving, let along thriving, within it.

The predilection of European powerhouses for a common currency is easy to understand.[13] But what of the penchant of weak societies, like Greece, for a hard currency that threatens to squeeze the living daylights out of them? Following the Nixon Shock, and the great inflationary bouts that followed in the 1970s, the elites in places like Milan and Athens grew tired of currency devaluations. Their yachts, smart town houses, countryside mansions, shares in local businesses, as well as the contents of their domestic bank accounts, constantly lost value when accounted for in dollars and deutsche marks.

Every time they visited London for the theater season or went skiing in Switzerland, they realized the net worth of their domestic fortune had diminished. Their recourse was to liquidate assets at home and find ways of violating their nation's capital controls to export capital to Geneva, London, Wall Street or Frankfurt. If only there was a single currency and free capital movement; if only the hard deutsche mark were everyone's currency, all these cares would disappear.

The working-class in Greece, Italy, Spain and elsewhere also grew impatient with their national currencies, as they did with their nations' ruling classes. Disproportionate effort had to be invested into collective bargaining with employers to secure higher wages—the costly industrial action, the tiresome organizing, the fatigue and bitterness involved in mobilizing fellow workers and so on. Then, the moment the nation's central bank announced yet another devaluation, any gains that came through these endeavors went up in a puff of smoke as inflation burgeoned in response to increases in the imported oil that, in turn, caused most prices to rise. While devaluations allowed workers to keep jobs that would otherwise fizzle out, protecting the products of their labor from being swamped by competing imports from places like Germany, devaluation weariness set in and was ably exploited by elites eager to enlist their working classes to the cause of monetary union.

Politics came into the equation too, differently but forcefully in each member-state. Ireland's government was keen to do something that made little economic sense but which packed political and symbolic power: to decouple the Irish punt from the British pound and have it shadow the deutsche mark instead. The German government, as a vote of thanks for Dublin's endorsement of the EMS, offered financial help. That aid did not compensate for the fact that most of Ireland's trade continued to be with Britain, but added political utility to a government seeking independence from London and a backdoor through which to bring the European Union's influence into Northern Ireland.

Italian, Spanish and Portuguese politics were also crucial to the monetary union project. Chancellor Schmidt had invested enormous political capital, in collaboration with Washington, to ensure that the Left failed in its bid for power in the Iberian peninsula[14] and, of course, in Italy where a resurgent communist party, under the enlightened leadership of Enrico Berlinguer, was working on a "historic compromise" with progressive elements of Italy's Christian Democrats.

Monetary union, and the prospect of a common currency, were political gifts of great value to conservative forces in the periphery. But the lure of EMS was used also with dexterity by French and German leaders to circumvent peripheral European governments, offering lucrative contractual arrangements to local businessmen on behalf of

French and German multinational corporations. The combination of
Brussels-sourced monies and business links was pressed into the service of monetary union with zeal, preventing serious challenges to the
logic of monetary union. Together with their political agents, employers reaped great utility from these deals, placating hitherto unruly labor unions along with national intelligentsias seeking reasons to rebel
against what they saw as European homogenization.

In countries such as Italy and Greece, domestic kleptocrats used
the monetary union card admirably to extend their rule. Cheekily
confessing to their culpability for the inflation, administrative incompetence and corruption besetting their nations, they asked for more
time until Rome, Athens, Madrid and Lisbon could be governed directly by Brussels and Frankfurt, as part of a monetarily united Europe. Greek and Italian politicians, representing shady local interests
(e.g., Gulio Andreotti and Betino Craxi, two of Italy's infamous prime
ministers, leading members of the New Democracy's and PASOK's
Greek governments, etc.) extended an intriguing offer to voters fed up
with them:.

> Keep voting for us and we shall soon rid you of . . . our rule! Once
> monetary union is complete, our country will be administered de facto
> by Northern Europeans. So bear with us for a little while longer and we
> shall deliver you from . . . us! Modernization is coming. Calvinist admin-
> istrators will take over our nation's reins, turning it into a Germany, or
> perhaps a Denmark, on the Mediterranean!

Most Greeks I know deep down welcomed that offer, even if they
protested for show and for the benefit of their wounded pride and
guilty conscience. I suspect the same applied in Italy, Spain, Portugal,
even in Ireland.

Northern Europe was different, only not much. Here too political factors determined attitudes toward monetary union. Belgium is a
good example. Before the Great War, Belgium was in France's sphere
of influence, tied for decades to the Latin Monetary Union (a nineteenth-century attempt to create a European common currency around
the French gold franc) that caused it to fall behind the Netherlands and

Germany at a time when these two countries were industrializing rapidly. Later on, in the 1930s, Belgium's fate was again bound to France's,
as both nations foolishly remained tied to the dying gold standard
until the high value of their currencies decimated their economies.
For decades Flemish areas were up in arms against the damage done
by Belgium's overreliance on France. So, when the United States reconfigured Europe after the Second World War, the Benelux Treaty
tied Belgium with the Netherlands and pegged its franc to the deutsche mark. Still, given ethnic divisions between Dutch- and French-
speaking communities, a Franco-German monetary union was exactly
what the proverbial doctor ordered for Belgium, independently of economic arguments and realities.

After the Berlin Wall came tumbling down, a different species of
member-state was invented. Former soviet satellites, having undergone
massive retrenchment, deep recession, unprecedented poverty levels
and often outright desolation, queued up to join the European Union.
They arrived at a time when monetary union was the main game in
town. Keen to be let in, and to leave behind the memory and fear of
the Soviet bear, they embraced the new mantra enthusiastically.

A tradition of following faithfully the geopolitical hegemon's party
line, coupled with the extensive use of recession as a way to regulate
social conflicts, meant that countries such as Slovakia and Latvia were
prepared for the logic, such as it was, of a monetary union lacking the
politically administered surplus recycling necessary to properly stabilize it. German politicians eager to spread the deutsche mark's reach as
far as possible seized the opportunity.

At the same time, the inclusion of even weaker and more impover-
ished member states allowed Germany to justify a reduction in state
support for aspirational riffraff in countries such as Greece and Italy.
"How can you argue for Greek monthly pensions of seven hundred euros when Lithuanians and Slovenians have to do with three hundred
euros?" was a question I was repeatedly berated with in Eurogroup
meetings in 2015. My response was that this should preclude allowing
Albania into the European Union, lest Lithuanians and Slovenians
suffer a 60 percent pension cut (to fall into line with their Albanian
counterparts)—in other words, the logic of their argument would be a

race to the bottom. But it cut no ice. While arguing my case, though, I could discern the French finance minister's worried posture. For he knew that the pressures, exerted upon me by a German-led alliance of predominantly Eastern European finance ministers, to accept inhuman cuts on low pensions and ridiculous hikes in the sales tax on basic goods[15] would soon be applied on him—with the French government being placed increasingly under pressure to reduce pensions and benefits and the like as well.

What was it that diminished France's power so significantly since the days when Helmut Kohl and François Mitterrand were plotting together to push forward the Maastricht Treaty, at which the EU was formally established, and create the euro? In the 1980s and 1990s, despite many standoffs between France and Germany over control of their bold project, there was close collaboration between German and French officials. Immediately after the creation of Europe's monetary system in 1978, France's position was bolstered by the first phase of European Union expansion in which nations with strong left-wing opposition parties (Greece, Spain and Portugal) were inducted. However, the second phase of expansion, which saw the European Union move eastward into a vast ex-communist dominion ravaged by recession and used to deferring to a hegemon, altered the balance of power at France's expense.

The Eastern entrants—for example, the Baltic states and Slovakia— were also deficit countries (like France) but had no social security systems to protect (unlike France), had already practiced severe austerity and were keen to demonstrate their credentials as worthy followers of Berlin's lead in the Eurogroup. Fast-forward to 2010 and France was suddenly outnumbered at precisely the point in time when the euro crisis was pushing its national budget into the red.[16]

FRANCE'S SLOW-MOTION DEFEAT

Being the deficit partner of a deficit-phobic Germany, whose budget was moving into the black precisely because of the same crisis,[17] undermined France's position immensely. Its finance minister's failure

to make a difference in the Eurogroup was an almost natural repercussion of the expansion of the eurozone. But the libretto of France's
defeat was written back in 1983, even though it took another ten years
to be performed fully on the stage of Europe's monetary union.

As we have seen in chapter 2, in the 1960s, President de Gaulle
had the idea of a common currency to smother a resurgent Germany
and remove it from Washington's direct control. And as we have seen
in chapter 3, in the 1970s, President Giscard d'Estaing had signed the
EMS treaty to energize a wider European federation and use a franc-
mark peg to place the powerful French trade unions under the moder-
ating power of the Bundesbank's disciplinarian clout.

A decade later, President Mitterrand combined de Gaulle's and Giscard's projects into a new daring plan: to use the Bundesbank as an
instrument for achieving at the European level an economic program
that was impossible at the level of France's nation-state. To see the logic
in this outrageous plan, which ultimately failed fabulously and led to
the great diminishing of French power, we must return to the beginning of his administration.

François Mitterrand was elected in May 1981 on a ticket to form
a socialist-communist coalition government with the express purpose
of ending austerity, restoring equality and promoting growth. Trust-
ing that the new government would place growth and jobs above the
maintenance of the (relatively high) franc's value within the EMS arrangements (that Giscard, Mitterrand's predecessor, and Schmidt had
agreed to in 1978), City of London and Wall Street speculators started
taking out bets that Mitterrand's administration would allow the franc
to slide. The power of the speculators' prophesy was taken seriously
even by small investors who, anticipating a fall in the franc–deutsche
mark exchange rate, sent their cash to Germany. Thus, shortly after
Francois Mitterrand moved into the Elysée Palace, an exodus of capital from France, heading to Frankfurt, Germany's financial center,
was on.

Mitterrand was not keen to tear up the EMS treaty with Germany
on the first week of his presidency. Hoping to buy time, he authorized
France's central bank, the Banque de France, to push interest rates up

to 25 percent as an incentive to French savers to keep their cash in the country but also to attract foreign money into France. Meanwhile, his finance minister, Jacques Delors, introduced a price freeze to contain inflation. Neither worked, and Mitterrand instructed Delors to negotiate with Germany a devaluation of the franc within the EMS. German authorities agreed on condition of an immediate wage freeze throughout the French Republic.

France's Left was outraged and demanded immediate exit from the EMS, lest France's government be reduced to the agent of the German government's policy choices for . . . France. Mitterrand's government had to choose between dropping out of the EMS, with a unilateral devaluation of the franc, and dropping its anti-austerity program in order to stay within the EMS. Sticking to that proto-euro, the EMS, necessitated attracting foreign money into France which, in turn, meant higher interest rates, lower public expenditure and, in essence, shrinking the French economy in order to maintain a stable franc-mark exchange rate.

It was the first time a left-leaning government was unceremoniously to discard its anti-austerity agenda in favor of remaining true to the iron logic of Europe's monetary union.[18]

However, Jacques Delors, a master tactician, convinced his president that their socialist agenda was compatible with their U-turn on austerity. His point was that to fight austerity they first had to . . . embrace it, in the context (and this is my term, not Delors's) of an "enhanced anti-austerity" stratagem. Delors's argument was as follows:

For as long as France insisted on pro-labor policies, such as targeting unemployment through public works and protecting wages, the Anglosphere's financial markets would bet against the franc, drive the state's borrowing costs up, cause a flight of capital to Germany and elsewhere, and force a devaluation of both the French currency and the French state. Inflation would follow and, before they knew it, the government would fall.

Did that mean that they should give up, though? No, answered Delors. It meant that their anti-austerity policies, which could not be implemented at the level of France's nation state, should instead be implemented at the level of the EMS area, today's eurozone. As the currency of a deficit country, the City of London and Wall Street could treat the French franc as their plaything. But not if the franc was indivisibly connected to the formidable deutsche mark. The trick for implementing their 1981 agenda, concluded Delors, was to "capture" the Bundesbank and somehow convince the German government to adopt the socialists' agenda at a European level.

Merely stating this proposition today is enough for its implausibility to shine through. Germany's elites would never roll over and adopt the French socialists' agenda. Nevertheless, in 1983 this outrageous ambition seemed to carry significant weight in Parisian circles. French elite administrators of all political persuasions believed deeply that France's nuclear capabilities (both peaceful and military), their superior administrative systems, their relatively (to Frankfurt's) more sophisticated banks, plus a divided Germany's reluctance to lead Europe, sufficed to keep them in Europe's driving seat. Jacques Delors's crusading mindset just added an anti-austerity veneer on this sense of entitlement, leading him to persuade himself that German officials could be convinced of the wisdom of French Keynesianism as long as Paris demonstrated to the Germans a capacity to discipline itself sufficiently to keep the franc as strong as the deutsche mark, whatever the cost of doing so.

And so President Mitterrand's socialist government abandoned anti-austerity policies on the dubious grounds that austerity could only be defeated Europewide, once the French economy was subjected to doses of austerity sufficiently large to placate the money markets and to convince Germany's elites to bow to the superior wisdom of French economic policy making.

French "socialist" austerity would, according to this ill-fated plan, lull the Bundesbank into a false sense of security that would deliver it into Delors's arms, allowing French bureaucrats to erect the European Central Bank in France's image. From there the single European currency would spread Mitterrand's and Delors's expansionary, growth-oriented, anti-austerity policies, the same ones they had just abandoned at home, throughout the union. Or so the fairy tale went.

By 1983 Helmut Kohl was in the chancellery and liked what he saw over the border—Jacques Delors's readiness to prop up the franc in particular. The two governments embarked on a project that is with us to this very day: to convince German voters that monetary union was Germanizing France, turning Latin grasshoppers into ants and exporting Teutonic discipline to Latin Europe, rather than importing French sloth into Germany. Two years after Kohl's election and Delors's abandonment of his anti-austerity stance, Delors moved from Paris to Brussels as perhaps the European Union's most powerful commission president ever.

One of history's curious habits is the tendency to be influenced more by our failures than our desires. François Mitterrand entered the Elysée with the best anti-austerity intentions. But it was his failure, and subsequent volte-face, that left an indelible mark on Europe and, of course, France. Today's Eurogroup meetings, in which the French finance minister carries next to no weight, are the direct repercussion of that failure.

The importance of the Delors-inspired recourse to French austerity, as a ramming rod with which to batter down the Bundesbank's gates, was amplified by Mitterrand's unique achievement of co-opting much of the traditionally recalcitrant French Left to Delors's cause—effectively into support for the conservative North-Central European cartel.

Instead of the socialism-in-one-country that he had promised French voters in 1981, he ended up espousing cartelized corporatism-on-one-continent, or along the Paris-Berlin axis to be a little more precise. And yet, a large number of French Marxists were impressed by Mitterrand's crushing determinism, which surely reminded them, subliminally, of the Stalinist enthusiasm for being on the right side of an inevitable historical process. Some would become his loyal runners on the path to monetary union.

Between 1983 and 1986 the EMS worked to the Bundesbank's satisfaction, allowing the Mitterrand-Kohl relation to flourish. Volcker's vacuum cleaner continued to function as planned, siphoning off excess German capital to the United States, keeping the dollar strong and permitting, as Chancellor Schmidt had anticipated in the late 1970s, the franc-mark peg to survive, aided occasionally by a new austerity dose in France.

But things began to go awry after 1986 when American authorities decided to wind back their vacuum cleaner, limiting the rate at which US deficits grew. The recession in the early 1980s, caused by Volcker's sky-high interest rates and Ronald Reagan's early budget cuts, frightened the Reagan administration into action. Using the US military budget as its main instrument, Washington effected the most Keynesian macroeconomic expansion in America's history. It was quite extraordinary. The president, who had won the 1980 election by preaching against public spending and in favor of shrinking the state, won reelection in 1984 declaring, "It is morning in America again" on the basis of a massive public spending spree.

The Minotaur, subsequently, went crazy—in fact a little too crazy, with imports ballooning and US exports severely hampered by the dollar's high value. Keen to keep foreign money flooding into America, Washington did not wish to reduce interest rates significantly. How could the US authorities force the dollar's international value down (to boost US exports and somewhat limit the import spree) without reducing the dollar price of borrowing and lending (that the Minotaur needed to be kept at high levels)? Washington's answer was typically American: it employed brute political power on the world stage.

In the so-called Plaza Accord that was struck in 1985, Tokyo was forced substantially to appreciate the yen in relation to the dollar, with the deutsche mark also forced to follow suit. Japan's exports took a major hit, Germany's less so. Washington's objective was achieved except that the "correction" proved larger than desirable. By 1987 the dollar had devalued to levels that were jeopardizing Wall Street. In the same year, in 1987, a G7 meeting was held in Paris where American officials pushed in the opposite way, toward a strengthening of the dollar. In that meeting, which is now known as the Louvre Accord, Washington bullied the Europeans into accepting coordinated efforts to strengthen the dollar.

The Bundesbank was unhappy that politicians out of its direct control were messing about with the deutsche mark's international value.

It was not long before it made its unhappiness shown in the form of destabilizing the EMS-ERM system, at the expense of France. To do so, the German central bank simply had to signal to markets (through rumors or small adjustments in a variety of the interest rates it controlled) that it was not going to act when necessary to stabilize the value of the franc, a reluctance that had caused so much tumult in the days of Bretton Woods (recall chapter 2).

The French government did its best to continue to demonstrate to the Bundesbank its austerity credentials by using every available lever with which to push French inflation below Germany's, bringing France's interest rates in alignment with those prevailing in Frankfurt and showing that the franc was on par with the deutsche mark. French officials were in the process of adopting a new refrain: they spoke as if monetary union between France and Germany had already been attained, save perhaps for the fact that the French and German banknotes looked different and carried different pictures on them. The more the Bundesbank's gathering unhappiness, the greater the show of harmony French officials put on.

France's treasury director at the time, a certain Jean-Claude Trichet,[19] phrased the French authorities' hubris admirably. In a bid to refute the plain truth that the deutsche mark was the anchor keeping the EMS-ERM system grounded, he denied the predominance of the German currency with the extraordinary statement that "the anchor of the [EMS] system is the system itself."[20] Incapable of grasping the finer aspects of French postmodern sophistry, Bundesbank officials were aghast. "No fixed regional exchange rate system can anchor itself!" they must have thought, correctly. Even Bretton Woods required the gold-greenback link to do the anchoring. Trichet's denial that the German mark anchored Europe's monetary union would not go unpunished.

Punishment had, however, to be delayed because of Germany's reunification. Chancellor Kohl instructed the Bundesbank to sit tight while the Soviet Union, under President Mikhail Gorbachev, and President Mitterrand were indicating willingness to let West Germany absorb the German Democratic Republic. France had to be allowed its illusions for the foreseeable future, even if this required that the Bundesbank be caged like a wild animal in case it pounced on Delors and Trichet.

Frankfurt got its chance after Germany's reunification was safely in the bag. The Bundesbank's pretext was the cost of reunification, which gave it the opportunity to push German interest rates up to such an extent that Paris was forced into a fresh dilemma not so different from the earlier one Delors and Mitterrand had faced in 1983: Devalue, and therefore confess that the franc's permanent parity with the deutsche mark was a soothing lie? Or push French interest rates to a level that would double unemployment in a few months?

Confess to the deutsche mark's EMS leadership or go into recession?

That was the choice Frankfurt gleefully gave Paris after long months of biding its time and suffering silently the self-congratulatory statements of French officials.

Humbling France, however satisfying in itself, was not the Bundesbank's sole concern. Its mission was to exact revenge upon German politicians, Kohl in particular, who had disregarded its objections to a monetary union between the two Germanies that granted East Germans one (West German) deutsche mark for each worthless East German mark they handed over. Under Helmut Schlesinger, its new boss, the Bundesbank soon struck both birds with one stone. This is how:

The European Exchange Rate Mechanism, the EMS's main engine, was Berlin's and Paris's pet political project, its "glidepath" toward a single currency. By early 1993 the Bundesbank had blown up that particular glidepath. Why? Because it never forgave Berlin's federal politicians for reaching an agreement with Paris to effect a monetary union behind its proverbial back and without its full approval. And how did the Bundesbank scuttle this glidepath? Through an interest rate policy, and subterranean machinations, that intentionally disemboweled the EMS-ERM system.[21]

Once Berlin politicians had got their comeuppance, and had learned (again) the hard way that sidelining the Bundesbank in their dealings with Paris was a terrible idea, the Bundesbank was happy to consider a common currency. But under its terms and direct control.

Only after Berlin and Paris had acknowledged Frankfurt's authority and priorities, and even then with considerable reluctance, did the Bundesbank feel ready to grant politicians their wish to replace the EMS-ERM with something even more ambitious: the single currency known as the euro.

As for France, it had been subjected to yet another politically engineered recession during which a large section of the population saw their prosperity and prospects sacrificed on the altar of a flimsy monetary union between France and Germany. That recession was particularly hard to take since it did not even succeed in keeping alive Delors's and Trichet's dream of a monetary union between equals.

When the euro's time came, after Europe's pitiful attempts at fixed exchange rate regimes were abandoned, it was evident that the franc and the deutsche mark were not entering into a romantic marriage. "Takeover" came closer to describing the proceedings than "union." Indeed, the eurozone's formation smacked of the two versions of German reunification: the one in the nineteenth century, dominated fully by Prussia, and the second one in 1990, when East Germany was absorbed into West Germany.

Perhaps the only silver lining for France's politicians was that, at the end of the day and at the dawn of the euro project, their German colleagues were also nursing Bundesbank-inflicted wounds.

CRUEL GLIDEPATH

On December 8, 1991, the Soviet Union expired. On that same day, European leaders began their journey to the Dutch city of Maastricht where, in the next couple of days, they were to draft the euro's birth certificate: the Maastricht Treaty. As the red flag was being lowered for the last time at the Kremlin, Europe's currencies were committed to a new glidepath meant to guide them smoothly onto a common landing strip; a common currency that would end twenty years of turmoil caused by the 1971 Nixon Shock. Unfortunately, the path to the single currency proved more of a botched bungee jump than a glidepath.

The original idea was that the fluctuations between the value of Europe's "other" currencies and the deutsche mark would be eliminated within a few years with a view to locking them securely together. Once they began to move in a perfect synchronicity, all rising and all falling at exactly the same rate vis-à-vis the dollar, they would be replaced by the euro. At least that was the plan, to be completed by 1997.[22]

It is a remarkable trait of the Brussels commentariat that its professional success seems to be inversely related to its predictive capacity. Daniel Gros, an economist and commentator whose opinion is fêted to this day as the ultimate conventional wisdom regarding the European Union, had this to say on the agreed process: "Overall, there is therefore little reason to believe that the EMS would be destabilized by random self-fulfilling attacks in the 1990s . . . the basic ingredient for exchange-rate stability [is] a firm and credible commitment to subordinate domestic policy goals to the defense of the exchange rate."[23]

Could anyone really expect France or Germany to subordinate its goals to the defense of indefensible exchange rates? The events of 1992 would soon demonstrate that such faith was misplaced.

To qualify for the euro, a nation would have to eliminate all controls in the movement of money in or out of the country for at least two years and, during that time, prove that its currency's deutsche mark value could stay within a narrowing band of upper and lower limits—until it stabilized fully. Additional criteria, also known as the Maastricht criteria, specified common rules on the total amount of public debt and the maximum budget deficit the member-state was allowed.[24] So Germany would give up the deutsche mark, or allow the rest to use a version of it, if the rest of Europe committed to fund their deficits without counting on Germany or the new central bank.

Once drafted, the Maastricht Treaty was signed a couple of months later, in February 1992, foreshadowing the creation of a European central bank whose charter would mirror that of the Bundesbank and whose job would be to ensure that grubby politicians from Paris, Athens, Rome and Madrid had precisely zero control over Europe's money.

Any illusions that the glidepath to the new currency would be smooth were dashed immediately, despite the Maastricht Treaty's strict rules. Nine days after the treaty was drafted, and before it was signed, the Bundesbank dished out some pain to Paris, lest the French begin to imagine that they had co-opted Germany's central bank in accordance to Jacques Delors's original plan. Pushing a main interest rate to the highest level since the war, Frankfurt was signaling to deficit nations that the single currency was extended to them on condition of their constant readiness to be beaten back into their recessionary pen. If they failed to increase their interest rates too, at the cost of more unemployment and lower investment, their currencies would suffer and they would be knocked off the agreed glidepath. They could choose the path leading to the euro or they could opt for growth-oriented policies. They could not choose both.

Pierre Bérégovoy, France's prime minister, openly spoke of a "victory of German selfishness over international solidarity,"[25] and Italian newspapers published condemnations of what they referred to as the Bundesbank's "axe-job." By June 1992 Denmark, whose economy had suffered from a long recession as a result of its government's desperate attempts to keep its currency within the EMS-ERM band, held a referendum to ratify the Maastricht Treaty. When the Danes unexpectedly voted against it,[26] in a bid to maintain the relative independence from the Bundesbank that their national currency made possible, Brussels officialdom was in disarray, the glidepath was put into question and markets began to turn against the currencies of the deficit nations.

Italy, France and Spain reacted first by telling their central banks to spend all their reserves to keep the lira, the franc and the peseta on the agreed glidepath. And when this proved insufficient in the face of the speculators' fervor, they turned to more austerity. Meanwhile at the Bundesbank, President Schlesinger began to plan further interest rate hikes, fearing a rise in German inflation.

Chancellor Kohl used every trick in the book, and every possible threat against the Bundesbank, including the prospect of legislating less autonomy for Frankfurt, to prevent a fresh interest rate increase that would turn the glidepath into a free fall. On July 16, 1992, the Bundesbank reacted to Kohl by increasing one, but not all, of its rates—a signal, albeit a dismal one, that it wanted peace with the federal government.

MARGARET THATCHER MADE two errors regarding Europe. The first error, a common one among British politicians and commentators, was to imagine that a single European market was possible without something resembling a single European state.

Tariffs can be lowered and quotas abolished without affecting Parliament's sovereignty. But a single European market requires a lot more: it demands a single rulebook. But this means that the member-states lose all power to set particular quality standards, environmental controls tailor-made for specific habitats, or protections for workers and pensioners from cross-border races-to-the-bottom. A single market may not need a single currency, but it needs a single federal-like state to function properly. But then again, if a single federal-like state is in place, then we might as well have a single currency too.

Margaret Thatcher was dazzlingly astute in her criticism of the idea of a single currency in the absence of a democratic state to back it. She correctly foresaw that the euro project would not lead to "harmonious circumstances" when the common central bank behaved as if it were possible to depoliticize the most political of economic entities: money and its price (the rate of interest). But she was wrong to imagine that the euro was a Trojan horse for ushering federation through the back door.

Thatcher's second mistake was, in short, to confuse the Central European, traditionalist, conservative tendency toward a Europe of states with a desire for actual federation. Mitterrand's mistake, however, was more of a moral and political failure in that he, like de Gaulle, Pompidou and Giscard before him, chose not to distinguish between "we the governments" and "we the people"—a crucial difference since only the latter can vest institutions, like those in Brussels, with the power to legislate on their behalf, whereas governments cannot.

A Europe of states provided the right conditions for the dominance of the heavy industry cartel on which United Europe had been erected in the 1950s. To Europe's elites and establishment politicians, therefore, the notion of a federal republic—in which the sansculottes of France, of Spain, heavens forbid of Greece, would have real influence upon Europe's collective decisions, independently of the national elites—was anathema. It simply did not compute.

So, unable to learn from history, and unwilling to forget their petty agendas, Europe's ruling class set out to re-create the gold standard, demonstrating a grandiose failure of perception of what they were doing. Keynes had described the gold standard as "a dangerous and barbarous relic of a bygone era." Little did he know that Europe would re-create it in the late 1990s, thus replicating circumstances ripe for another Great Depression in the 2010s; an economic crisis that ended up, as Nicholas Kaldor (another Cambridge economist) had predicted in 1971, preventing the very political union that was to have been its antidote.

CHAPTER 5

THE ONE THAT GOT AWAY

I had a friend once who would attend parties only to whine about how boring they were. It is not difficult to draw a parallel with Britain's attitude to the European Union. Both major parties, Labour and the Tories, have for years been tearing themselves in shreds over the European question. To this day, the imperative of maintaining open communication lines with Euroloyalists and Eurosceptics across Britain's political spectrum makes British officials visiting Brussels behave like my friend: they would attend everything in order to declare their permanent dissatisfaction.

Margaret Thatcher, from the Right, and Tony Benn, from the Left, both demonstrate why Britain's opposition to the European Union is founded on a great deal more than whimsical British snobbishness: despite being at opposite ends of the political spectrum, both were opposed to further integration with Europe on the grounds that it would result in an undemocratic dilution of the powers of the British parliament.[1]

Traditionally a trading nation, Britain needs to be part of the large marketplace on its doorstep. At the same time, a homogeneous, single, market requires rules, standards and regulations that cannot be decided at the level of the nation-state.[2] The very sovereignty that Britain's political forces, of both Left and Right, want jealously to preserve within their cherished House of Commons is put under pressure by the exigencies of its most powerful social groups: traders, manufacturers and, of course, the City of London, for which "Brexit" is fraught with dangers.

This tug-of-war, between sovereignty on the one hand and the forces of financialized capital on the other, has led to a precarious halfway house: Britain is inside the European Union, constantly threatening to leave, maintaining its monetary independence but bamboozled by the sight of a eurozone whose crisis gives rise to developments outside London's control.

Its institutionalized dithering on matters European notwithstanding, there is no doubt whatsoever that Britain was spared large-scale economic pain by having got away from the euro in the nick of time. The nature of its close escape from the euro, and the reasons Britain remains permanently dissatisfied in its relation with Brussels, throws useful light on the state of Europe's union.

MAJOR'S FOLLY, LAMONT'S BATH

The 1980s were a terrible time for the Left. Trade unions were defeated, the working class began to shrink in numbers and in influence, inequality was seriously on the rise for the first time since the Great War, the Soviet Union was collapsing under the weight of its moral and economic decline, and social democratic parties the world over were being lured by the beast of financialization.[3] At the same time, the 1980s struck a mighty blow at the simplistic monetarism that Margaret Thatcher and her New Right warriors had brought into vogue.

The monetarist mantra that London adopted in 1979, with Thatcher's elevation to power, was simple. Inflation, it insisted, was due to more and more money chasing after the same, more or less, quantity of commodities within an economy like Britain's. When this happens, the sum of money available to be spent per commodity (i.e., its price) increases, thus maintaining inflation at a high rate.[4] If this is right, the monetarist remedy for inflation was to keep a lid on the rate at which the so-called money supply grew. To bring back the price stability that the Nixon Shock had destroyed in 1971, all that was necessary was to ensure that the pace at which the quantity of money grew was in sync with the growth rate in the production of goods and services.

Monetarism went hand in hand with legislative moves and economic policies that devastated organized labor and its political agent, the Labour Party. But, at the same time, it devastated the labor market, depleted Britain's manufacturing base and put the country into a trajectory of increasing social conflict. By 1983 it became clear to Thatcher's economic team that targeting the quantity of money[5] would quicken their political demise. The period between 1983 and 1987 was an interregnum of sorts. Crude monetarism was abandoned and the economy recovered. Only it recovered on the back of new bubbles in housing and finance—bubbles that soon spearheaded a debt-fueled growth utterly at odds with Thatcher's Victorian values.

Meanwhile, rising prices were beginning to put paid to the Tories' credentials as the party of sound money and low inflation. Some new target had to be discovered with which to replace the quantity of money in order to rein in inflation without returning Britain to the 4 million unemployed of 1981–1983. It was at this time that the European Monetary System (EMS), with the deutsche mark at its heart, appealed to several Tories in Thatcher's government. From 1987 onward, London began to target its exchange rate with the deutsche mark, testing to see if pound sterling could be hitched to the EMS-ERM[6] bandwagon in a manner that kept inflation on a leash while allowing Britain's economy some breathing space. The problem with this strategy was that the interest rates necessary to keep sterling pegged to Germany's money would have to be so high as to make them politically toxic. And so the pound failed to keep up with the deutsche mark, the result being that, by 1990, Britain's rate of inflation was three times Germany's.[7]

By the end of the 1980s Margaret Thatcher was on the wane politically, after more than a decade at the helm. In October 1990, she was hoodwinked into accepting Britain's membership of EMS-ERM[8] by John Major, her chancellor of the exchequer, who convinced her that the EMS-ERM was the only available anti-inflationary device. A month later she was to be ousted by Tory Euroloyalists (see the previous chapter) for refusing to take the next step from acceptance of the EMS-ERM to embracing the euro project.

Thatcher was, eventually, replaced by Major who, in turn, appointed Norman Lamont in his place as chancellor. Lamont thus inherited Britain's place in the EMS-ERM fixed exchange system and tried to make the best of it, seeing it also as a bulwark for pushing down Britain's inflation rate from 12 percent at the time Lamont became chancellor to about 2 percent in 1992.[9]

In April 1992, Major won the Tories' fourth successive general election. Buoyed by his largely unexpected victory, and the pound's subsequent rise in response,[10] Major felt confident enough to make a proclamation he lived to regret: sterling was to become the EMS-ERM's strongest currency, its anchor maybe. Lamont must have bitten his tongue, knowing full well that such an outcome was just as unlikely as it was undesirable. A few months later Britain's very place in the EMS-ERM was in jeopardy.

The early 1990s, like the early 1980s before, were years of global recession. America's Federal Reserve, whose genes are happily free of the Bundesbank's deficit phobia, responded by pushing interest rates down to less than half the level prevailing in Europe. As the dollar fell, British trade with the United States suffered and sterling struggled to keep up with a deutsche mark that was rising as the Bundesbank was ratcheting up German interest rates to deal with the cost of the two Germanies' reunification.[11] Everyone expected Chancellor Lamont to bump up British interest rates to keep sterling within its EMS-ERM band.

Lamont's conundrum was that his natural loyalty to his prime minister clashed with his pessimism about Europe's monetary project. By August 1992 he thought that it was game over: the EMS-ERM had helped Britain rid itself of the high inflation rate that 1980s monetarism had bequeathed them, but had nothing more to offer the United Kingdom, except the unnecessary recession and social pain guaranteed by any attempt to push interest rates through the roof to keep up with the deutsche mark.

On August 26, 1992, pressures on the pound caused the City of London and all market players to expect from Lamont an interest rate increase that would keep sterling above its EMS-ERM floor. Lamont understood that there existed no interest rate level that could keep Britain in the EMS-ERM without crushing its real economy. Instead of making a clear-cut announcement that he would increase interest rates, Lamont made a strong but vague statement to the effect that he would do whatever was necessary to support sterling. The markets sensed a reluctance to push interest rates up and assumed that only the support of the Bundesbank could keep Britain inside Europe's problematic monetary system. But would the Bundesbank come to the party?

Over the next week, Britain's and Italy's currencies were under enormous pressure, at the glidepath's edge, inches from a crash. On September 3 Lamont announced that, rather than push interest rates up, he would borrow more than 10 billion pounds to prop up the pound. All eyes were, once more, on the Bundesbank: would it climb off the fence and come to the Anglo-Italians' aid? It was on the following day that the die was cast in response to a television debate in Paris.

France was about to hold a referendum on the Maastricht Treaty. Unexpectedly, due to the "yes" recommendation of the main parties, the "no" vote was polling strongly, echoing the surprising "no" result of the earlier Danish referendum. If the French too were to reject Maastricht, the euro would be dead in the water. Mitterrand knew this well and used that night's remarkable television debate to secure a victory for the "yes" campaign.

The debate was extraordinary because alongside Mitterrand arguing for the "yes" vote there was Helmut Kohl, the German chancellor. On the opposite side there was "no" campaigner Philippe Séguin, who launched into a tirade against Mitterrand's acquiescence to an unaccountable, anti-democratic European Central Bank (ECB). Indeed, his arguments were not far from Margaret Thatcher's critique.

Stung by the criticism, and fearful that it might lose him the referendum, the president went a few steps beyond what the Bundesbank could stomach. His argument was that

> the technicians of the ECB are charged with applying in the monetary domain the decision of the European Council . . . One hears it said that the ECB will be master of its decisions. It's not true! Economic policy belongs to the European Council and the application of monetary policy is the task of the ECB, in the framework of the decisions of the European Council . . . The people who decide economic policy, of which monetary policy is no more than a means of implementation, are the politicians . . . [The members of the ECB would be like members of the Commission

who] no doubt cannot help feeling a certain tenderness for the interests of their country.[12]

It was only a matter of moments before the good folk in Frankfurt would pounce upon the insinuation that the European central bank they were about to defer to would be a plaything of France's politicians. Sensing that the Bundesbank was not keen to stand behind the existing exchange rates—yet another bid to teach politicians a lesson—money traders tested the "system" by betting against the lira. As they had expected, the Bundesbank did not come to the Italian currency's rescue and the lira was pulverized. Nothing that the Italian central bank could do, not even raising interest rates from 1.75 percent to 15 percent, helped restore the lira's deutsche mark value.

A few days later, in an informal meeting held in Bath involving Europe's central bankers and finance ministers, Lamont attempted to elicit from Schlesinger, the Bundesbank's head, a commitment to reduced German interest rates. That would have taken some of the pressure off sterling and the lira, and perhaps keep the glidepath dream alive. To no avail. The Bundesbank was determined to humiliate the French by having Mitterrand's government request a formal devaluation of the franc within the EMS-ERM. It demanded a formal French "concession," in the form of a requested devaluation that would have ended the smooth, inescapable glidepath narrative.

For President Mitterrand, who had invested so much in the myth that the franc was already locked into the deutsche mark, this would probably spell defeat in the all-important referendum. For the Italian government, agreeing to devalue when France would not was equally poisonous. Britain also resisted the idea of devaluation, keen to keep Britain's interest rates at a level not far off Germany's. In the end, despite pressure from all quarters, Schlesinger conceded nothing and even gave an interview to announce the Bundesbank's intention to sit on its hands.

John Major, Britain's prime minister, attempted to outdo King Canute with a speech in which he committed to shun "the soft option, the devaluer's option that would be a betrayal of our future and our children's future."[13] It was the signal speculators needed, with George Soros famously ahead of the pack, to take the British government to the cleaners: a once-in-a-century opportunity to profit from a commitment to an exchange rate with the deutsche mark that the Bundesbank had signaled it would not defend. In horse racing terms, it was as if he had known the name of the winning horse (the deutsche mark) while some very rich punter (the Bank of England) was committed to bet huge sums that the wrong horse (the pound) would win: the more money Soros could beg, borrow and steal to bet against the rich punter, the greater his profit. To this effect, he led a syndicate of speculators, pooling $10 billion, with which he took his wager against the Bank of England and sterling. His estimated profit was in the vicinity of $1 billion for a few hours' "work."

Lamont knew that his prime minister's supercilious public commitment would end in disaster. There simply existed no interest rate, below stratospheric levels, that would do the trick. On September 16, 1992, in a cabinet meeting at 10 Downing Street, he recommended to Major leaving the EMS-ERM forthwith.[14] His counsel was put aside and he was instead "ordered" to raise interest rates to 15 percent. "That was an expensive mistake by Major but of course the blame was pinned on yours truly," Lamont put it to me recently in a private communication.

That same evening, also known as Black Wednesday, and after all attempts to stay the course had failed, Major was forced to make the announcement that Britain was exiting the EMS-ERM, with the media ridiculing his government's spectacular failure. A few days later the media reported that Lamont, instead of being downhearted, sang in the shower. As always, the media had got it wrong: Lamont was taking a bath![15]

FALLOUT

Britain was the only nation whose finance minister sang in the bath when the EMS-ERM fell about his ears, but London did not surrender alone to the speculators. Rome followed and, very soon, the whole of

Europe was forced to surrender to the impossibility of its EMS-ERM glidepath.

London's open acceptance that it had all been a terrible mistake was unique and largely due to Chancellor Lamont's determination to use Black Wednesday to nip in the bud any thought of Britain getting trapped again in Europe's monetary schemes. While some cabinet ministers, those at the forefront of overthrowing Thatcher, entertained hopes of returning to the EMS-ERM, Lamont would have none of it.[16]

Sweden and Finland, non–European Union countries that were not even meant to join the ERM-EMS, but who tracked its currency settings, and paid a hefty price for it,[17] followed Britain's lead and put clear blue water between themselves and Europe's monetary experiment. In contrast, Europe's South, Rome and Madrid in particular, were loath to admit defeat. In the Mediterranean, EMS-ERM had become acronyms synonymous with the local elites' strategy to maintain their hold over their populations by promising eventually to forfeit that control and to transfer it to a competent technocracy of experts who would run Europe from Brussels.

France's establishment had a particular reason to pretend it was business as usual; that the EMS-ERM was alive and kicking. During Mitterrand's long presidency (1981–1995), the dominant center-Left and center-Right parties alternated in government,[18] taking it in turn to impose austerity in pursuit of the "franc fort," continuing Delors's original blueprint of 1983 in which austerity at home would capture the Bundesbank and, thus, end austerity at the continental level. A whole decade of political capital, based on this fanciful strategy, was at stake and some fudge was better than outright admission of failure.

To avoid admitting to the EMS-ERM's debacle, a fig leaf was invented quite typical of European Union fabrications: the EMS-ERM would remain in place except that it would not be really binding, as currencies within it would be allowed to fluctuate by up to a whopping plus or minus 15 percent. In other words, if the currencies could not be made to stay within the original glidepath, then the glidepath's definition would be broadened to include anything—even falling out of the sky and crashing on a faraway hill would now be considered evidence confirming that the glidepath remained operational.

The only European institution that saw the events of late 1992 as a vindication was Germany's Bundesbank. Hans Tietmeyer, who soon after replaced Schlesinger at the head of the Bundesbank, had a simple agenda. Monetary union was to be given a go as long as any notion of symmetry between France and Germany was replaced by an ironclad commitment to the Bundesbank's unfettered domination of European economic policy. Paris and the riffraff had to be taught whatever lessons were necessary to make them toe enthusiastically Frankfurt's line and bow to its authority.

France knew it had no option. While the 1992 referendum was won (even if only by a whisker),[19] its elites' grand plan was in tatters. For a decade they had played second fiddle to the Bundesbank and subjected their economy to a long, slow-burning recession, thinking it a fair price to pay for instituting a French-dominated European central bank that would ultimately defang the Bundesbank and render it obsolete once and for all. This plan had been stood on its head by Frankfurt's well-judged periodic backlashes, the intended captive turning into supreme schemer.

The German central bank's coup de grâce was the way it had engineered the collapse of the EMS-ERM in 1992. It was a masterstroke with which the Bundesbank ensured the European Central Bank would be created in its image, that it would be located in Frankfurt and that it would be designed so as to impose periodic, variable austerity upon weaker economies, including France.

After a stormy 1992, 1993 looked like a benign year. Recession in Germany, aggravated by the high interest rates with which the Bundesbank had undermined the EMS-ERM, opened the door to looser money from Frankfurt.[20] And looser German money worked like oil poured over the troubled waters of the normally tempestuous Franco-German canal. Except that every time calm returned, ambition got the better of some French official who would issue a statement that the Bundesbank felt it had a duty to react to in its inimitable way.

Right on cue, in April 1993 the governor of France's central bank thought it wise to repeat the outrageous (and not just to the Bundesbank) claim that the French and German currencies were equals and would provide comparable support to the single currency. It was as if France were demanding a few more smacks from the Bundesbank before Germany shared its money with the French. Within hours, German interest rates rose and the French central bank paid the price.

FINANCIALIZATION'S HELPING HAND

As France eventually learned the art of submission the hard way, the Minotaur was going berserk in the guts of the American economy, gobbling up enormous imports of foreign goods and foreign money. This helped stabilize Germany's economy by sucking out of it oodles of idle cash that were accumulating in Germany due to the country's large trade surplus.

The Clinton administration, and especially Robert Rubin and Larry Summers in the National Economic Council and the US Treasury Department respectively, were busily working toward maintaining the Minotaur's feeding frenzy. America's deficits kept global capitalism effervescent, creating the illusion of a Great Moderation when, underneath the surface, markets were increasingly addicted to America's growing imbalances. If the American Minotaur's frantic consumption of other people's products and money were to end, markets would take a hit, banks would go under and the global economy might keel over. Precisely as it did in 2008.

To prevent this, and to keep the Minotaur satiated, the Clinton administration felt the need to emancipate finance from the last remaining shackles tying it down since the New Deal. To sustain the illusion of a stable global equilibrium, constant boosts of financial energy were necessary. But that meant unshackling the bankers and letting them loose to create gigantic paper "value" out of capital moving in and out of Wall Street and the City.

In this brave new world of financialization, of bankers creating new so-called products that soon after their birth behaved like privately minted money, the world of finance and banking decoupled from planet Earth in ways that the world came painfully to grasp in late 2008. A worldwide spending and investment spree was powered by private money created within the private banks and financial institutions

(Lehman Brothers, Goldman Sachs, AIG and the like) whose activities became exotic and distant to that which common folk, including German manufacturers, understood as banking.

In the mid-1990s, European bankers and their political friends realized that something "big" was going on in the Anglosphere and Europe ought either to embrace it or to reject it. Except that European officialdom lacks the political courage to do either and is bereft of the analytical capacity to take a stand on anything controversial. Their natural tendency is to fudge; to try to do both at once; to have their cake and eat it. So Brussels did nothing. Instead of regulating Europe's banks, to stop them from loading up on the toxic paper that they were buying in droves, they whistled in the wind.

The Bundesbank, meanwhile, could also see financialization coming. Its specter frightened the good men and women in Frankfurt because they knew well how primitive the German banks were. The Bundesbank liked them that way, weary of all-singing–all-dancing Anglo-style banks that paid little notice to the needs of midsized manufacturers of the type constituting Germany's industrial backbone. Would German banks mutate into something inimical to the German way of (economic) life?

German banking, even today, comprises a small number of Frankfurt-based global banks and a grid of numerous small banks, many of them regional and intimately connected to state governments as well as to local manufacturers. The Bundesbank based its power on maintaining strong links with both types of bank.

Since the Nixon Shock, Germany's central bank would intervene ferociously in defense of small banks that foreign speculators tried to take over. The rise of financialization in the Anglosphere gave Frankfurt serious cause to worry about both the smaller banks, which were the blood vessels of German industry, and the multinational German banks that were running the risk of decoupling from Germany's economy or doing silly things that jeopardized it.

With these worries in mind, the Bundesbank found a further reason[21] to warm to the prospect of a European central bank located in Frankfurt, with a charter copied from its own, and with Bundesbank genes determining its policies: greater German sway in determining the pace and nature of financialization throughout Europe and the maintenance of the Bundesbank's control over Germany's global banks.

By the end of 1993, the French authorities' capitulation to the Bundesbank was complete and the road was open for the completion of a monetary union that Paris had first imagined as a means of capturing the Bundesbank but which Frankfurt eventually embraced after it shot the French stratagem out of the sky. Mitterrand, his government and officials in France's central bank knew they were defeated but decided to look on the bright side.

Once locked in the Bundesbank-dominated euro, France's ruling class, and the technocrats it was so good at producing, could at least look forward to maintaining their power within France and along the Paris-Brussels corridor. They might not have won Europe but at least they did not lose France—at least not yet.[22] Their government could better resist pressures from organized labor. Apparatchiks could take solace from exercising their skills in the European Commission, which Jacques Delors was beefing up into something resembling a European government. And despite France's failure to capture the Bundesbank, the European Union remained capable of promoting Paris's "planification," which was code for looking after large French companies through bailouts (such as the rescue of Air France) and steps to help them expand across European borders (such as when a state-owned French company, aided and abetted by Brussels, purchased the largest part of Britain's privatized electricity industry).[23]

And so it was that, with a little help from Anglo-centric financialization, and given the Bundesbank's successive victories against politicians both in Paris and in Berlin, the euro was allowed to be born. Even before the euro had entered our wallets, pockets and ATMs, a glimpse of what Euroland would look and feel like (especially after its honeymoon period was over) could be had by recounting, as this chapter has done, the almost forgotten history of the 1990s.

Lacking a political surplus recycling mechanism, Europe's monetary union meant that the weakest nations and their frailest citizens had to suffer a sharp contraction the moment Europe's capitalism went into a spasm in response to financialization's inescapable seizures. Only

Mitterrand's original hope (that a future global financial crisis would force upon the eurozone a federal solution) offered any respite from the pitiless reality. By 2010, two years after the type of crisis Mitterrand had in mind, that hope had died out too.

ENTRANCE ETIQUETTE

The single European currency, the euro, can be thought of as a club whose rules of entry were meant to be violated and whose functions were designed as mind-boggling paradoxes.

Its entry rules, the so-called Maastricht criteria of quantifiable thresholds (e.g., a limit on a country's public debt of no more than 60 percent of its national income, or a government annual budget deficit no greater than 3 percent of national income), would function as the members' book of Psalms. To be recited at regular intervals, the "criteria" were the eurozone's Decalogue, prescribing essential dos and don'ts, exuding a Protestant disdain for loose finances. They were the texts of ritualistic incantations, promoting the new ode to Europe's "apolitical" money—the type of money that Margaret Thatcher had warned against.

Of course, the Maastricht criteria's real purpose was to allow into the eurozone countries that did not meet these criteria and then force them to do whatever it demanded to meet them. Greece is world famous for its "statistics," and the creative manner in which they were massaged to allow my country into the fold. But it is Italy that we must turn to to grasp what happened.

Italy had to be admitted into the eurozone from the beginning (that is, from 2000), not least because German manufacturers were fed up with the falling lira, which periodically restored the car manufacturer Fiat's competitiveness vis-à-vis Volkswagen et al. A eurozone without Italy, but with France, made no sense in view of Northern Italy's strong trade links with France and Germany, its heavy industry's participation in the original cartel on which the European Union was founded as well as its full cultural integration with Central Europe.

But Italy's public debt was twice that specified by Maastricht as the maximum permissible level for an entrant, with its inflation rate languishing in the red zone too. Rome did its very best to push these numbers toward their Maastricht threshold. Smart officials, working with the best financial "engineering" Goldman Sachs could provide, indulged in creative accounting that shaved off some of the debt and a little of the government's budget deficit. However, the numbers budged very little even when Rome applied large doses of austerity with which to depress prices, suppress spending and generally give Italy a semblance of a nation in the process of acquiring Teutonic virtues.

Regardless of these efforts, it was clear that the Maastricht rules had to be visibly bent for Italy to trade its unloved, depreciating lira for the copper-plated euro. And bent they were. Brussels and Frankfurt offered a broad reinterpretation of their book of Psalms, of the Decalogue: as long as countries were moving in the direction of the Maastricht thresholds, Europe's authorities could decide that they had made the grade.

A year or so later, Greece was also, surprisingly, admitted into the euro. The financial presses went crazy with stories of cunning Greek officials pulling the wool over Northern European officials, with "Greek statistics" as their weapon of subterfuge. None of this was true. When I asked a friend who played a central role in Greece's induction talks how they managed to convince Germany to let Greece into the eurozone, his answer was fantastically unassuming: "We just copied everything the Italians had done, and a few tricks used by Germany itself. And when they threatened to veto our entry, we threatened them back that we would tell the world what Italy, and Germany, had been up to."[24] Once bent to allow Italy through, the Maastricht rules could not have kept Greece out—at least not without exposing in front of Europe's public what the officials had done.

COMMON CURRENCY, UNCOMMON FLAWS

The euro's design was built on three paradoxes and one fallacy.

The first two paradoxes were already embedded into the EMS-ERM system, Europe's attempted simulation of Bretton Woods. The first paradox dates to 1983, when France's socialist government espoused austerity as a means of ending . . . austerity at a pan-European level.[25] The second paradox was the Greco-Spanish-Italian oligarchy's promise to their own people that the euro would rob them of power over their people![26]

The third paradox was designed exclusively for the euro. The common currency was equipped with a European central bank lacking a state to support its decisions and comprising states lacking a central bank to support them in difficult times.[27] To fill this institutional lacuna, the Maastricht Treaty and its successor treaties created a panoply of noncredible rules to constrain states. Of course noncredible rules end up as violated rules. Seeing its rules being violated, Brussels and Frankfurt made up new, even stricter, ones (see chapter 6) that ended up suffocating those who tried to implement them.

As for the fallacy at the euro's foundation, it is one that humanity ought to have grasped between the wars when it led unforgettably, one would have hoped, to depression and war. Encouraging free trade by removing tariffs and quotas may be combined profitably with attempts to fix exchange rates (in order to make long-term prices more predictable for buyers and sellers). But to do this and at the same time allow for free movements of money across the borders is to ask for serious trouble.

The reason for this is that when money is free to travel, during the good times it chases after higher interest rates. Deficit countries offer higher rates and, in view of the fixed exchange rate, are very attractive for the excess money of the surplus states. But this causes a buildup of debt in the deficit regions that goes bad at the first sign of an economic downturn. It is, for this reason, one of the few things economists tend to agree on, that freedom of goods and money to travel unimpeded cannot be combined with fixed exchange rates, unless a political surplus recycling mechanism is also part of the deal.[28]

Fixing exchange rates between disparate economic regions always brings benefits in the short term. But it resembles past invasions of Russia: a brisk beginning full of enthusiasm and hope, rapid progress that seems unstoppable, followed by a heart-wrenching slowdown as a Cruel Winter takes its toll, ending up with blood on the snow and ceaseless retributions thereafter.

The Americans learned that lesson in the 1930s, with the 1920s gold standard, and applied it during the Bretton Woods era, until they ran out of surpluses to recycle. The moment men like Paul Volcker saw that political surplus recycling was beyond the American economy's capacity, they brought the whole damned system down—with the 1971 Nixon Shock. For they understood the fallacy that Europe refuses to grasp: if you set up a free trade, free capital and single currency system without a political surplus recycling mechanism, you will end up with something like the 1920s gold standard.

After the Nixon Shock, European leaders set out to fix the exchange rates between Europe's currencies, brushing aside the certainty of the ensuing asymmetrical recessions (with the largest loss of income afflicting the weaker economies). In 1978 Chancellor Schmidt and President Giscard d'Estaing inaugurated Europe's monetary system. Then again in the early 1990s Chancellor Kohl and President Mitterrand oversaw the construction of their glidepath to the single currency. And finally, the euro—the mother of all fixed exchange rates—was inaugurated in 2000. Each one of these heartrending attempts at monetary union led to the same pattern: a promising beginning that soon degenerated into tears and recriminations as economic warfare erupted in the face of recessionary winds that felled the weakest of Europeans.

The reason Europe seemed to be prospering in the late 1990s and until 2008, despite having introduced an unsustainable gold standard in its midst, had little if anything to do with its single currency's awful design. The reason was that, during that time, there was no need for political surplus recycling, as the world of private finance was doing plenty of fair-weather recycling on the back of the American Minotaur.

In 2008, following Wall Street's collapse under the weight of its hubris and of the mountains of risk that financialization had amassed (while pretending that it was . . . risk free), America could no longer provide the European Union with the demand for its exports that had, until then, stabilized it. The Minotaur had been wounded mortally. Europe would soon discover that its private banks were replete with

Wall Street–sourced toxic debt and that countries like Greece had insolvent states. The death embrace, or doom loop, between insolvent banks and insolvent European states had begun. The rest is history.

The eurozone's architecture was incapable of sustaining the shockwaves of the 2008 earthquake. Since then it has been in a deep crisis reinforced largely by the European Union's denial that there was anything the matter with its currency's rules, as opposed to their enforcement.

EUROPHILIA, GERMANOPHOBIA, AND THE FRENCH ELITES

Why did Europeans create the euro? An analytically wrong but entertaining answer goes like this:[29]

> The French feared the Germans.
> The Irish wanted to escape Britain.
> The Greeks were terrified of Turkey.
> The Spanish wanted to become more like the French.
> Southern Italians craved migratory rights to Germany.
> Northern Italians wanted to become German.
> The Dutch and the Austrians had all but become German.
> The Belgians sought to heal their sharp divisions by merging into both Holland and France under the auspices of a reconfigured deutsche mark.
> The Baltic states shivered at the thought of a resurgent Russia.
> Slovakians had nowhere else to go after separation from their Czech brethren.
> Slovenia was escaping the Balkans.
> Finland had to do something Sweden wouldn't.
> And, finally, the Germans feared the Germans!

Like all big lies, this account contains small but important truths. The corrupt ruling classes of Greece, Italy, Spain and their ilk were empowered by pledging to transfer their power over to Brussels and

Frankfurt. The French elites did indeed fear the Germans. And the German people had reason to fear that fear, as well as their own nation-state's capacity to self-destruct through extreme belligerence.

It is almost a natural instinct of those who are critical of the euro to blame its ill effects on Germany and "the Germans." I have always opposed this tendency for two reasons. First, there is no such thing as "the Germans." Or "the Greeks." Or "the French" for that matter. "You are all individuals," as Brian famously told his unwanted followers in Monty Python's classic comedy. The serious point here is that there is a great deal more divergence in character, virtue and opinion among the Greeks and among the Germans than there is between Germans and Greeks.

The second reason I oppose the habitual censure of Germany is that, if the debate is allowed to stoop to this stereotypical level, Paris bears greater responsibility than Berlin for the euro's moldering. Recall the awful article in French conservative daily *Le Figaro* which I first mentioned in chapter 2's ending comments. Published two days after Black Wednesday and two days before the French voters were to deliver their verdict on the Maastricht Treaty, it said: "The opponents of Maastricht fear that the common currency and the new Central Bank will fortify the superiority of the Deutsche Mark and the Bundesbank. But the exact opposite will happen. If it comes to Maastricht, Germany will have to share its financial might with others. 'Germany will pay,' they said in the 1920s. Today Germany does pay. Maastricht is the Treaty of Versailles without a war."[30]

No German, indeed no European, could forgive such callousness and none would expect anything less from the Bundesbank than a plan for making France's conservative establishment, of which *Le Figaro* is a distinguished part, eat its words. The desperate struggle French elites were caught in to persuade a skeptical French electorate to vote "yes" in the Maastricht referendum (which almost produced a "no") is no excuse. The 1919 Versailles Treaty condemned Germans to unspeakable misery, humiliated a proud nation and prepared it to be taken over by Nazi thugs. The Nazis would have remained a historical footnote if it were not for impossible reparations the victorious

Allies had no right to impose and the German government no moral right to accept.

And it was not just a wayward editorial of some French newspaper. President de Gaulle, as I mentioned in chapter 2, had envisaged monetary union with Germany as war by other means, precisely in the spirit of *Le Figaro*'s article. Even Delors's 1983 U-turn was nothing less than a French plan to usurp an institution cherished by the German people (the Bundesbank), subsume it in a French-dominated central bank, and extend into Germany and the rest of Europe policies close to Paris's heart.

From a German perspective, Delors and *Le Figaro* were on, more or less, the same page. The fact that civilized Frenchmen like Delors and Mitterrand truly believed that their policies would prove good for Germany too is neither here nor there. After all, most Bundesbank officials also believe that their strict monetary posture is good for France, indeed for the Greeks too.

The fact that German politicians, like Wolfgang Schäuble today, tend to speak incessantly about the sanctity of rules, whereas their French counterparts are prone to terminology more redolent of the French Enlightenment, is not evidence that Europe's problem is too much German power. As a younger person I would listen to well-bred representatives of the French ruling classes appeal to Europe's general will or common interest, and my Greek heart fluttered with joy. But the effect of such fine words changed once I learned to translate them into what they really meant.

Before the euro was introduced, de Gaulle, Mitterrand, Delors and their kin would talk of Europe's common good when they were, under the surface, demanding that the rest of Europe should make sacrifices in support of the costly illusion that the franc was as "hard" a currency as the deutsche mark.[31] And whenever France's better-laid plans crashed on the shoals of reality, it was common practice to blame it all on uncivilized foreigners who could not appreciate the finer aspects of France's plan.[32]

The euro changed all that. Locked into its steel embrace, France's sophisticated administrators sipped little by little the bitter realization that monetary union would not deliver them Germany on a plate. Indeed, that they were losing France. It was a natural and not unfair outcome of a monetary experiment egged on, with panache, by Paris, with Germany a reluctant participant.

THE CHRONICLE OF the path toward the euro should have made clear to any reader that it was never going to sail smoothly across the high seas of the global economy. In the event, the Europeans' failure in the 1990s to understand that the value of money can never be depoliticized led to an agonizing struggle for dominance within a sinking ship of a monetary system.

Since the Nixon Shock, European currencies stubbornly refused to move in sync, despite the authorities' best efforts. The euro was meant to abolish such stubbornness. Except that, instead of abolishing the headaches caused by exchange rate fluctuations, it engendered a series of real economy migraines. After an initial period of irrational optimism, which erected new mountain ranges of private and public debt, the new currency fed the old problems with steroids and let them loose upon unsuspecting Europeans.

In the 1990s, even as the American Minotaur was easing Europe's passage toward the euro, observing Europe's high officials at work was a little like watching Macbeth or Othello, wondering how supposedly smart people could be so gullible. After the American Minotaur's serious wounding in 2008, reality pulled the rug from under the euro's feet. Unsurprisingly, Europe's leadership descended from tragic incompetence to a comedy of errors.

How could so many top journalists, academics, functionaries and politicians believe that they could sustainably bind together the French franc and the deutsche mark, let alone the Italian lira, the Spanish peseta and the Greek drachma, without a political mechanism for recycling German and Dutch surpluses and managing the various private and public sector deficits? Did they not see that German surpluses, left to the Frankfurt and Parisian bankers to dispense throughout Europe's periphery, would flood the deficit regions, causing massive bubbles? How did they expect the eurozone, bereft of any mechanism for coping, to handle the preordained bursting of these bubbles?

Much of the blame must go to the word "union." One puts the words "monetary" and "union" together and immediately imagines some prospect of convergence, of economies and peoples coming together. Except that the last two chapters' tale on the 1980s and 1990s reveals the opposite. Forcing all the costs of adjustment on the deficit economies repeated the cardinal sin of the gold standard. But, unlike the gold standard, where states could just leave by severing the peg between their currency and gold overnight, once in the eurozone member-states had entered a "Hotel California" they could never leave.

This is the beauty and the curse of the eurozone. Once in, you lack a currency to unpeg from, and cut loose of, the euro: you have only the euro. To get out of Europe's monetary union Greece or Italy, for example, would have first to create a new drachma or a new lira and only then unpeg it from the euro. But creating a new paper currency, distributing it around the country, recalibrating the banking and payment systems to function with it and doing everything else that would be required takes a minimum of twelve months.

Given that the purpose of going through the palaver of re-creating a lost currency is to devalue it vis-à-vis the currency in people's hip pockets,[33] leaving the euro is tantamount to announcing a major devaluation twelve months before it happens. At the drop of a hint of a devaluation twelve months hence, a frightful race is on. Every Tom, Dick and Harriet will rush to liquidate whatever wealth they have, convert it to euros, take their euros out of the banking system and either stash them under the bed or carry them across the border to Germany or Switzerland for safekeeping. Before you say "panic," banks fail, the country is drained of all value, the economy collapses.

The Hotel California clause embedded in the eurozone's design was, therefore, always going to prevent exit for the economies that needed to be out of the euro the most. Once in the euro, deficit countries are caught in the common currency's enormous gravity, condemned to ever-increasing depression the moment the global economy turns bad. At that point, governments face three options: a death by a thousand austerity cuts, a lethal exit from the euro or a campaign of disobedience versus the edicts of Brussels and Frankfurt, in order to force Europe either to reconsider its currency's architecture or violate its own laws by forcibly pushing a member state out of the eurozone. As Greece's minister of finance, I advocated the third option and resigned in July 2015 when my prime minister accepted the first option in the belief that Brussels was about to impose upon Greece the second option—a forced exit.[34]

Seen from some emotional and historical distance, it is as if Europe had turned its own Balkanization into an objective, into an art form. What would have otherwise been benign recessions ended up dividing Europeans and ruling over them, deepening divisions in living standards and causing different life prospects in different parts of the union. This was the natural repercussion of attempting to keep currencies locked into one another before establishing any mechanism for recycling the surpluses of those who produced them by investing part of those surpluses into countries and regions in serious deficit.

Prior to the final lockdown of exchange rates in the late 1990s, which preceded the euro's launch, Europe's fixed exchange rates had a tendency to unfix themselves regularly following political pressure from the suffering populations. Instead of learning from this, the powers-that-be decided to up the ante: to fix the rates in an irreversible manner, to replace all currencies with a single one, while doing nothing to provide the missing, the essential, political recycling mechanism.

Had Norman Lamont inherited not the EMS-ERM but the euro itself, he would not have had to worry about devaluation of his nation's currency. With the pound abolished, he would, instead, be facing a collapse of his country's real economy, a buildup of unsustainable debt, plus demands from a ferocious European Central Bank for more austerity that would feed back endlessly to more recession. In short, the euro replaced the fear of devaluation with the certainty of depression.

During the late 1990s, as the euro was appearing over the horizon, I remember heated debates with other economists internationally as well as with Athenian friends. However hard I tried to explain to them that the euro was badly designed, it was in vain. I used analogies from driving, from sailing, from any walk of life I could imagine, to warn that not only Greece, but also France, Italy, Spain, had much to lose by entering a half-baked euro.

"It is as if we removed the shock absorbers from a car and then drove it straight into the largest pothole," I would say, my voice entirely muffled by their well-upholstered certainties. "It is like sailing a fine riverboat on a calm, majestic ocean, knowing that it is not designed for stormy weather," was another metaphor that produced the same degree of indifference. The lure of the euro was proving capable of overpowering the most rational of economic arguments.

Some argue that this is evidence of Europe's virtue. They are wrong. Totalitarianism is underpinned by ideologies impervious to reason and perfectly capable of luring perfectly sensible people into its grasp. István Szabó's film *Mephisto* is perhaps the best depiction of a good mind's takeover by a totalizing, sinister ideology. As the protagonist, played by Klaus Maria Brandauer, loses his critical faculties, he replaces them with an increasing hunger for power that he embellishes with an incantation of senseless certainties. My conversations with friends in the late 1990s revealed considerable evidence that Europe was in the grip of a similar trend.

In Europe's polite society, as well as among my friends and colleagues, doubts over the mechanics of the fledgling system of European central banks were regarded as "anti-European." Subordination to the elites' agenda for squeezing wages and to Brussels's automatic right to dictate the answers to genuinely political questions was considered "modernization." "Europeanism" became synonymous with the relegation of parliaments to rubber-stamping agencies, and with the subjugation of the weak to the superior opinion of the strong. Using self-defeating austerity as the sole macroeconomic policy instrument emerged as "common sense." And so on.

The common folks who liked the idea of sharing a currency with other Europeans, as a first step to a mythical federation, could not have known that they would be the first to be sacrificed on the altar of Europe's inane handling of the euro's inevitable crisis. But their elected representatives had no such excuse, except that they were busily engaged in sharing in the immense discursive power, and material rewards, that the euro project distributed to the many thousands of bureaucrats and administrators who contributed to its genesis.

Margaret Thatcher feared that, behind the euro, a federation was being snuck in through the back door. If only she were right! But if the euro was a Trojan horse it begat something far less heroic: a clueless, inefficient bureaucracy, complete with its own mystical beliefs, working tirelessly for politicians with an infinite capacity to recite unenforceable rules. Democracy is too fragile a flower to survive such sadness.

CHAPTER 6

THE REVERSE ALCHEMISTS

As the Iron Curtain was coming down, one movie elegantly captured the emotional impact of Europe's postwar division, but also
conveyed a brooding angst about the transforming European Union.
It was Krzysztof Kieślowski's *The Double Life of Veronique* (1991).

Kieślowski's device was the overwhelming bond between two
identically looking strangers, Weronika in Poland and Véronique in
France (both played by Irène Jacob). Their paths cross only once, as
Europe is about to be reunited. Jubilant because she has just been in-
vited to audition for a major singing part, Weronika is rushing home
through Kraków's main piazza only to find herself in the midst of a
demonstration. A protester accidentally knocks her bag over and her
sheet music falls on the ground. As she is picking it up, she notices
Véronique boarding a tourist bus. The two women's eyes meet for a
fraction of a second. After a successful audition, Weronika lands the
solo singing part but, while singing her heart out in the concert's premiere, she collapses on stage and dies. At precisely the same moment,
in Paris, Véronique is overwhelmed by deep, inexplicable grief.

Véronique's emotional and musical bond with her Polish double
(they share a love of the same music), and the radical absence she feels
upon Weronika's death, symbolize the solidarity and cultural-cum-
spiritual connection between Western Europeans and those left behind the Iron Curtain, even with the southerners in Greece or in Spain
who were not released from fascism until the mid-1970s. Films like
Veronique epitomized a European cultural unity that not only survived
but actually grew in the shadow of harsh divisions. It was also part

of the cultural oeuvre that helped drive the idea of a single European currency.

As borders receded and the single market triumphed, deeper unification became synonymous with the monetary union that began life in 1972 (with the ill-fated snake), begat the EMS agreement between Giscard and Schmidt in 1978, and took its final shape in 1993 under the firm guidance of Mitterrand and Kohl. The bitter irony, as the present demonstrates, is that the new push toward European unification backfired, producing unprecedented discontent.

Today, Weronika might get a recording contract in Paris or in London but her music would be homogenized within a European marketplace for music and art that knows no boundaries and lacks a heartland. Instead of being bonded by melody, emotion, guilt and culture, Véronique and Weronika would, today, be bound by a contract drawn out by some global legal firm. Indeed, Véronique would probably be worried that Weronika will move to Paris and take her job. In this harsh world of ours, there is no longer room left for films like Kieślowski's *Veronique* to romanticize Europe's unity.

In centuries past, alchemy was the expression of an infinite optimism that lead could, somehow, be turned to gold. That something precious could be made out of the mundane. Before Europe set a course for its single currency "glidepath," Weronika's optimism struck most Europeans as more than alchemy. It felt like a realistic prospect. The European Union was a precious source of hope. A gleaming attractor of dreams. But then came the reverse alchemists. Committed to exploiting the magnificent opportunities for profit and power made available by the folly of depoliticizing Europe's money, they set out systematically, even if unwittingly, to turn Europe's gold into lead.

FRENZY

Franz worked for a major German bank for twenty-five years. In November 2011 we sat next to each other on a long-haul flight from Frankfurt to New York. After the first few hours, in which we exchanged a couple of nods and sat in silence, as is typical between perfect strangers, we struck up a conversation about the euro crisis that had begun, in Greece, a year earlier. Within minutes, Franz confided in me that the euro's "good" years, by which he meant from the late 1990s to just before 2008, had been the worst of his life.

Before 1998 his job entailed flying around European capitals, assessing the credit worthiness of governments, local authorities, utilities, developers, local banks, large businesses. Prospective borrowers would take him to the nicest restaurants, give him long presentations of their business plans, caress his ego, take him to the opera, put on a mixed display of subservience and superiority and, importantly, make an effort to illustrate their creditworthiness. Franz would remain noncommittal, fly back to Frankfurt and, at some leisure, pour over the data and the documents he brought back to reach his final decision as to who got how much of his bank's money. "Before the euro," he told me, "I felt like royalty."

Things changed abruptly the moment markets realized that the euro was going to happen, and that even Greece would be joining. Around 1998 Franz's charmed life was suddenly transformed into a nightmare. The pressure from his bosses became relentless. "Lend, lend, lend!" was their new creed. From a relaxed purveyor of scarce money he had become an angst-ridden, overpaid proletarian. A weekly quota of loans that he had to make independently of the creditworthiness of his clients robbed him of the discretion that had previously made him feel important.

The tremendous bonuses for exceeding his lending target were no compensation, he insisted, for the fact that his clients soon realized he was no longer the boss. They were. When Spanish businessmen, Irish developers, Greek bankers, Italian industrialists caught on to the pressure Franz was under to lend to them, their attitudes changed. They grew cockier the pushier he was becoming, under pressure from HQ's orders to unload more of the money sloshing around in their Frankfurt lair.

For a time, Franz tried to caution the bank's board members against the tide of lending to iffy customers whom the bank would not have touched with a barge pole a little while back. His reports were soundly ignored and he felt a cold draught of disapproval emanating from the body language of his superiors on the odd occasion he would spend time in Frankfurt. Soon he realized that his reports had clashed with senior management's business plan. He was running a serious risk of being labeled disloyal and an unsafe pair of hands.

In strategic sessions organized to galvanize the workforce around the senior management's new logic, Franz and his colleagues found that their job description had, indeed, changed dramatically. They were no longer there to pass judgment on clients. Risk "assessment" and "management" had been taken away from them altogether. They were there to peddle loans, to reach their quota in a manner not dissimilar to encyclopedia salesmen whose success and bonus depended on how many units they shifted.

"But what about the risk involved?" Franz told me he had once asked. Unlike encyclopedias, which can be ignored by their seller once transferred to the customer, loans have a nasty habit of biting back their supplier. Bankers like Franz were made to feel important because they were responsible for assessing the riskiness of every loan they granted. It was what gave them their kudos, their sense of self-importance, their mojo. Alas, a new "division of labor" within banking had brought all this to an abrupt end.

Loan deliverers, like Franz, were now instructed to turn a blind eye to risk. "Leave risk to our risk managers," they were told. "Your job is to chase yield[1] and maximize the sums you lend" were their fresh instructions. Once the client signed up, and received a loan from Franz, the contract was immediately turned over to the risk managers who would begin a process first developed on Wall Street. Just as in the United States, Franz's loans would be sliced up into small pieces, mixed and matched with slices of other loans, bundled together into new products, known as "derivatives," and sold on to other financial institutions in the four corners of the planet. And so the risk that Franz had created by lending to unscrupulous Europeans was, supposedly, cast off on the vast archipelago of global "riskless" risk.[2]

Franz's new circumstances were clearly not specific to the eurozone's banks. They were born on Wall Street, as a result of the financialization built on the American Minotaur's back. Later they made their way to the City of London and to Frankfurt and Paris. What was different about Franz's experience, compared to his colleagues in the Anglosphere, was a most particular folly to do exclusively with the form that "chasing for yield" took in the euro area.

Maastricht had declared that monetary union was forever. To cement this thought, the 1993 treaty specified conditions for entering the single currency but made no provision for exiting. Thus the Hotel California doctrine was enshrined in European law. Once markets had come to believe that no one would ever leave the eurozone, German and French bankers began to look at an Irish or a Greek banker as equivalent to a German customer of the same creditworthiness. It made sense. If the Portuguese, Austrian and Maltese borrowers all made their income in euros, why should they be treated differently? And if the risk involved in lending to particular individuals, firms or governments did not matter, as the loans would be dispersed throughout the known universe immediately after being granted, why treat differently prospective debtors across the eurozone?

Now that the Greeks and the Italians earned money that could never be devalued again vis-à-vis German money, lending to them appeared to the German and to the French banks as equivalent to lending to a Dutch or German entity. Indeed, once the euro was invented, it was more lucrative to lend to persons, companies and banks of deficit member-states than to German or Austrian customers.

This is because in places like Greece, Spain and southern Italy, private indebtedness was extremely low. People were of course poorer than Northern Europeans, lived in humbler homes, drove older cars and so on, but nevertheless they owned their homes outright, had no car loan and, generally, displayed the deep-seated aversion to debt that recent memories of poverty engender. Bankers love customers with a low level of indebtedness and some collateral, in the form of a farmhouse or an apartment in Napoli, Athens or Andalusia. Once the fear of devaluation of the lira, the drachma or the peseta in their pocket passed, these became the customers that bankers like Franz were instructed to target.

Franz went to some length to impress upon me the suddenness and force with which his bank targeted the European periphery. Its new business plan was straightforward: to secure a higher share of the eurozone market than other banks, the French banks in particular, which were also on a lending spree. This meant one thing: extend loans to the deficit countries, which offered the bankers a triptych of advantages.

First, the low level of private indebtedness left enormous room for a lot more lending. Back-of-the-envelope calculations made French and German bankers salivate at the room for lending in the Mediterranean, in Portugal and in Ireland. In contrast to British or Dutch clients who were mortgaged up to their ears, and were hardly in a position to borrow more, Greek and Spanish customers could quadruple their borrowing, given that they had so little debt to begin with.

Secondly, the surplus nation's exports to deficit countries welcomed into the euro were now immune to the devaluation of the defunct, weaker currencies. In what the bankers considered a virtuous circle, their increasing loans to deficit nations foreshadowed more domestic growth, which in turn justified the loans they were extending to them.

Thirdly, German bankers drooled over the large difference between the interest rate they could charge to German customers and the going interest rate in places like Greece. The chasm between the two was a direct repercussion of the trade imbalances. A large trade surplus means that cars and washing machines flow from the surplus to the deficit country, with cash flowing the opposite way. The surplus country becomes awash with "liquidity," with cash accumulating in proportion to the net exports pouring into its trading partners. As the supply of cash increases within the surplus nation's banks, in Frankfurt to be precise, it becomes more readily available and therefore cheaper to borrow. In other words, its price drops. And what is the price of money? The interest rate! Thus interest rates in Germany were remaining much lower than in Greece, Spain and their equivalents, where the outflow of cash (as the Greeks and the Spanish purchased more and more Volkswagens) maintained the price of euros in Europe's south above its equivalent in Germany.[3]

It was this burgeoning chasm of lending interest rates between the eurozone's core and periphery countries that wrecked Franz's life, for Franz's task was to lend wherever he could charge the highest interest rate (so-called chasing yield). The euro's creation had inadvertently saturated the German banks with liquidity that men like Franz were then forced by their bosses to reexport to every nook and cranny of the deficit nations—nations typified by a hitherto low level of indebtedness. Franz's mission: to boost debt in the deficit countries for the purpose of reaping the huge rewards that were springing from the chasm between interest rates in the weaker and stronger eurozone nations.

Towering above all other lending, courtesy of the larger sums involved, was public debt: the borrowing of governments. Even a small difference between the interest rates bankers charged the Greek state relative to the German government was a license to print money. As long as the assumption that the monetary union was forever held, these differences in interest rates (also known as "spreads") ensured that a banker taking money out of Germany or France (at a rate of, say, 3.5 percent) and lending it to the Greek state (at, say 4 percent) would make risk-free money. How much? The difference between the two rates (i.e., 0.5 percent) multiplied by the amount lent to the Greek government.

The more money was lent to the Greek government (or the Irish banks for that matter) the lower the "spread"[4] and, therefore, the more loans the banker had to shift in the direction of the Greek government (or the Irish banks) in order to maintain his profits. Frenzy is probably too mild a word for conveying what was going on.

"I lived the life of a predator lender," were Franz's words as the airplane touched down. Picking up our carry-ons we headed for the customs area, Franz shook my hand, adding, "Greece was our subprime market. Good luck, mate." Little did either of us know that four years later I would be struggling to explain to my fellow finance ministers that Greece's unpayable debt was a symptom of our collective eurozone folly.

"*NEIN*" CUBED

It is September 2008. Dick Fuld, Lehman Brothers' last CEO, begs Hank Paulson, the US treasury secretary, for a gigantic credit line to keep Lehman afloat. Paulson famously turns him down. The best he can do, he tells Fuld, is to ask other investment bankers to help shoulder some of Lehman's bad trades. But that would be all: no bailout! "File for bankruptcy, if you must."

Imagine a slightly different, entirely fictional, exchange in which the US treasury secretary were to say to Fuld, "No bailout for you and you are not allowed to file for bankruptcy!" What? Surely a figure of authority cannot demand of a bankrupted entity that it refrain from insolvency while, at once, denying it a bailout. It couldn't happen. Except that it did happen. Not in the United States, of course, but in Europe eighteen months later.

Toward the end of 2009, George Papandreou, the newly elected Greek prime minister, had all the indications that Greece was another Lehman Brothers. By January 2010 there was no doubt left. The Greek state stood no chance of servicing its gigantic debt of more than 300 billion euros. Locked into the eurozone, there was no drachma to devalue and no Greek central bank to assist. Desperate for a bailout before markets and citizens became fully aware of the situation, he contacted Greece's European partners for help.

There were two key people with a capacity to answer his distress call: Chancellor Angela Merkel of Germany and Jean-Claude Trichet, a Frenchman presiding over the European Central Bank and terribly keen to maintain the French elites' façade that France and Germany were speaking with one voice, and shared a single agenda, on matters monetary.

Merkel's answer, enthusiastically seconded by Trichet, will go down in history as the world's oddest reply: "*nein*" to a bailout for Greece, "*nein*" to interest rate relief[5] and, stupefyingly, "*nein*" to Greece defaulting on its debts Lehman style. Denial has never appeared more vividly nor been delivered with greater aplomb. The leader of a bankrupt country, whose currency was issued in Frankfurt and controlled by Mr. Trichet, was instructed by the German chancellor to not even think of declaring his state's bankruptcy, even as he was being denied assistance.

The Greece-Lehman analogy is justified in more ways than one, despite the fact that one is a country and the other a defunct merchant bank. Both Lehman and Greece were bound to collapse as soon as financialization got into trouble. Tasked with feeding the American Minotaur's enormous appetite for the surplus nations' exports and money, financialization was bound for a sharp reversal once the mountain of derivatives it built reached a tipping point. Like a vicious tide that goes out without warning, credit and money disappeared from America's and Europe's financial circuits.

Deprived of the piles of private money the financiers conjured up daily, the entities with the greatest burden of debt would be the first ones to crash. Lehman and Greece were possibly the most famous of them. But behind the headlines, and beyond the tragic figures of Mr. Fuld and Mr. Papandreou, something larger and more terrible was unfolding: the illusory certainties upon which the eurozone had been erected were about to be dispelled.

Of all the economic blocs and macroeconomies, the one least prepared to sustain the shockwaves of this violent fin de siècle was the eurozone. Prodigious architectural faults begat a grand denial. The German chancellor's triple-"*nein*" to Mr. Papandreou summed up the determination with which the eurozone's established order would deny the truth about its flimsy foundations. The eurozone's rules, agreed in Maastricht, resembled Band-Aids keeping together the creaking edifice.

SUBTERFUGE

Financialization's house of cards (or derivatives, to be precise) began to subside in 2007, under the weight of its hubris. With private money minting wound down, as the bankers would no longer trust each other's paper products, liquidity dried up fast everywhere. The first bank run hit Britain's Northern Rock and the first taxpayer-funded bailout of US investment bank Bear Stearns followed. American officials, like Paulson, Fed chairman Ben Bernanke and New York Fed chief Timothy Geithner, began a frantic sequence of trying to contain the "contagion."

In the course of the next twelve months they authorized the manufacture of as much public money as they deemed necessary with which to replace the private money that was disappearing from the system. But how many of their banker friends should they rescue, and whom should they abandon to the raging market forces? In September 2008 they opted for a nuanced response.

They would allow one bank, Lehman, to fail, as a morality tale for the rest of the bankers, and as a signal to the American people that they, their public representatives, were not entirely under the bankers' spell. Meanwhile, they were preparing to bail out all other financial institutions if Lehman's insolvency got out of hand. The result was the largest ever transfer of private losses from the banks' books onto the public debt ledger.

Wall Street's troubles instantaneously infected the City of London. Thus the Anglosphere went from financial supremacy to global basket case. Officials in Brussels, Paris, Frankfurt and Berlin rejoiced, confident that the "Anglos," who had been lecturing them regarding the flimsiness of Europe's monetary union and social market model, had got their comeuppance. Until, that is, they realized that Germany's and France's banks were in a state worse than Lehman's, with their asset books weighed down with US-sourced derivatives that had lost 99 percent of their value.

Germany's federal government panicked into action. In 2009 the Bundestag, Germany's federal parliament, was bamboozled into setting aside 500 billion euros of credits and transfers to save German bankers. Similar action was taken in France, where the top four financial institutions faced an immediate wipeout. Parliamentarians in both nations were told in no uncertain terms: cough up ridiculous sums for the banks or the world as you know it comes to an end.

And so it was that politicians used to quibbling over a few million euros to be spent on pensioners, health or education gave their governments carte blanche to transfer hundreds of billions to bankers hitherto awash with liquidity. "Solidarity with bankers" helped Germany's and France's banks survive the collapse of their foolish derivative trades. However, another calamity beckoned: the remaining loans that bankers, like Franz, had granted to the deficit regions of the eurozone were sizeable enough to bankrupt those nations if stressed Irish,

Spanish, Greek banks were to default. Before the ink of their own bailout agreements had dried, a second bank bailout was in progress: a bailout for the bankers of deficit countries whose governments could not afford to rescue them.

France's and Germany's governments were loath to go back to their parliaments to ask for fresh money for Irish, Italian, Spanish and Greek banks. So the task was passed on to the European Central Bank (ECB).

In the absence of the powers that a proper central bank ought to have, the ECB allowed the eurozone's banks to do something remarkably dicey: to issue IOUs that no one would want to buy[6] (given that the banks were insolvent), take these IOUs to their government's finance minister, have the minister stamp on the IOUs a state guarantee (which everyone knew the state could not honor) and, finally, have the banks deposit these IOUs back with the ECB as "collateral" in exchange for money that the ECB created to lend to them.

In effect, the eurozone's central bank, whose Maastricht-era charter bans it from lending to member-state governments or to insolvent banks, was lending indirectly to the government of each deficit nation the money insolvent banks required to pretend they were not insolvent.[7] The banks thus pretended to be solvent, the deficit states pretended they had the money to guarantee that the banks were solvent, and the ECB stood by pretending that these sad pairs of insolvent banks and insolvent states were perfectly solvent and, thus, eligible, under the ECB's charter, for ECB liquidity.

The strangest ritual I had to endure during my five months as Greece's minister of finance, in the first half of 2015, concerned this shenanigan, almost eight years after it was first invented. My most trusted aide and good friend, Wasily Kafouros, would come to my office bearing the contracts according to which my ministry, and by extension the Greek state, was guaranteeing IOUs on behalf of Greece's bankers. Mindful of my contempt for this arrangement, Wasily would approach me with the utmost care and only at times he deemed relatively stress free. Both of us shook with rage at the sad fact that my signatures were guaranteeing more than 50 billion euros of private bank debt while our state could not rub together a few hundred million euros to pay for our public hospitals, our schools or Greece's old-age pensioners.

Placing my signature on these pieces of paper, week in and week out, was probably the oddest and, at once, the ugliest thing I had to do. The closest "competitor" to it, for the prize of My Most Disagreeable Ministerial Chore, was the obligatory repetition of the lie that Greece's banks were solvent and that the government would honor all its commitments to every one of its creditors, including these guarantees that I was signing in the full knowledge that I could not honor them if the need arose.

My only solace was that I was not alone: eurozone finance ministers and central bankers had been engaged in this type of gross subterfuge since the heady days of the fall of 2008.[8]

DENIAL

The reason Greece became the first eurozone country to go manifestly bankrupt was simple enough. From the moment it looked likely that the drachma was history and Greece's place in the euro was safe, bankers like Franz went into a frenzy of lending for the reason he explained to me so eloquently as we were flying to New York.

The part of the story that Franz had left out, probably because he had missed its significance, was the labor market reforms (known as the Hartz reforms[9]) that the German Federal Republic enacted as soon as euro notes began to circulate. At a time of US-led growth, these reforms aimed at enhancing German exports and their competitiveness (i.e., making them cheaper) through reducing German workers' average take-home pay significantly, both by cutting hourly wage rates and pushing large numbers of workers into so-called mini-jobs.[10]

The result was that German workers could not afford the goods they produced as their share of their employers' profits fell. Deprived of domestic demand, surplus German products thus flowed to places like Ireland, Greece and Spain where demand for them was supported by the loans Franz and his Frankfurt banker colleagues shifted to Europe's periphery, dipping into the German corporate profit glut.

The result of this export of German goods and German profits to the rest of the eurozone was debt-fueled annual growth of 5 percent in Greece and in Ireland, making these fragile, deficit-ridden societies look like miracle economies, in contrast to a laggard Germany growing at a feeble 1 percent rate. Was it any wonder that financially stressed German workers visiting Greece in the summer months would rub their eyes at the sight of rising living standards they could only dream of? And is it a mystery that when the German loan-driven bubble burst in Europe's south, this bewilderment turned into hostility toward Greece's, Spain's, Italy's grasshoppers?

Of course what the German tourists never saw was that Greece was full of hard-working ants struggling to survive during those years of miraculous growth rates. Low-wage workers and pensioners were being told that they'd never had it so good; that their real wages and living standards were rising. Only they did not feel that way. And they were right.[11] Whereas richer Greeks, who lived well off the back of German and French bank loans, prospered, poorer Greeks fell increasingly into a poverty trap. In the good times! And when the bad times came in 2010, they were told that they had been profligate grasshoppers who had caused the crisis and now had to pay the price.

Many ask, "Did the authorities in Brussels, Berlin and Athens not recognize that Greek public debt (and the rich Greeks' lifestyle) was unsustainable?" The startling answer is, "They did not!" Here is why. If you think of a nation's public debt and its national income as two growing mountains, debt appears manageable as long as the income mountain grows at a greater pace than the debt mountain. And the debt mountain grows automatically as interest is piled up on top of it, at a rate that is, naturally, equal to the interest rate. In Greece that rate had fallen to 3 percent, courtesy of the foreign-sourced lending spree (that Franz explained so eloquently). At the same time, the national income mountain (measured in euros) was growing much faster, at 8 percent (3 percent of this growth was due to rising prices and another 5 percent resulting from higher production). Thus it seemed that Greece's public debt, while large, was serviceable due to much faster rising incomes. But when the 2008 events spread the credit crunch everywhere, two terrible things happened at once to put paid to this illusion.

First, the cessation of new credit to all and sundry meant that the Greek state could no longer refinance its debt unless it was prepared to pay the few risk-loving investors left in the money markets interest rates exceeding 10 percent. Secondly, Greek national income went into reverse growth, its level falling due to a global recession that depressed tourism and the incomes of the countless Greeks trading in debt-financed imports. Once the debt mountain's growth rate (i.e., interest rate) shot up from 3 percent to 10 percent and the income mountain, instead of growing, started shrinking (first by –3 percent, then by –5 percent), Greece's "debt sustainability" became a contradiction in terms.

Against these brutal facts, the triple-"*nein*" in reply to George Papandreou's request for help in early 2010 was devastating in its inanity. It was as realistic as suggesting to him that he ought to beam Greece up to another galaxy were it was possible to avoid declaring bankruptcy without devaluation, without debt relief and without new loans. The triple-"*nein*" was a knee-jerk expression of Europe's gross denial that it was facing an architectural, a structural, crisis. That it had created a monetary union featuring states without a central bank to back them at a time of global crisis and a European Central Bank without a state to have its back. That the Maastricht rules were impossible to abide by.

The eurozone's triple-"*nein*" was upheld from January 2010 until May of that year, when at last Berlin and Frankfurt could no longer avoid the fact that Greece was about to default on its debts to German and French banks. At that point, in May 2010, Europe's denial mutated into another form: into Greece's so-called bailout, which was to become the blueprint for equivalent action in Dublin, Lisbon and Madrid and that left its mark on Rome, even on the Netherlands and on France, pushing the whole continent into a new recessionary phase.[12]

The gist of the bailout deal offered to Greece was simple: as you are now insolvent, we shall grant you the largest loan in history on condition that you shrink your national income by an amount never seen since the grapes of wrath. It would take a smart eight-year-old to see that such a "bailout" could not end well.

But this was not a bailout. Greece was never bailed out. Nor were the rest of Europe's swine—or PIIGS as Portugal, Ireland, Italy, Greece and Spain became collectively branded. Greece's bailout, then

Ireland's, then Portugal's, then Spain's were rescue packages for, primarily, French and German banks.

In bending its rules to rescue the PIIGS's private banks (with the issue of the aforementioned IOUs), the ECB had given Chancellor Merkel and France's President Nicolas Sarkozy some respite from having to go back to their parliaments for more taxpayers' money for French and German bankers. But much more was now needed.

By May 2010 Greek government bonds had lost 82 percent of their value. Put differently, a bank or private investor owed 100 euros by the Greek state could only sell this debt on for 18 euros. This was a disaster for the French and German banks that were owed up to 200 billion euros by Greece. It was also only the tip of a huge iceberg. In 2009 the exposure of German banks to Greek, Irish, Spanish, Portuguese and Italian debt amounted to a dizzying 704 billion euros.[13] Much, much more than the total capital base of Germany's banking system. If Greece went under, and contagion brought down some of the other peripheral banks, Germany's banking system would be toast.

Suddenly, it became imperative to save Greece. But with the Greek state cut off from money markets, as no sane investor would lend to the Athens government, the German and French banks feared the worst: Greece would have to default and they would be at the mercy of regulators whose rules said they had to declare the insolvency of venerable banks like BNP Paribas or Finanz Bank.

Another German and French bank bailout had become unavoidable. The second one in less than two years.

The problem here was that Chancellor Merkel and President Sarkozy could not imagine going back, once more, to their parliaments for more money for their banker chums. So they did the next best thing: they went to their parliaments invoking the cherished principle of solidarity to Greece, then to Ireland, then to Portugal and finally to Spain. Thus Mr. Papandreou was pushed into accepting the largest loan in history of which the bulk, more than 91 percent, went to make whole the French and German bankers, by buying back from them at 100 euros bonds whose market value had declined to less than 20 euros.

A cynical ploy that transferred hundreds of billions of losses from the books of the French and German banks to Europe's taxpayers was presented to the world as the manifestation of European solidarity. What makes this transfer sinister, rather than just cynical, was that the Greek loan came not only from French and German taxpayers but also from the Portuguese, the Slovaks, the Irish taxpayers—from countries whose banks had nothing to gain. In essence, the private losses of French and German banks were spread around throughout the eurozone, forcing even the weakest citizens of the weakest of member-states to chip in.

The idea of the Greek bailout did not go down well in the sixteen parliaments where it was tabled. Nationalists and anti-Europeans were salivating at the opportunity to lambast their government for daring to ask their people to cough up money for the worst of the Mediterranean's grasshoppers, when they themselves were suffering from the post-2008 recession. Behind the scenes, the government would inform them that the Greek bailout was all about saving their own banks. But, still, the opportunity for putting on a show of nationalist fervor was too tempting to ignore. So they demanded to see some Greek blood before signing off on the largest loan in economic history.

The Greek loan thus came with vicious strings attached—strings designed to cause visible pain to the weakest of Greeks. The "conditionalities," as the strings were called, boiled down to the dismantling of basic social welfare provisions to be supervised by officials representing the ECB, the European Commission and the International Monetary Fund.[14]

This is how the troika—meaning the triumvirate of the ECB, the EC and the IMF—was born. It comprised a small group of bailiffs, disguised as technocrats, who acquired powers that Europe's governments cannot dream of. With every visitation by the troika, the dream of shared European prosperity was dealt another blow.

FISCAL WATERBOARDING

My use of the term "fiscal waterboarding" back in 2010 was, after I became finance minister in 2015, used as evidence that I was a provocateur. In fact it was a perfectly apt and reasonable term by which to describe the troika's practices in Athens and elsewhere. What does the term "waterboarding" imply? You take a subject, you engulf his head with water until he suffocates but, at some point before death comes, you stop. You allow the subject to take a few agonizing breaths and then you continue to engulf his head in water again. You repeat until he confesses.

Fiscal waterboarding is obviously not physical, it's fiscal. But the idea is the same and it is exactly what happened to successive Greek governments from 2010 onward. Instead of air, Greek governments nursing unsustainable debts were starved of liquidity while, at once, they were banned from defaulting to creditors. Facing payments to their creditors that they were forced to make, they were denied liquidity till the very last moment, just before formal bankruptcy. Instead of confessions, they were forced then to sign further loan agreements, which they knew would add new impetus to the crisis. At that moment, the troika would provide just enough liquidity in order to repay members of the troika (the ECB, the IMF).

Exactly like waterboarding, the liquidity provided was calculated to be barely enough to keep the subject going without defaulting formally, but never more than that. And so the torture continued with the effect that the government was kept completely under the troika's control.

This is how fiscal waterboarding functions and I cannot imagine a better and more accurate term to describe what has been going on since 2010. During my five months in the finance ministry I came to know this most interesting process intimately and at first hand. Such as, for instance, when the European Central Bank connived to reduce our government's access to liquidity by preventing Greece's banks from purchasing our treasury bills.

Of course, the problem with waterboarding is that, even when successful, it is a terribly unsafe method of eliciting the truth, as subjects will confess to anything the interrogator wants to hear just to stop the suffocation. Similarly with the troika's fiscal waterboarding. Successive governments of indebted eurozone member-states conceded to troika "programs" they knew would deepen their societies' crisis.

PONZI AUSTERITY

Franz and his banker colleagues had been, in effect, running a huge Ponzi scheme in the deficit nations of Europe's monetary union. This is what Franz meant with the sad admission, "I had become a predatory lender." And when those pyramids crashed, as Ponzi schemes inevitably do, "Ponzi growth" metamorphosed into what I once called "Ponzi austerity."

Standard Ponzi schemes are based on a sleight-of-hand that creates the appearance of a fund whose overall value grows faster than the value of the investments made in it. In reality the opposite is true. The schemer behind a Ponzi scheme usually helps himself to some of the incoming capital, but the fund itself is not creating any new capital with which to replenish these leakages, let alone pay the returns it promises. Any dividends that are paid to maintain the illusion of growth simply come from new investments. And this appearance of growth that does not really exist is, of course, the lure that brings into the scheme new participants whose capital is utilized by the Ponzi scheme's operator to maintain that façade.

Ponzi austerity is the inverse of Ponzi growth. Whereas Ponzi growth schemes are based on the lure of a growing fund, in the case of Ponzi austerity the attraction to bankrupted participants is the promise of debt reduction for the purposes of defeating insolvency through the combination of austerity "belt tightening" and new loans that provide the bankrupt with necessary funds to repay maturing debts (such as bonds). As it is impossible to escape insolvency in this manner, given austerity's depressing effect on income, Ponzi austerity schemes, just like Ponzi growth schemes, necessitate a constant influx of new loans to maintain the illusion that bankruptcy has been averted. But to attract these loans, the Ponzi austerity's operators must do their utmost to maintain the façade of deficit reduction.

Ponzi growth has been around for ages. But it took the collective wisdom of Europe's great and good to create history's first Ponzi austerity scheme. The Greek, Portuguese, Irish, Spanish and Cypriot loan agreements are splendid examples. Bankrupted states, in a death embrace with bankrupted banking sectors, were forced to take in

ever-increasing loans (mainly from European taxpayers) on condition
of belt-tightening austerity.

As the scheme progressed and more loans were agreed, public debt
as a proportion of national income only rose. Again, as in Ponzi growth
schemes, where more and more investments are required to maintain
the pretense of growth, in the case of Greece, Portugal, Ireland, Spain
and Cyprus, more and more loans were necessary in order to maintain
the pretense of debt reduction.

Here is an example of eurozone-style Ponzi austerity at its worst.
It is spring 2012. An interim Greek government that signed up to the
country's second bailout[15] has collapsed under popular anger at the nation's sad state. A fresh election is due in May 2012 and Syriza, the radical left-wing party that advocates rescinding the bailout agreement, is
rising fast in the polls. Horrified at the prospect of an anti-troika party
in government, the troika suspends the disbursement of loan payments
to the interim Greek government.[16] The caretaker Greek government
is left with no alternative other than to suspend its own payments to
Greek institutions and individuals. Hospitals, schools, wages, pensions
all suffer. But the concern of the great and the good is about Greece's
debt to the European Central Bank—the ECB.

You see, dear reader, a year before, in 2010, an ill-fated attempt to
shore up Greek government bonds by the ECB's president, Monsieur
Jean-Claude Trichet, involved the purchase by the ECB of a bunch
of Greek bonds at low, low prices. The stated objective was to prop
up their value and thus help prevent the Greek state from losing its
market access; that is, its capacity to borrow from private investors.[17]

Trichet's ploy failed, as did Greece.[18] Regardless, the ECB held
these bonds and they started maturing. Had they not been purchased
by the ECB in 2010 they would have been given a haircut together
with the rest of the Greek government's bonds in private hands a few
months earlier, in early 2012. But no, the ECB cannot accept write-
downs from member-states because it is against its Maastricht charter, which prohibits it from doing anything that resembles financing
member-states (except, of course, when it bends its own rules in order
to rescue assorted bankers—as we saw earlier).[19]

This means that the caretaker Greek government, while putting Greece's social economy through the wringer, has to find 5 billion euros in a few days to repay the ECB for one of these maturing bonds. Where will the money come from? The troika had suspended loan payments and no privateer is ready to go where even the troika refuses to tread.

The obvious thing to do, under the circumstances, would be for Athens to default on the bonds that the ECB owned or for the ECB to offer the Greek government longer maturities, a debt swap or something of the sort. But this was something that Frankfurt and Berlin rejected with venom. When it came to countries like Germany and France, the rules were meant to be broken.[20] But for countries like Greece, the rules are the rules are the rules! Even if they are unworkable, unenforceable rules. The Greek state could default against the weakest of Greek and non-Greek citizens, against pension funds and the like, but its debts to the ECB were sacrosanct. They had to be paid come what may. But how?

This is what they came up with in lieu of a solution: The ECB allowed the Greek government to issue worthless IOUs (or, more precisely, short-term treasury bills), that no private investor would touch, and pass them on to the insolvent Greek banks.[21] The insolvent Greek banks then handed over these IOUs to the European System of Central Banks[22] as collateral in exchange for loans that the banks then gave back to the Greek government so that Athens could repay the ECB.

If this sounds like a Ponzi scheme it is because it is the mother of all Ponzi schemes. A merry-go-round of Ponzi austerity which, interestingly, left both the insolvent banks and the insolvent Greek state a little more insolvent while, all along, the Greek population was sinking deeper and deeper into despair. And all so the European Union could pretend that its inane rules had been respected.

This is but one example of the vicious cycle of Ponzi austerity that was replicated incessantly throughout the eurozone. Its stated purpose was to reduce debts. But debt rose everywhere.[23] Is this a failure? Yes and no. It is a failure in terms of Brussels's stated objectives but not in terms of the underlying motives. For, in reality, the true purpose of the bailout loans was to effect a transfer of the periphery's bad debts from the books (mainly) of the Northern European banks to the shoulders of Europe's taxpayers at the cost of increasing debts and a recession caused by the strings, or conditions, attached to the new loans.

These toxic transfers, effected in the name of European solidarity, led to a death dance of insolvent banks and bankrupt states, sad couples that were sequentially marched off the cliff of competitive austerity. Deflation, ultra-low investment, social fragmentation and rising poverty ensured that large sections of proud European nations, mostly the weakest of their citizenry, were dragged into the contemporary equivalent of the Victorian poorhouse.

IMPOTENCE

It is 2011. The contagion of default and collapse is spreading via the common currency from country to country. The minister of finance of a major European nation, with an economy that dwarfs Greece's, is keen for ideas on how to stop the domino effect taking his country down. He agrees to see a friend of mine who wishes to convey to the minister a proposal on how the eurozone debt juggernaut could be stopped in its tracks.

The minister hears the idea and likes it a lot. Immediately he asks his aides to organize meetings between his visitor and Brussels officials, members of the European Parliament and the like with a view to helping his visitor lobby these important European policy makers in favor of this interesting proposal. At that point his visitor turns around and says:

"Minister, what is the point? Why should I try to convince all these officials if I have convinced you? You are the finance minister of a major European nation. You sit on the Eurogroup and Ecofin (the European Union's council of finance ministers). If you like my proposal, why don't you table it as your own at that lofty forum?"

The minister smiles. He sits back in his plush armchair and responds in a manner that, tragically, makes perfect sense:

"Do you know what will happen if I table your splendid proposal? SMSs will stream out of the room while I am talking. The press will shortly be reporting that I am tabling a proposal for the central management of a part of the debt of every eurozone member-state. Seconds later the money markets will refuse to lend to my government, except at usurious interest rates, as the rumor spreads that, for me to be proposing such ideas, my government cannot refinance its debt. My dear friend, I shall cease to be minister the next day. How exactly will that help promote your proposal?"

A year later that minister was gone anyway, and so was his government. What never went away, judging by my own more recent experiences, is the terrible disconnect between the eminently sensible things some ministers say behind closed doors and the inanity of their statements in the Eurogroup, other official bodies and when the television cameras are switched on.

FALLING DOMINOES OR TUMBLING MOUNTAINEERS?

As the Greek disease began to spread, infecting Ireland, Portugal, Spain, before reaching Italy and threatening to bring the whole house of cards down, the metaphor of falling dominoes became rather oversubscribed in the media. A better analogy would be that of a ridiculous mountaineering club.

Imagine a group of disparate mountaineers perched on some steep cliff face, some of them more agile, others less fit, all bound together in a forced state of solidarity by a single rope. Unbelievably, the members of our mountaineering club abide by an irrevocable rule: the common rope would not be pinned to the rock face they were climbing.

Suddenly an earthquake hits (such as the collapse of Wall Street) and one of them (of, let's say, a certain Hellenic disposition) is dislodged, her fall arrested only by the common rope. Under the strain of the stricken member's weight, dangling in midair, and with some especially loose rocks falling from above, the next weakest (or "marginal") mountaineer (Irish perhaps?) struggles to hang on but, eventually, has to let go too.

The strain on the remaining mountaineers greatly increases, and the new weakest, or marginal, member is now teetering on the verge of another mini–free fall that will cause another hideous tug on the remaining circle of saviors. Will the stronger members hold on? Will they manage to reach the peak, carrying the hangers-on with them, before the ruthless dynamic plunges the whole group into the underlying ravine? Or will the strongest members cut themselves loose with their sharp knives (and revert to something akin to the deutsche mark)?

The reason why the mountaineering analogy is far better than the domino effect has to do with the eurozone's architecture and, in particular, the Maastricht rule that no member-state should count on financial aid from other member-states or from the union—the so-called no-bailout clause that was meant to deter governments from getting into trouble in the first place.[24] Could this rule (the equivalent of not pinning the common rope on the cliff) be respected while at the same time prohibiting countries like Greece from declaring bankruptcy and defaulting on the bankers? Ordinary minds would answer in the negative. But Brussels functionaries are not ordinary people.

Aided ably by financial consultants, who had made a fortune out of bending logic to their advantage, they came up with an ingenious alternative. They created a new fund, which they called the European Financial Stability Facility (EFSF), that would bail out the fallen member-states, lending them the money necessary to make the bankers whole. It was the financial equivalent of binding our mountaineers more tightly together but still without pinning the common rope to the cliff face.

The trick that allowed member-states to lend to other stricken members while still apparently respecting the no-bailout clause was hidden in the devilish structure of the bonds that the EFSF would issue. At the beginning, when only one country, Greece, needed bailout money of, say, one billion euros, the EFSF would issue a bond with a face value of one billion euros, sell it to the money markets and pass the monies on to the Greek government (which would, promptly, pass it on to Europe's bankers).

This new one billion euro liability now fell upon Greece, but it was backed by the remaining eurozone member-states that remained solvent and that had, suddenly, become Greece's creditors, each one of them bearing a proportion of this new debt equal to its relative national income.[25] To preserve the no-bailout clause and to ensure that there was no common debt whatsoever (i.e., that every euro of debt corresponded to one and only one member-state), the slice of that one billion euro bond belonging to, say, France would bear a rate of interest payable to the bond's owner (i.e., to the investor that purchased it) equal to the interest rate France paid to borrow for its own purposes. The Spanish slice would bear a different interest rate, so too the Italian, and so on.

So each nation participating in Greece's rescue, or later in Portugal's, Ireland's and the rest, paid market interest rates depending on its own creditworthiness, which reflected its country-specific risk of bankruptcy. The member-state with the higher probability of going Greece's way paid more interest for the slice of the EFSF bond it guaranteed so that Greece could receive the one billion euros of new debt.

Those familiar with the structured derivatives that brought down Lehman, and Wall Street along with it (the so-called collateralized debt obligations, or CDOs), will recognize in the EFSF bailout bonds the same form of synthesized risk. Except that the EFSF bonds were even more toxic than Wall Street's noxious derivatives! To see this, consider what happened when Ireland went bankrupt and needed an EFSF-funded bailout.

The EFSF had to issue new debt on behalf of all eurozone countries, except Greece (which had already fallen into insolvency) and of course Ireland, to lend to Ireland. This meant that, with Greece and Ireland out of the group of creditor EFSF members, a greater burden was to be shared by the remaining pillars of the EFSF. The markets immediately focused on the next marginal country: the one that was currently borrowing at the highest interest rates within the EFSF in order to loan the money to the "fallen" Greece and Ireland: Portugal.

Immediately, Portugal's own interest rates shot up, pushing it over the edge. And so on, until the band of nations within the EFSF would become so small that they would become either unable or unwilling to bear the burden of the fallen states' combined debt. At that point, led by Germany, the remaining solvent nations would have to signal the euro's bitter end and withdraw. Or the ECB would have to invent another trick to violate its impossible rulebook.

IGNORANCE

Europe's finance ministers traditionally gather at least once a month in the context of the Eurogroup. During the worst of the eurozone crisis, their meetings produced one calamitous decision after the next. By 2011, as markets learned to dismiss the Eurogroup's upbeat communiqués, the half-life of their positive impact on market sentiment dropped to a few hours at best.

In the fall of 2011, the Eurogroup was meeting in Poland. Timothy Geithner, the US secretary of the treasury, was in attendance with some solid advice to Europeans on how to sever the death embrace between insolvent banks and bankrupt states. Geithner's chief recommendation was that the European Central Bank should, somehow, signal a readiness to underwrite part of the debt of key countries, like Italy, to give markets a sense that Europe was ready to draw a line under the domino effect threatening to topple the eurozone. He was not just ignored. He was attacked.

As the meeting ended, Ms. Maria Fekter, the Austrian finance minister speaking on behalf of the other ministers, opined that the Americans had no business telling Europeans how to deal with the debt crisis when America's debt was higher than the eurozone's. "We need no lectures from the United States," she said defiantly.[26]

When I saw her on television speaking those words I must admit I despaired. I despaired because her words revealed the deep ignorance of our European leadership and their unwillingness to understand the simple, useful advice that the US treasury secretary was bringing. She and the other eurozone finance ministers seemed on a mission to misunderstand their problem. To believe that Europe's problem was debt. Not the architectural design of the eurozone. Not its unenforceable rules. But debt.

Debt was never Europe's problem. It was a mere symptom of an awful institutional design. Our finance ministers resembled doctors who misdiagnose a cancer patient in severe pain as afflicted with a pain crisis. No wonder the medicine they prescribed was worse than the disease.

PONZI AUSTERITY SPREADS

By the end of 2011, ECB president Jean-Claude Trichet, arguably the world's worst central banker, was replaced by Mario Draghi, a frightfully smart former chair of Italy's treasury and central bank and, not insignificantly, a former Goldman Sachs International vice president.

Draghi could see that his own country, Italy, had a few months left before falling into the same rut as Greece, leading to Spain's and France's incapacity to service their multitrillion euro debt. In effect, the euro was about to dissolve as the eurozone's mountaineering club members went about falling sequentially, and in slow motion, into the abyss. So Draghi decided to take immediate action.

His first move, a couple weeks after taking over the ECB's helm, was to "print" a trillion euros and lend them to the eurozone's stricken banks. As long as the bankers could find some sheets of paper lying around, Draghi would accept them as collateral and hand over the cash.[27]

As is Europe's habit, this simple operation was given a complex acronym: LTRO (Long Term Refinancing Operations). Draghi's real intention, with the LTRO, was to lend to the banks for next to no interest so that the banks would, in turn, do what the ECB's charter did not allow him to do: lend to the faltering states, in particular to the Italian government that was on its way to the poorhouse.

Meanwhile the concept of a democracy-free zone, which had begun life in Brussels in the 1950s, had just been given a new twist in Rome, and indeed Athens. Two prime ministers, George Papandreou in Greece and the inimitable Silvio Berlusconi in Italy, had been deemed, by Chancellor Merkel (with France's President Sarkozy in tow), unfit to maintain the pace of austerity necessary to justify in the Bundestag the propping up of Italy's and Greece's unsustainable debts either via the EFSF or the ECB. It is hard to believe that prime ministers of European nations can be pushed aside, or selected, at the whim of some other European leader. But this is exactly what happened when Papandreou was replaced by the ECB's former vice president, a certain Mr. Loukas Papademos, and Silvio Berlusconi by Mario Monti, a former European commissioner.[28]

Monti's mission was to put Italy's public finances in some kind of order. He knew that Berlin was keen to put Italy through the same ordeal as Greece, with the hated troika invading Rome's ministries and imposing hyper-austerity. So he tried to prevent this by introducing milder austerity himself, hoping to contain Italy's debt before needing to go to the Eurogroup cap in hand. In this task, he looked to the other Mario, the ECB's Mr. Draghi, for badly needed help. It was to arrive in the form of the aforementioned LTRO trick.

At the time, all of Europe's banks were on the verge of collapse while frontline states, like Italy, were faring just as badly. The ECB hoped that its LTRO loans to banks, at almost zero interest, would net them a nice little profit from lending to the states at higher interest rates which would, nevertheless, be far, far lower than the usurious rates private investors were demanding from those same governments. Both banks and states would thus be reprieved, at least for a while.

One morning in February 2012, the CEO of one of Italy's largest banks informed Monti's government that his bank was about to fail unless it received 40 billion euros there and then. A state that was about to collapse under its own debt burden, Greek style, was put in an awful dilemma: fork out a sum it could not afford or sit idly by as the nation's banks closed their doors one after the other. Thankfully, Draghi's LTRO was at hand.

So this is what happened: The failing bank issued IOUs worth 40 billion euros on that very morning that no investor would buy, given its parlous state. The Italian minister of finance guaranteed this private debt by committing future taxes to it, thereby adding a fresh 40 billion euros to Italy's public debt. Finally, the bank took these IOUs to the ECB and received cash from Mr. Draghi's generous LTRO program.

At the end of the proverbial day, Draghi's plan to prop up the Italian banks and the Italian state had failed. Instead, his scheme supported the banks but plunged the Italian state deeper into unsustainable debt.

DESPOTISM

Mr. Klaus Masuch was, until recently, the ECB's representative in the troika delegation that spreads panic everywhere it goes. It is early 2012 and the troika passes through Dublin. In the press conference after his meeting with Irish officials, Mr. Masuch felt comfortable enough (among mostly sycophantic journalists) to relate his view that the Irish people were sophisticated because they understood that the troika's endeavors were tough but necessary. His precise words were: "The attitude [of the Irish people] as far as I can see, and I have a limited perspective, is very good. I am impressed by the depth of the discussion in Ireland and by the understanding of complex financial and economic arguments . . . When I come from the airport by taxi the taxi drivers are very well informed, so I think this is a very good sign that here we have an open discussion. It's a difficult adjustment process but there is an economic debate and this is how it should be."

At which point Vincent Browne, the seasoned Irish journalist, asked a killer question that set off a fascinating exchange:

> BROWNE: Klaus, did your taxi driver tell you how the Irish people
>   are bewildered that we are required to pay unguaranteed
>   bondholders billions of euros for debts that the Irish people
>   have no relation to, or no bearing with, primarily to bail out
>   or to ensure the sovereignty of European banks? And if your
>   taxi driver were to ask you that question what would have been
>   your response?
> MASUCH: I would say I can understand that this is a difficult de-
>   cision that was made by the government but there are a num-
>   ber of different issues to be balanced against each other and
>   I understand that the government came to the view that the
>   cost for the Irish people, for the stability of the banking system,

the confidence in the banking system, would have been much greater for the taxpayer than the action you mentioned . . . So the financial sector would have been affected, the confidence in the financial sector would have been negatively affected, and I can understand that it was a difficult decision which was taken in that direction.

BROWNE: That does not address the issue! We are required to pay on behalf of this defunct bank, in a way that has no bearing on the benefit of the Irish people at all, billions on unguaranteed bonds in order to ensure the health of the European banks. How would you explain that situation to the taxi driver that you referred to earlier?

MASUCH: I think I have addressed the question.

BROWNE: No, you have not addressed the question. You referred to the viability of the financial institutions. This institution that I am talking about is defunct. It's over. It's finished. Now, why are the Irish people required, under threat from the ECB, why are the Irish people required to pay billions to unguaranteed bondholders under the threat of the ECB?[29]

MASUCH: . . . [Muttering something inaudible]

BROWNE: You did not answer the question the last time, maybe you will answer it this time.

MASUCH: . . .

BROWNE: This is not good enough! You people are intervening in this society causing huge damage by requiring us to make payments not for the benefit of the people here in Ireland but for the benefit of European financial institutions. You must answer the question: Why are the Irish people inflicted with this burden?

MASUCH: I think I have addressed the question . . .

BROWNE: You have nothing to say? There is no answer, is that right? Is that it? No answer?

MASUCH: I have given an answer . . .

BROWNE: You have given an answer to a different question.

MODERATOR: This is your view.

BROWNE: This is my view and it will be the view of the taxi driver!

Unable to silence the indefatigable journalist, Masuch gathered his papers and left the room with his tail between his legs. If anyone wants a visual depiction of Europe's democratic deficit, or an explanation of why a majority of Europeans are increasingly reporting to pollsters that they have no confidence in European institutions, put "Vincent Browne versus ECB official" in your search engine, watch the clip and weep.

Berthold Brecht once quipped, through one of his characters, that "Brute force is out of date—Why send out murderers when you can employ bailiffs?"[30] In the era of the troika, Europe gave his quip another spin, employing well-groomed technocrats, like Mr. Masuch, in that capacity.

Three years later, in February 2015, I was to come face to face with Mr. Masuch. He in the same role, as the ECB's troika point man, me as the finance minister of a Greek government elected to say no to the irrational misanthropy that passed as official European policy.[31]

As I sat opposite Klaus, in a drab Brussels office, exchanging niceties prior to beginning a tough negotiation, those images from the YouTube clip featuring the gutsy Vincent Browne came flashing back in my mind. Our meeting led to impasse because, unlike the Irish government in 2009, I had the authorization from my cabinet, our parliament and the prime minister to say no to him. Vincent Browne would have been pleased, I like to think.[32]

MONTI'S MUTINY

Meanwhile, as the winter of 2012 was passing the baton to a troubled spring, Italy was on its knees, a short step away from ruin, and a struggling Mario Monti was feeling the strain of collapsing state finances and banks with burgeoning black holes on their books.

Most Italians saw Monti as a safe pair of hands, courtesy of a successful tenure in Brussels, a strong academic background and a basic human decency. However, he was unelected and owed his meteoric rise to Italy's highest office to Chancellor Merkel's insistence that he replace the elected, albeit obnoxious, Silvio Berlusconi—not the best of credentials for endearing him to an Italian public skeptical of the German leader's right to decide who ruled their nation.

Chancellor Merkel had charged Monti with the impossible task of reining in Italy's burgeoning debt at a time when the interest rates the state was paying were going through the roof due to the contagion that had begun in Greece. Monti's own priorities were different. Having observed the ignominy that Greece suffered at the hands of the troika, his patriotic duty, as he saw it, was to exploit his good relationship with the German government to implement a type of austerity-light that would keep Mrs. Merkel at bay, and thus to avoid a troika-administered state of occupation in his country.

Soon after his appointment, Mario Monti could see that his task was becoming increasingly impossible. Italy's banks were reaping all the benefits of the other Mario's efforts, without even getting out of the woods themselves. But the bond markets, where Italy had to borrow daily to service its 2 trillion euro debt, were going feral, asking for extortionate interest rates and, thereby, pushing Italy's total debt into the stratosphere.

The prime minister predicted that, as long as investors saw Italy's problematic banks relying on his problematic government, there was no level of mild austerity that would placate them. Sensing the impossibility of his situation, his critics, both those on the Left, which disdained his austerity, and those fuming at his predecessor Berlusconi's ousting, were sharpening the knives, while his few admirers were losing faith in his magic.

MONTI KNEW HE HAD TO ACT. AND ACT HE DID!

In the June 2012 European Union Summit, as the meeting was drawing to a close, and Chancellor Merkel was preparing to exit the room, Monti demanded the floor. With his mild voice he came up possibly with the most jagged statement of his life. The chancellor sat down again, realizing that for Mario Monti to be taking such a stance something of significance must be up.

Monti's statement was simple: unless a radical agreement were reached there and then on the financing of eurozone banks, no one was to leave the room as he would veto the summit's communiqué. His obvious point was that it was absurd to expect stressed states, like Italy, to borrow money on behalf of insolvent banks while expecting the same insolvent banks to fund the state through loans from the ECB.[33] Things had to change.

In particular, Monti demanded that banks in need of further capital injections should borrow directly from Europe's bailout fund, the European Stability Mechanism (ESM), which had, in the meantime, succeeded the temporary EFSF. Monti's key demand was that these loans, from the ESM to banks, should bypass totally the national governments and not count as part of the member-states' national debt. A commercial bank in Italy, in Spain or in Greece that needed taxpayers' money to stay afloat should, Monti insisted, get it from Europe's bailout fund—not from the stressed governments of Italy, Spain or Greece.

Monti had just broken protocol by doing something dreadfully radical (by European standards) that happened also to be radically sensible: he had demanded a proper banking union, like the one in the United States. If his demand had been approved, Italian banks that got in trouble would be Europeanized; that is, managed and funded directly by the eurozone exactly as a Nevadan bank in trouble is recapitalized, resolved and handled by Washington, without asking the state government of Nevada to borrow on the bank's behalf in Wall Street or the City of London.[34]

For a few moments, Monti's intervention was met with an eerie silence. Then, moved by his own yearning for a similar solution for Spain's failing banks, Prime Minister Rajoy of Spain dared second Monti's proposal. And then perhaps the meekest of leaders, President Hollande of France, in his first summit intervention, joined in.

Faced with a united Latin front, comprising Spain, France and Italy, Chancellor Merkel relented but added a precondition: okay to direct bank recapitalizations, for Italy's and Spain's banks, but only after member-states agreed to form a formal banking union within Europe's monetary union.

Who could ever disagree with such a sensible suggestion? I, for one, would have agreed enthusiastically. The idea that all banks should be under the same regulatory regime, supervised by a single supervisor (sitting in the ECB's Frankfurt offices), answerable to Europe as a whole, and with a unionwide common recapitalization fund (the ESM according to Monti's proposal), was a rare display of rationality by the standards of European Union summit meetings.

So had Mario Monti managed to push the German chancellor into accepting the first, and possibly most significant, step toward a proper economic union? To a union willing and able to treat a bank failure in Italy or in Greece or in Germany as a European financial sector insolvency to be addressed by a European institution, without referring the failed banker to a member-state's stressed government?

For a moment it looked that way. Except that it was an all-too-fleeting moment.

IN THE BREACH

When the June 2012 summit meeting ended, the press rightly hailed Mario Monti as a European hero who had saved the eurozone, or at least succeeded in imposing upon the German chancellor and her finance minister a policy that created the first, important shock absorber.[35] It was the first time that, as a commentator on the euro crisis, I went on television praising a European leader and had good things to say about a European Union summit's decision.

Except that a few weeks later, Monti's triumph dematerialized. The first signs of what was to come appeared in a letter Germany's finance minister, Wolfgang Schäuble, published in the *Financial Times* in August 2011. In that letter,[36] Dr. Schäuble hailed the decision to form a banking union but added, ominously, that he could not imagine how such a union of more than six thousand banks could be effected in practice. It was the beginning of a process, directed from Berlin, of instituting a banking union in name only. The purpose of setting up a banking union in name only served the purpose of paying lip service to the June 2012 agreement, of seeming to move in the right direction, when in reality the Monti proposal was being defanged.

The process would require several careful steps. First, Berlin insisted that banking union concerned only the "systemically significant" financial institutions, meaning 124 banks. The purpose? To leave out the many smaller, state-based German regional banks whose network of political and corporate vested interests the German government, and the Bundesbank, wanted to keep to themselves and outside any European supervision.

The second step was to limit the banking union to common supervision of the large banks, by the ECB, but leave most of the costs of resolving failed banks at the national level.[37] The third step was to create a collective insurance fund, to which everyone would contribute, to be drawn on in the event of another meltdown but that would in fact be hopelessly inadequate if another crisis like that of 2010 were to hit.

Taken together, the second and the third steps meant one thing: the nexus of failed banks and bankrupt member-states, this hideous death embrace, was to be preserved fully. When crisis threatened a German or a Dutch bank, depositors would be safe. If it hit a Greek or Portuguese bank, depositors with more than 100,000 euros in the bank would probably take a large hit[38] and insured deposits (less than that sum) would burden the stressed state's finances.

In short, Monti's excellent idea was to be confirmed in the breach, not in the observance. Europe's celebrated banking union lives in name only while, in reality and in practice, our banking disunion is as toxic as ever. Ultimate proof of this came in my last weeks in office as Greece's finance minister, when the ECB closed down the Greek banks even though, in its capacity as the banking union's sole supervisors, it considered them to be solvent. What sort of banking union allows for the closure of banks it considers solvent in order to pressurize a member-state government to accept more fiscal austerity, more pension cuts, higher sales taxes and the like?

With Monti's last-ditch effort in tatters, his days were numbered. That same summer, in 2012, the burden of Italy's salvation, which was tantamount to the euro's own survival, was to be passed on to the other Mario: the one presiding over the European Central Bank.

WHATEVER IT TAKES?

As the summer heat of 2012 began to build up, the euro's fault lines grew to the breaking point. Italy and Spain were the frontline states, their defenses buckling under the bets taken out by emboldened bond dealers against Rome's and Madrid's capacity to avoid a fate similar to that of Greece, Portugal and Ireland. Berlin recognized it was facing a simple dilemma: exit the monetary union itself or allow the ECB to save the euro by violating the spirit, possibly even the letter, of its Bundesbank-imposed charter.

In mid-July, Christian Noyer, representing France's central bank, spoke hitherto unspoken words in an interview with German financial daily *Handelsblatt*: "We are currently observing a failure of the transmission mechanism of monetary policy. From the markets' perspective, the interest rate facing individual private banks depends on the funding costs of the state where they are domiciled and not on the ECB overnight interest rate . . . Hence the monetary policy transmission mechanism does not work."[39]

This was an admission equivalent to a pilot picking up the intercom and saying to the passengers: "The landing gear has failed and the wings are about to crack."

On July 26, 2012, Mario Draghi took matters into his own hands with an elegant speech in London, addressing frazzled investors: "The euro is like a bumblebee. This is a mystery of nature because it shouldn't fly but instead it does. So the euro was a bumblebee that flew very well for several years. And now—and I think people ask 'how come?'—probably there was something in the atmosphere, in the air, that made the bumblebee fly. Now something must have changed in the air, and we know what after the financial crisis. The bumblebee would have to graduate to a real bee. And that's what it's doing."

Undoubtedly, Draghi wanted to see the euro graduate into a proper currency, complete with surplus recycling mechanism and the kind of political legitimacy that only liberal democracy can yield—the very liberal democracy that the eurozone was designed to lack. His hopes rested on a political investment from all involved in not allowing the single currency to die, the way that the ESM-ERM had died in the early 1990s.

He said so in no uncertain terms: "When people talk about the fragility of the euro and the increasing fragility of the euro, and perhaps the crisis of the euro, very often non–euro area member states or leaders, *underestimate the amount of political capital that is being invested in the euro*" (emphasis added).

Having reiterated that the euro was a political project, albeit a paradoxical one in that it was erected as a politics-free zone, Draghi came to the one sentence that did more to save the euro, in the summer of 2012, than all the hundreds of billions the ECB had poured into stabilizing it put together: "Within our mandate, the ECB is ready to do whatever it takes to preserve the euro. And believe me, it will be enough."[40]

What did he mean by "whatever it takes" and "within his mandate"? In the next few weeks, an official ECB announcement explicated Draghi's commitment: Italy, Spain and, of course, France would not be allowed to go Greece's way. "Whatever it takes" meant that these frontline states in the battle to save the euro would not have to borrow from other European taxpayers but their debt would be bolstered by monies printed by the ECB. But how could that be done "within" Draghi's "mandate"? His answer came in the form of announcing the so-called OMT (Outright Monetary Transactions) program.

The simple idea of the OMT was that, at a time of the ECB's choosing (i.e., when the going in Italy and Spain got really tough), the ECB would step into the money markets to buy unlimited numbers of Italian and Spanish bonds in order to stabilize their value—and with them stabilize the interest rates that the Italian and Spanish governments paid to refinance their public debt. And how would the ECB finance these purchases? By creating digital euros from nothing. But was this "support" of member-state debt permissible by the ECB's charter? Did it not violate the no-bailout clause that the Bundesbank had insisted would be the centerpiece of the ECB?

Draghi's ingenious argument was that his OMT (or Outright Monetary Transactions program, as this operation would be called) had nothing to do with propping up Italy's and Spain's state finances. That it was all about restoring the broken-down circuits through which the ECB's monetary policy was transmitted throughout the eurozone.[41]

True enough, even though the ECB's interest rates had fallen to less than 1 percent, companies in Italy and in Spain were having to borrow at 9 percent, while equivalent companies in Germany or Holland were borrowing at less than half that rate. So Draghi's argument was that OMT did not aim at helping monetarily the governments of Spain and Italy, since such an intention was explicitly banned by the ECB's charter. No, the purpose of buying Italian and Spanish public debt (i.e., government bonds), claimed Draghi, was to restore the ECB's control over the interest rates businesses paid throughout the eurozone; to recover the ECB's capacity to do that which its charter asked of it: maintain full control over the interest rates that businesses and households paid. Except that, as Draghi explained, to do this the ECB had first to push down the interest rates the states paid in the hope of a therapeutic spillover that would bring down commercial interest rates too.[42] In other words, Draghi presented OMT as a mechanism for restoring the central bank's control over interest rates, with any assistance to the state finances of Italy and Spain as an unintended consequence of his OMT policy: as a means, not an end in itself.

While it was true that the transmission mechanism of the ECB's monetary policy was broken and needed fixing, it was also true that Draghi's real intention was to prevent the Italian and Spanish governments from going bankrupt, Greek style. And the only way of doing this was to do that which the ECB's charter banned: the "monetization"[43] of member-states' public debts.

With the Bundesbank waiting in the wings to denounce Mario Draghi as an apostate and a violator of the Maastricht Treaty, the ECB president had to take an important legal precaution: he had to make any purchase of Italian and Spanish public debt conditional on the acceptance by Rome and Madrid, respectively, of a program of harsh, Greek-style austerity, to be administered by the hated troika. It was the price Mrs. Merkel made Mr. Draghi pay to be allowed to save the euro by announcing his OMT program.

Even before OMT was announced, Draghi's London speech and the "whatever it takes" phrase had worked. Interest rates fell sharply, giving Italy and Spain a welcome reprieve. So thirsty were the money dealers for a good news story from Europe that they lapped up Draghi's commitment, ignoring all evidence that it was a noncredible commitment—a threat, or a promise, that the ECB president would not be allowed to carry out if it became necessary to do so.[44]

Draghi, however, knew better. He knew precisely that which those of us with a sense of the euro's faulty architecture had been fearing all along: the OMT program was based on a noncredible threat by the ECB against bond dealers planning to "short" Italian and Spanish debt (i.e., to bet serious money that their value would fall). As Mario Monti and Luis de Guindos, Spain's minister of finance, confirmed in conversations we held years later during my tenure as finance minister, neither Rome nor Madrid was prepared to sign a Greek-style Memorandum of Understanding with the European Commission, the European Central Bank and the International Monetary Fund. For if they were to sign a deal with the troika, the Italian and Spanish governments would not last for more than a few weeks.

OMT will go down in history as an unlikely success story. It quelled the market for the bonds of Italy and Spain, later on of Portugal and Ireland too, based on the ECB's noncredible promise to buy these bonds in large numbers. The only reason it worked was that, like a winning bluff, the ECB was never tested. Draghi's word was taken on trust (or fear, to be more precise). Bond dealers began purchasing Italian and Spanish debt in order to lock in the gains from rising bond prices (following Draghi's speech). And so Draghi never had to put his money where his mouth was, the result being that Rome and Madrid never had to sign a Memorandum of Understanding with the troika.

Thus Mario Draghi bought precious time for the euro. Rome and Madrid imposed upon themselves mild austerity to exorcise the troika's much harsher version; interest rates fell steeply, but so did average prices and nominal incomes, making those countries' debt as unsustainable as ever.

Italy, in particular, found itself in a rare bind. The country exported more than it imported and its government reported a healthy surplus, not including interest and debt repayments, of more than 2 percent of national income. And yet its public debt increased considerably as a proportion of national income. Why? Because overall national income was still falling, while debt was still rising—even if slowly as a result of the ECB's OMT program.

Draghi knew that OMT had bought him at most a year. He would have to do a lot more monetizing of member-states' debt if the illusion behind the euro's salvation were to be maintained. Unfortunately for Draghi, Jens Weidmann, the Bundesbank president, knew that too. In OMT he saw a violation of the rules the Bundesbank had dictated as a condition for giving up the deutsche mark. And he would also foresee that this violation would have to get far, far worse if Draghi's quest to save the euro were to succeed.

NORTH AND SOUTH

The Irish and the Greeks are, in many ways, very different people. And yet the euro crisis merged their fortunes significantly as the weakest of Greeks and the weakest of the Irish were forced to cover the private losses of German and French bankers.[45]

Vincent Browne's pounding of Klaus Masuch at that poignant press conference put the hapless ECB official in the impossible position of having to defend the ECB's indefensible behavior toward the people of Ireland. In his aggressive questioning, Browne alluded repeatedly to the ECB's blackmail of the Dublin government, forcing it to transfer private debts to the public purse of a bank that was dead and buried and, thus, posed no threat to Ireland's financial stability. Little did Browne know, however, that the ECB's dirty job was not fully done.

Beginning at the beginning, when the Anglo-Irish Bank and other such financial time bombs exploded in 2009, the ECB forced the then Irish government, without the consent of the Irish electorate, to offer the bankrupt bankers so-called promissory notes (another type of IOU), which, as every Irishman and Irishwoman knows, bankrupted the nation, brought mass emigration back and condemned the majority to untold hardship.

The promissory notes specified regular payments by the Irish treasury to the bearer of the notes that were steep and to be paid in a few years, thus causing both the liquidity crisis of the public sector and the insolvency of the Irish state. The defunct Irish banks took these promissory notes and deposited them as collateral with Ireland's central bank, drawing liquidity to repay their (mostly German) uninsured bondholders.

That government collapsed, under the weight of its hubris. But the new Irish government bowed too to the ECB's pressure not to haircut, or restructure, these promissory notes. Instead Dublin adopted the "model prisoner" strategy: "We shall do as we are told in the hope of a later reprieve."

From then on the promissory notes were sitting on the books of Ireland's central bank and the Dublin government was struggling to pay them as they matured in short shrift. For two years the new Irish government petitioned Brussels and Frankfurt to elongate the promissory note repayment schedule, while subjecting the weakest of Irish citizens to the worst cuts Northern Europe had seen since Ireland's potato famine. Alas, the ECB was adamant: the Irish central bank was not allowed to give better terms to its own government because that would be considered a violation of the no-bailout clause of the Maastricht Treaty.

In other words, the uninsured private bankers had to be bailed out illegally and utterly unethically. But the taxpayers who were forced to carry that can should not even be given better terms for repaying the odious, private debt they were forced to acquire in order to bail the bankers out.

After months and months had passed, in 2014 the ECB relented, accepting that the notes could be swapped for new, longer-term, interest-bearing Irish government bonds. The ECB, in effect, accepted that this repulsive debt should be restructured, lessening a little the strain on the Irish state. Thus Ireland's central bank swapped the hated promissory notes[46] it was holding for fresh Irish government bonds that promised their bearer significant interest payments in the long term. And, as long as the bearer was the Irish central bank, which kept these bonds to maturity, the government would pay this interest to its own central bank that would, in turn, pay it back to the government as dividends. In a sense, the long-term beneficiary would be the Irish tax-payer, receiving benefits that would compensate her, to a small extent, for the pain the ECB and the bankers had put her through.

But, no, the ECB would have none of that. "What?" its Frankfurt functionaries thought. The Irish state benefitting from the swap of the promissory notes for government bonds? "We can't have that! This would be a gift to Ireland's taxpayers. Monetary financing by the ECB of the Irish state. What will the Bundesbank think?" And so, the good people of Frankfurt pressured Ireland's central bank to unload these bonds, to sell them to private bankers who would then, in the fullness of time, collect the interest from the Irish taxpayers. If anyone was to benefit, it ought to be the bankers and the hedge funds again. Never the citizens.

Something similar was happening at the same time in Greece. In the spring of 2012 Greece's public debt did, eventually, take a haircut, confirming that an unpayable debt will receive a haircut whatever the dogmas of European officials. The question was, who would lose and who would gain from the haircut's timing and makeup? In the case of Greece's 2012 haircut it was the bonds held mostly by Greek banks, Greek smallholders and pension funds that took a hit. The troika insisted that the Greek government do nothing to compensate the small-holders or the pension funds but that it fully reimburse the bankers.

Greek bankers had, indeed, lost 38 billion euros from the haircut and were, to all intents and purposes, bankrupt.[47] So Greece's second bailout (which accompanied the haircut in the spring of 2012) set aside 50 billion euros that the government would borrow from Europe's bail-out fund (the EFSF-ESM) to recapitalize the banks—a sum that would, in contrast to Mario Monti's insistence, further increase Greece's public debt.

In effect, the bankrupt Greek state was forced by Europe to borrow from Europe on behalf of the bankrupt Greek bankers and ensure that the latter receive these capital injections without losing control of their banks (i.e., without their being nationalized). To allow the bankers to keep control of the banks, Greek parliament had to legislate that, if the bankers could show that they could raise 10 percent of the additional capital, the Greek state would put in the remaining 90 percent of required capital (i.e., the money that the taxpayer would borrow from Europe) but have no control over the running of the banks.[48]

And as if that were not enough, the same piece of legislation specified that the private buyers of bank shares would receive (with their shares) something called "warrants." Warrants are, essentially, options to buy more shares at the original low share price. Put differently, the state was not only allowing the bankers to remain in control of the banks they bankrupted, but it was also committing itself to passing on whatever benefit there was from an increase in bank share prices to the bankers. Heads the state lost, tails the bankers won. Simple!

Naturally, these insanely generous terms, especially the warrants, caused a whirlpool of speculative interest in Greece's banks. To seal in the bankers' gains, in April 2014 a change in the bank recapitalization rules was slipped through Greece's parliament in a manner that almost no parliamentarian noticed. An innocent emendation to some bill prevented the Greek state from buying new shares the banks were about to issue.

By allowing for new shares to be issued at prices well below those that the Greek state had paid (during the injection of almost 40 billion euros into the banks), and at once banning the state from buying into these shares, the state's shares lost value and its equity in the banks was diluted substantially. In short, the public was shortchanged, in ways not dissimilar to those that transpired in Ireland that very same week, when the Irish central bank was forced to unload the Irish government bonds it had received for its promissory notes.

And what was the common thread between these fresh assaults on the Irish and the Greek people? Europe's custodian of the euro, the defender of the monetary realm, the pursuer of Europe's common interest: the European Central Bank.

THE EMPIRE STRIKES BACK

In December 2012 Germany's central bank, the unyielding Bundesbank, struck back with a deposition by the bank's president, Jens Weidmann, at the country's constitutional court against the ECB's and Mr. Draghi's OMT program.[49] Three statements make this a bombshell of a deposition.

The first openly questioned whether the ECB has a mandate to prevent the currency's collapse. The second questioned the joint decision (in the summer of 2012) of Chancellor Merkel and ECB president Draghi to keep Greece in the eurozone. And the third challenged Mr. Draghi's oft-stated conviction that the ECB's broken monetary transmission mechanism should be mended as quickly as possible.

Taken together, these three statements constituted an act of war against the euro as a coherent currency, especially in view of the fact that these were official depositions by the Bundesbank to the German Constitutional Court for the purpose of invoking a constitutional ban on Mr. Draghi's last remaining monetary instruments by which he was trying to keep the eurozone together.

One wonders, if it is not the ECB's job to keep the euro together, as Mr. Weidmann suggested, then whose role is it? By challenging the notion that the euro's survival was the ECB's remit, the Bundesbank adopted an interesting new position: the eurozone's salvation was not paramount, even if Europe's political leadership thought it was. The Bundesbank's tendency to be a backseat driver in Europe's evolution had evidently not been laid to rest with the passing of its cherished deutsche mark. Even if it had gone to sleep for a while, with Jens Weidmann on the rear seat, it had now returned.

Reading the Bundesbank president's deposition more closely, though, it acquires an eerily plausible rationale. The deposition attempted to blast out of the water the credibility of Draghi's OMT program, with which Mr. Draghi strove for the euro's irreversibility, using Greece as its dynamite. Weidmann argued that the ECB's determination to keep Greece in the eurozone could not be squared with its charter. If preventing sequential fragmentation of the monetary union necessitated a willingness to do "whatever it takes" to keep Greek banks open, then the ECB was declaring to the world a determination to buy debt owned by Greek banks even after the Greek banks had lost genuine claims to being solvent. But such a declaration was equivalent to an ECB statement that it was prepared to violate its charter to save the euro!

Weidmann was, of course, correct. To keep the eurozone intact, the ECB repeatedly had to find shrewd excuses for bending its own ridiculous Maastricht-era rules. No one has done this better, or with more panache, than Mario Draghi. If the euro is alive today, for better or for worse, it is down to the ECB president's dexterous handling of this potentially explosive game: subverting the ECB's rule book in a manner neither obvious nor excessively coy.

Jens Weidmann could see this and knew that Draghi would have to up the ante. That once OMT was established as a bona fide policy, he would have to go further in order to keep ahead of the bond dealers. Livid at the prospect of further violations of the charter it had so painstakingly imposed upon the ECB, the Bundesbank was, and remains, prepared to do "whatever it takes" to stop Mario Draghi in his tracks.

The fact that Herr Weidmann has, so far, failed is testimony to Chancellor Merkel's determination not to have the euro crumble on her watch. But, as Draghi knows too well, neither he nor Berlin can afford to ignore either the Bundesbank's wrath or its preference for a "smaller" euro area.

UNEASY EASING

Mr. Draghi's OMT was the perfect weapon in that it worked because it was never fired. The ECB president, nevertheless, knew that if his bluff were called by bond dealers, and he had to fire it, the result would be underwhelming.[50] He could also see that the austerity that had first been imposed upon Greece, before being exported to most of the rest of the eurozone, was causing a vicious deflation that threatened to push the whole of the eurozone into a postmodern version of the Great Depression of the 1930s. In this sense, OMT had merely bought him time to bring out the big guns: quantitative easing, or QE.[51]

QE was invented in Japan in the 1990s and was adopted in the United States after the 2008 disaster. Once a crisis proves so large that everyone is trying, against all hope, to pay off debt in conditions of shrinking incomes, no one wants to borrow even if interest rates come down to zero. At that point, central banks run out of means to stimulate the economy in their usual way; that is, by reducing interest rates. Zero is, indeed, a radical number, and any interest rate below it means that depositors, who must now pay for the banks to hold their money, will rush to take every penny out of the bank, causing the banking sector's collapse.

John Maynard Keynes, back in 1936, had to quote Ibsen's *Wild Duck* in order to convey to his readers the problem that the central bank faces when interest rates fall to zero but the economy is still in the doldrums: "The wild duck has dived down to the bottom—as deep as she can get—and bitten fast hold of the weed and tangle and all the rubbish that is down there, and it would need an extraordinarily clever dog to dive after and fish her up again."[52]

QE was meant to be Keynes's "extraordinarily clever dog"—an alternative way by which central banks could stimulate the economy.

The idea is simple: the central bank buys from commercial banks other people's debts. Who are these "other people"? They can be families that owe mortgages to the bank, corporations, or even the government itself that has sold bonds to the bank. In exchange for these debts that banks own (together with the stream of income they produce) and transfer to the central bank, the central bank deposits dollars or euros to an account the commercial bank keeps at the central bank.

Where does the central bank find the money? From thin air, is the answer: they are just digital numbers that the central bank conjures up and adds to the commercial bank's account held at the central bank itself.

Why do this? In the hope that the bank will now use this money to pass it on to businesses wishing to invest and to families wanting to buy houses, cars, gadgets and so on. If this happens, economic activity will rise and all boats will begin to float again as liquidity rushes in. At least this is the theory of how QE stimulates a flagging economy.

QE works but, even under the best possible circumstances, it works neither very well nor in the manner it is intended to. The reason is that, for QE's virtuous wheel to start spinning, a multiple coincidence of impossible beliefs must occur.

Jack and Jill, who are Bank Y's customers, must trust that the real estate market has bottomed out in the medium term and that their jobs are secure, so as to dare ask Bank Y for a mortgage. Bank Y must be willing to take the risk of stretching its already large assets column (i.e., its list of income-generating loans) by lending Jack and Jill the money to buy a house in the hope that some other bank, Bank X, will buy that iffy mortgage from it using its QE-funded reserve account at the central bank. Companies that are thinking of employing people like Jack and Jill (in the medium to long term) must believe that Bank X will indeed buy Jack and Jill's mortgage from Bank Y and, moreover, that this sort of transaction will increase demand for their products, thus justifying more hires.

To cut a long story short, a great deal of believing must occur before QE delivers on its promise to boost the real economy. But given the state of self-confirming pessimism that prevails in the depths of a severe crisis, to expect that these beliefs will flood into the different agents' minds at once is to believe in miracles. More likely, as we witnessed in Japan and in America, where QE was tried out with a vengeance, banks tend to lend the monies conjured up by the central bank not to other banks or to Jack and Jill but to companies. Except that these companies do not invest the borrowed money in machinery and workers, fearful that the demand will not be there for extra output produced.

No, what they do is to buy back their own shares in the stock market in order to increase their shares' price and collect a nice bonus for having "added value to the company." While this process does boost, to some extent, high-end house prices and the demand for luxuries, the only genuine beneficiary is gross inequality.

In Japan and in the United States, QE failed to bring about recovery[53] but at least it ensured that the recession was not allowed to turn into depression. In the eurozone, QE was always going to prove more problematic as a result of the eurozone's shoddy architecture, reflected in the Maastricht Treaty's incongruities.

President Draghi knew this but felt he had no alternative except to implement QE. He had two main reasons. First, because he knew his OMT bluff would, sooner or later, be called. And, second, because he expected that, once the Federal Reserve and the Bank of Japan began to curtail their own QE, sometime in 2014, volatility would return and his OMT ploy would certainly need bolstering.

The ECB, as the Bundesbank keeps reminding Mario Draghi, does not have the right to monetize member-state debt. It cannot, thus, buy Italian bonds at will from Italian or Spanish banks in the way that the Fed buys treasury bills.[54] To stay as much as possible within the strictures of its Maastricht-era charter, the Draghi-led ECB governing board came up with the following plan: bonds would be purchased from every member-state in proportion to its shares in the ECB; that is, in proportion to the relative size of its economy. Draghi was clearly banking on the excuse that, if everyone's debt was monetized by the ECB in proportion to their economy's relative size, no one was being bailed out.

Further, to counter Jens Weidmann's claim that by buying the bonds of insolvent states the ECB was edging toward buying debt from insolvent banks (which were connected to them), Draghi accepted that nations that had fallen into the arms of the troika would have to be omitted from QE. This meant that the country with the greatest need of the ECB's QE, Greece, was to be excluded from it. Moreover, it meant that member-states that least needed QE, indeed economies that might be damaged by QE, would get the largest QE dose.

The German case illustrates this well. The ECB's economists calculated that, for the ECB's eurozone-wide QE program to work (i.e., to stop the deflationary spiral that threatened the euro), the ECB ought to purchase 60 billion euros' worth of bonds (i.e., public debt) per month. To stick to its rulebook, the ECB was obliged to ensure that 27 percent of these bonds were German bunds (as German bonds are called), as Germany owns 27 percent of the ECB (reflecting the fact that Germany's national income is about 27 percent of the eurozone's aggregate national income).

In short, in the first year of QE's operation, in 2015, the ECB was committed to buying more than 190 billion euros of bunds in a single year (16 billion euros' worth of bunds per month). Alas, in 2015 Germany's total bund issuance was going to come up to only 140 billion euros, because of the federal government's attempt to "deleverage"—to pay debt down and thus to borrow very little money. So the ECB found itself in a spot of bother as the German government was selling 50 billion euros of bunds fewer than the ECB was committed to buying.

The only solution was for the ECB to approach German pension funds and commercial banks begging them to part with their bunds, so as to make the 50 billion shortfall. The problem with this idea was that most German pension funds and insurance companies are obliged by German law to hold their reserves in . . . bunds. Consequently, the ECB had to offer outrageous prices to buy the remaining bunds from banks, hedge funds or private individuals that had hoarded them. To see how ridiculous these prices were, it suffices to point out that, on many occasions, a piece of paper promising its owner 1,000 euros in five years was purchased by the ECB for 1,010 euros! It is as if Jack were to pay Jill for the privilege of . . . lending to her. Negative interest rates thus became an everyday phenomenon in the surplus parts of the eurozone, offering a vicious reflection of the crisis that had begun in 2008 in Wall Street before migrating to Greece and then throughout Europe in 2010.

The problems negative interest rates created were legion. German savers and pension funds, who rely on decent interest rates to survive, face ruin. Additionally, speculators borrow at low rates in Germany and buy shares in the stock exchange, pushing stocks up, creating unwarranted financial profits for already rich Europeans, at a time when working men and women suffer low wages in Germany and devastation in places like Greece and Spain.

If Mario Draghi were allowed to act as a properly independent central banker, he would have had the discretion to buy only Spanish and Italian bonds, and no German bonds, reflecting the fact that deflation afflicts Spain and Italy and is virtually nonexistent in Germany. But no, the ECB must buy more German bunds in order to maintain the subterfuge that the ECB's silly charter is respected.

A VERY EUROPEAN COUP

Mr. Draghi's QE caused the price of shares and high-end real estate in surplus countries like Germany and Holland to go up. But it did not help mobilize idle savings in those countries by turning them into productive investments, and especially not in the crisis countries. And yet the financial press seems convinced that QE has worked.

What has happened is that a semblance of recovery appeared because QE pushed the euro's exchange rate down, as the quantity of euros manufactured by the ECB increased and a portion of it was exchanged for other currencies. For some countries, like Spain, this created a small export bonanza. But this was not the main driver of the claims that Spain's austerity drive, coupled with the ECB's QE, worked.

In fact, what has happened is that, as the quantity of euros manufactured by the ECB increased, a portion of those euros was exchanged for other currencies. As more euros were being sold in the foreign exchange markets for dollars, yen, Swiss francs, etc., the international value of the euro (its exchange rate) shrank. For some countries, like Spain, this created a small export bonanza. But one look at Spain's devastated labor market confirms that the only jobs that moved there did so because European corporations took advantage of the fallen Spanish at the expense of jobs in France, where wages have not yet fallen. The net effect on employment in the eurozone was negligible. The nonnegligible reality is that Europe is devaluing its own labor through internal competition, just as it devalued its own currencies through competition in the 1930s.

In this context, Mr. Draghi's QE stabilized the eurozone's deflationary forces only to allow this form of fruitless and integrity-busting beggar-thy-neighbor to take hold, without actually having what it takes to help overcome the crisis.

Ironically, the greatest success of the ECB's QE policy, from the perspective of Brussels, Frankfurt and Berlin, was that it allowed the troika to defeat the Greek government's effort to renegotiate the failed program that condemns our people to a never-ending depression. How did it do that?

Greece's two bailouts had by then completed the transfer of potential private losses onto Europe's taxpayers, thus shielding Europe's banks from the Greek drama. With the arrival of QE, the knowledge that Mr. Draghi could print up to 60 or 70 billion euros monthly to purchase the bonds of fiscally stressed nations (except Greece's) acted as a further shock absorber in the financial markets. This allowed the Eurogroup and the ECB to close down Greece's banks without any ensuing panic in the bond markets.

A policy that was meant to curb deflation across Europe first excluded the one country that needed such treatment the most—Greece—and, subsequently, strangled its newly elected government for daring to question the austerity program and unsustainable debt that had caused its depression in the first place.

Only the eurozone could create this despicable role for a monetary policy meant to ease its citizens' pain.

WICKEDNESS

A few years ago, long before a political career loomed, I found myself in Brussels, discussing the latest twists and turns of the crisis with one of the European Commission's high priests. It was, indeed, my first discussion with anyone so high and mighty in the Brussels self-regarding technocracy.

I asked an almost impertinent question to which I was surprised to receive an honest answer. "Why is the commission pushing Portugal to increase indirect taxes at a time of collapsing demand?"

Would these tax hikes not push sales and, by extension, the state's sales tax revenues down? So too with the doubling of taxes on heating fuel in Greece: "Why are you pushing for this?" I asked. "Don't you see that people will simply not heat up their homes and that government revenues from the fuel tax will fall?"

His answer was, "Of course. But, we are only pushing for higher sales and fuel taxes as a deterrent. The point is to demonstrate to Rome what it has coming its way if they do not comply with our demands for greater austerity there."

More recently, when I was negotiating on the Greek government's behalf with the commission, the ECB and the IMF, I came up against exactly the same form of rationale. When I asked an interlocutor whether he thought that the exorbitant sales tax rates he was trying to push down my throat would improve our state's tax revenue, he freely admitted that they would not. "So, why do you insist upon them?" I asked. His answer? "Someone whose views matter here wants to demonstrate to Paris what is in store for France if they refuse to enact structural reforms."

It is not, therefore, without justification that when I address Italian or French audiences on the subject of my recent experiences with the troika I tell them: "I have not come here to seek your sympathy or help. I am here to warn you that there is no such thing as a Greek or Irish or Portuguese crisis. We are in it together. Greece is just a huge laboratory where failed policies are tried before being transplanted to your backyard."

This is what the euro crisis has been doing to Europe. A clueless political personnel, in denial of the nature and history of a crisis whose roots go back to at least 1971, is pursuing policies akin to carpet bombing the economy of proud European nations in order to save them. Greece, Portugal, Ireland, Spain were beaten to a pulp in order to keep Italy and France in awe and the ECB in business. Meanwhile, these misanthropic policies are presented in the name of community, solidarity, efficiency, responsibility and, of course, heartfelt concern about the loss of the so-called credibility of European institutions.

REVERSE ALCHEMY IS no easier than regular alchemy. The transmutation of lead into gold, the alchemist's holy grail, proved impossibly difficult to achieve; turning gold into lead is no easier.

Europe's reverse alchemists—the bureaucrats, politicians, commentators and academics whose accomplishments this chapter has recounted—worked diligently, and over many years, to achieve something that ought to be just as impossible: the dissolving of decades of continental integration to be replaced with a leaden disunion that weighs heavily upon Europeans' hearts and minds. But they did so—by means of a single currency.

Looking down from the heights of the famous Ferris wheel at the Prater amusement park in Vienna, Harry Lime (played by Orson Welles in *The Third Man*, 1949) issues an impertinent theory of European civilization. Under the Borgias, he professes, three decades of bloodshed gave us the Renaissance. In contrast, five centuries of Swiss democracy and peaceful coexistence produced nothing more spectacular than the cuckoo clock.[55]

Impertinent though Lime's line certainly was (not to mention grossly unfair to Swiss history), European history and culture is drenched in blood and underpinned by conflict. It is the reason Europeans cherished the thought of a European Union. Art and music, realms in which Europe has contributed greatly to humanity, offer further evidence of our darker side: Picasso once said that a painting is not meant to decorate but to act as "a weapon against the enemy." Beethoven dedicated his Third Symphony to Napoleon, and then tore up the dedication in anger when Napoleon declared himself emperor. D. H. Lawrence sported a raging contempt for democracy, with a sprinkling of virulent anti-Semitism thrown in for good measure. Ezra Pound's poetry celebrated his immense love of European culture, which, alas, proved no impediment to his glorification of fascism.

Against such a rich and discontented cultural background, a common currency that works like a solvent of European unity seems less of a paradox. From the moment that Europe was discarded from America's comforting postwar dollar zone, European elites struggled to re-create the defunct dollar zone within Europe. Never having grasped the lessons that the New Dealers learned during the 1930s and 1940s, European officialdom repeated the same mistakes made during the 1920s, creating an ill-designed gold standard–like currency in the heart of Europe.

During the same period, from the late 1990s onward, Europe's banks were copying the practices of the Anglosphere's all-singing–all-dancing financial sector, without having the safety net of a Federal Reserve, or a Bank of England, or even a Bank of Japan to catch them when the inevitable fall from grace occurred. The combination of the eurozone's flimsy monetary architecture and the imperatives of Anglo-Saxon financialization, which infected the Parisian and Frankfurt banks under the noses of Brussels and Frankfurt, produced a reliance on money markets that Europe's monetary union could not withstand.

While the American Minotaur roared and kept German, Dutch and Chinese factories humming away nicely, Europe followed Britain and the United States in subordinating their industry to finance and converting society to the new creed that markets are ends in themselves, totems to be worshipped in their own right, temples whose sanctity is beyond rational scrutiny.

There was nothing wrong with the idea of a single market from the Atlantic to the Ukraine and from the Shetlands to Crete. Borders are awful scars on the planet and the sooner we dispose of them the better, as the recent Syrian refugee crisis confirms. And there is nothing wrong with a single currency either.

No, what was dangerously wrong-headed was the idea that we could create a single market and a common currency without a powerful demos to counterbalance, to stabilize, to civilize them.

Forgetting the mind-boggling economics of it all, a glance at the euro's aesthetic speaks volumes. Take a look at any euro bank note. What do you see? Decorative arches and bridges. But these are fictitious arches and nonexistent bridges. A continent replete with cultural treasures has, unbelievably, chosen to adorn its freshly minted common notes with none of these treasures.

Why? Because bureaucrats wanted to print nothing dangerous on the new money. They wanted to remove culture from our currency in the same way they craved for the depoliticization of politics and the technocratization of money. Even if one knew nothing of economics, and of the eurozone's hideous architecture, one glimpse of the cultural desert on the euro notes might have sufficed to guess what would transpire.

In place of a sovereign European people, with a shared culture that it proudly displays on its money, Europe continued along the path of the 1950s, transferring immense political power to a colossal, nominally technocratic, bureaucracy that ensured democracy and solidarity were more honored in the breach than in the observance.[56]

And here is the irony: Before the border fences were torn down between Poland, Germany, France and Britain, a film like *The Double Life of Veronique* resonated perfectly in Warsaw, in Paris, in London and in Stuttgart. Today, a similar film would not. Véronique and Weronika would have no bond, no mystical connection. They would be pitted against each other in the context of a ruthless European Union where solidarity has been reduced to predatory "bailouts" that increase debt, "reforms" that translate into savage cuts in the poorest Europeans' wages and pensions, and "credibility" that is synonymous with following failed economic recipes.

The Brussels-centric commentariat keeps pointing out that the demand for European Union membership has never been stronger. Is this not proof that "Europe is working?" They forget that the Roman Empire imploded when its inner core became too brittle while its borders were expanding eastward. A cultural degeneration, also known as the Middle Ages, was the result.

Today, the European Union is also seeing its core disintegrate at a time of eastward expansion. With one proud nation being subjected to fiscal waterboarding after the other; with one people turned against another; with Ponzi growth being replaced seamlessly by Ponzi austerity; with no serious discussion of how to create a rational economic architecture; and with some Europeans increasingly convinced they are more deserving Europeans than others, Europe's core is weakening perilously and the bonds of authentic solidarity are breaking up.

Meanwhile, across the Atlantic, Americans are watching in disbelief as the continent they helped save from itself all those years ago is now at it again: turning against itself, sowing the seeds of conflict in its midst and, in the process, jeopardizing America's and China's efforts to stabilize the global economy.

Is there anything that can be done to stop Europe's frightful reverse alchemy?

Can Europe snatch a democratic future from the jaws of a postmodern Dark Ages?

Or do Europeans, once again, need a helping hand from across the Atlantic, even if they do not want it?

One thing is for certain. Europe is too important to be left to its clueless rulers.

CHAPTER 7

BACK TO THE FUTURE

Every time I sat on the ministerial benches in Greece's parliament, immediately opposite me sat the democratically elected thugs of Nazi party Golden Dawn.[1] Each time I failed to avoid their gaze, or when friends from the United States, Britain, Australia, Thailand, China asked me to explain the Golden Dawn phenomenon, I was reminded of the figure of Kapnias.

The first time I met Kapnias was in December 1991, at the Southern Peloponnesian farm he shared with Grandma Georgia, his wife whom I was visiting[2] and whose life story deserves to be the centerpiece of some talented tragedian's labor of love. Having driven from Athens to spend a weekend with them, I caught my first glimpse of him standing next to his goats, a hawk hovering motionless overhead against the backdrop of an electric-blue sky.

A disheveled yet not undistinguished figure adorned in the work clothes poor Mediterranean farmers think of as their uniform, his octogenarian weather-beaten face, covered in white stubble, smiled at me. A friendly and, at once, ominous smile packed with the promise of disturbing yarns and indecipherable truths. "We meet at last! Welcome to my humble abode," he cried, spreading his arms.

Although Kapnias's reputation had preceded him, I was not prepared for the quiet ferocity of that night's welcome. After settling into the bedroom that Grandma Georgia had adoringly prepared, and having broken bread with them, I excused myself and drove to the nearby town to meet with local friends. Upon returning to the farmhouse, well after midnight, I could hear Kapnias's distant snoring and an array of excited cats. Exhausted, I was ready for a night's rest in the lap of the Peloponnese countryside. Then I saw them: two books resting on my pillow.

One was entitled *Memoirs of a Prime Minister.* Its author: Adamantios Androutsopoulos, the last prime minister of the military dictatorship that had darkened my youth, a puppet appointed by Dimitrios Ioannidis, the brigadier who took the neofascist junta further into neo-Nazi territory after the student massacre of November 17, 1973.

The second book was a small leather-bound volume in an advanced state of disrepair. Incredulous even after I had read the title, *Mein Kampf,* I opened it. It was an original German edition, published somewhere in Germany in 1934. Bedtime material to shock the visiting leftie with, I surmised. Courtesy of a semi-illiterate farmer who, clearly, wanted to make a point.

Upon awaking in the morning, I took my time getting out of bed, hoping that Kapnias would have headed out to tend to his animals and crops in the meantime. To no avail. He was never going to miss my emergence, overflowing with eagerness to gauge my reaction to his late-night offerings. And so we started talking.

Kapnias was once an "untouchable" farmhand bonded to Grandma Georgia's father, who before the war was something of a nobleman in the mountainous village of their origin—a beautiful village that was virtually depopulated later, once the 1944–1949 civil war took its toll. During the Nazi occupation (1941–1944), Georgia's father acted as a liaison between British intelligence and the local left-wing partisans, sabotaging in unison the nearby Wermacht brigade and several platoons of Italian soldiers. Georgia, the local beauty, fell in love and secretly married George Xenos, one of the partisans. Against the background of a harsh war, two young children were born to the defiantly happy couple.

Meanwhile, Kapnias, the teenage menial, decided to throw his lot in with the other side: he joined a paramilitary unit assembled by the local Gestapo and was sent to Crete for "training" in the art of interrogation and countersubversion. It was there that Hans, his instructor, gave him the leather-bound copy of *Mein Kampf,* like preachers who hand out copies of the Bible to illiterate natives before moving on to proselytize others.

The Second World War ended but the conflict in Greece intensified as the country sank into the mire of a nightmarish civil war. Allies turned against one another, brother against brother, daughter against father. Xenos, Georgia's partisan husband, found himself fighting the national army that was put together by the British and of which her father, having given his loyalty to the Brits, was now a local stalwart. Within two years, a modern Greek tragedy had concluded: Xenos was injured in battle against the national army and finished off by an American officer during the interrogation that followed his capture.[3] Georgia's father was killed soon after by her husband's partisan comrades for having also finished off an injured partisan who had sought refuge in his home. Thus Georgia was suddenly widowed by her father's nationalists and orphaned by her husband's partisans.

That was Kapnias's cue. Having made the transition from the Gestapo-organized paramilitary to the local gendarmerie, he was now in a position to exact revenge on the upper class of his small, quasi-feudal universe. He approached Georgia with a proposal: "You marry me and I shall stop my ilk from ridding the land of you and your communist seed," referring to her two young orphans.

Georgia acquiesced, hoping that Kapnias's uniform would provide safety for herself and her children, whom she shrouded in the "convenient" lie that their partisan father was murdered by the partisans. Alas, not long after their bleak wedding, Kapnias was dismissed from the brutal gendarmes for using excessive force during some interrogation—a little like being fired by Mephistopheles for excessive malice. His wrath and associated brutality then turned against his new wife, her seed and the whole world. Thus Georgia bought her family's survival at the price of a life of abuse, poverty, tears and terror under Kapnias's permanently cruel regime. She was never to find respite until her death in 2012.

Back then I had assumed that figures like Kapnias were a dying breed whose like would fade from the land of our parents. It was not to be, as the sight of the Golden Dawn deputies luxuriating in the Athens Parliament House confirmed some years later.

SERPENT DNA

Nothing prepares a people for authoritarianism better than defeat, followed closely by national humiliation and an economic implosion.[4]

Germany's defeat in the Great War and its humiliation due to the Versailles Treaty, coupled of course with the middle class's economic calamity a little later, played a well-documented role in the rise of the Nazis.

Greece suffered comparable defeat and humiliation in 1922, at the hands of Mustafa Kemal and as a result of its own nationalist government's hubris.[5] The political instability that followed the military and economic catastrophe, in unison with poverty's triumphant intensification after the 1929 global crisis, gave rise to our own variety of fascism: the regime of Ioannis Metaxas installed by a coup on August 4, 1936.

Of course, none of this was out of the ordinary. Only a few days before Greece's fascist regime was born, Spain was falling into the same crevasse with Generalissimo Franco's assault on the Republicans. Italy had turned to fascism ten years earlier, under Mussolini, as had Portugal under Salazar. Hungary, Serbia, Romania, Bulgaria, the Baltic states all fell to some variant of the serpent.[6] Even Britain had its brush with Oswald Mosley's blackshirts, not to mention several royals of a certain pro-Nazi disposition. Today we tend to forget that the specter of fascism was haunting most of Europe well before Hitler's first cannon shots, air raids and Panzer division advances kickstarted the Second World War.

We also forget that the dream of European Union did not begin after that war.

The spirit of Charlemagne, which French president Valerie Giscard d'Estaing and Chancellor Helmut Schmidt invoked decades later in support of Europe's monetary union, had a sordid history of earlier invocations. In late 1944, when it was evident to all with eyes to see and ears to hear that Hitler had already lost the war, between seven and eleven thousand Frenchmen enlisted in a new SS division, known as the Charlemagne Division or, to give it its full name, the 33rd Waffen Grenadier Division of the SS Charlemagne (1st French). In the months that followed they fought doggedly and were the last SS unit to defend the Führer's bunker to the bitter end.[7] Something motivated these Frenchmen to do this, and that something had to do with the idea of a Paneuropa worthy of Charlemagne's legacy that Hitler, in their deluded minds, represented. A potent reminder that the symbols of

European unity, having fallen prey to our continent's dark side once, may easily do so again.

Today, Europeans assume that our continent's dark side has been eradicated. That the European Economic Community, which evolved with the Maastricht Treaty of 1993 into the European Union, was conjured up as a bulwark against totalitarianism. While it is true that, after the war, Europeans most certainly imagined the new European institutions as defenses against another war, and another totalitarianism, it is not at all evident that the actual institutions we created were entirely consistent with this aspiration. If a grasp of history is a prerequisite for averting the resurrection of various forms of evil, this assumption must be interrogated. The short quiz below may help in this direction.[8]

Take a look at the following two quotations and try to imagine who, and in what context, might have uttered such stirring words:

> Above and beyond the concept of the nation-state, the idea of a new community will transform the living space given us all by history into a new spiritual realm . . . The new Europe of solidarity and cooperation among all its peoples, a Europe without unemployment, without monetary crises, . . . will find an assured foundation and rapidly increasing prosperity once national economic barriers are removed.

> The people of Europe understand increasingly that the great issues dividing us, when compared with those which will emerge and will be resolved between continents, are nothing but trivial family feuds . . . I am convinced that in fifty years Europeans will not be thinking in terms of separate countries.

The first of the two authors is Arthur Seyss-Inquart, an Austrian Nazi who, as Austria's newly appointed chancellor, signed the Anschluss before becoming minister of security and the interior in the post-Anschluss Nazi government. Later he was anointed prefect of (occupied) Holland. In the quote above he was addressing his Dutch "subjects" in 1940.[9] Seyss-Inquart was sentenced to death in the Nuremberg trials.

The second is Joseph Goebbels, speaking in 1940.[10]

Does the fact that the Nazis were the first to plan a European economic and monetary union that is too close for comfort to today's European Union imply that the latter was founded on Nazi-Fascist principles? No, of course it does not. The important point is not that the European Union was spawned by the serpent but, rather more constructively, that Europeans have a moral duty to dispel the dangerous illusion that the notion of a European union (within which nationalisms and the nation-state are supposed gradually to dissolve) is inherently incompatible with the autocratic, misanthropic, racist, inhuman warmongers who rose to prominence as a result of the interwar European crisis. A united Europe, based on free trade, free capital movements, common labor laws and a single currency is, unfortunately, as compatible with a Nazi agenda as it is with a progressive, humanist, internationalist one. A sobering thought, which Europe today has an obligation to keep in its collective mind.

Conferences on European integration, common agricultural policies, coordinated industrial policies, joint schemes to promote technological progress, monetary union and so on are not in themselves moves in the direction of a brighter European future. The first such conference, with the full participation of academics, government ministers and officials, to discuss (and I quote from the official program) "the formation of a European Economic Community" took place in Berlin in 1942, under the auspices of Walther Funk, Hitler's finance minister.

What this means is that a European union very much like the one that is administered presently by the Brussels technocracy is not incompatible with totalitarianism.

A multitude of evils can indeed hide behind the ideological veil of top-down European integration, especially when it is accomplished in the midst of (even by means of) a vicious, asymmetrical recession. Europeanists craving to imagine Europe as our common home, but who also sensibly fear that Europe is sliding into an unbearable authoritarianism threatening to turn our common home into a shared concentration camp, better beware: the slide into totalitarianism is not to be prevented by technical means to be applied by faceless bureaucrats primarily concerned with their own banal careers. It can be prevented only by a functioning, healthy democracy. By precisely the political process that Brussels and Frankfurt officials disdain so deeply and which every twist of the troika's screw depletes. With every toxic bailout, with each triumph of the Eurogroup over a democratically elected government, Europe is pushed further into a dark and arid future consistent with the serpent's plans.

The evidence is all around us. Today, as of this writing, France's National Front, with its roots deeply buried in a racist, Holocaust-denying mythology, is predicted to top the first round of the next presidential election. Hungary has a government with ultra–right wing credentials that make democrats cringe. In the Baltics, memorials to the local Nazis who joined the SS, and fought on Hitler's side alongside the 33rd French Charlemagne Division, are being held frequently, often attended by democratically elected government ministers. Political parties and paramilitary groups with allegiance to the memory of the Nazi's wartime collaborators remain influential in the Ukraine, in Serbia, Croatia, Albania.

Be that as it may, Greece remains a puzzling outlier. Only in my home country did an unashamedly Nazi party, Golden Dawn, manage to register impressive electoral results. Why are the Nazis back in Greece's parliament? The Spaniards, the Irish, the Portuguese, the Italians have also felt the ill-effects of the eurozone crisis in their bones. So why is it that only Greece has an out-and-out Nazi party, Golden Dawn, in parliament, while its storm troopers are terrorizing the streets?

The main reason is that Greece's economic collapse was far greater than that in the other eurozone countries. Having fallen first, after the 2008 global crash, Greece became the troika's laboratory. The most unsustainable public debt was dealt with by means of the largest bailout loans accompanied by the harshest austerity. The experiment failed disastrously, with almost a third of all incomes and jobs lost and debt casting an increasingly long shadow within which nothing flourishes but fear and loathing. So when it turned its attention to the other failed eurozone member-states the troika was already fearful of its own survival. To make some amends for the wastelands it had created in

Greece, it applied much lighter versions of austerity in Ireland, Portugal, Spain and Italy. Less austerity, shallower recessions, less room for Nazism to grow roots.

Another reason for the reemergence of fascism in Greece is hidden in Kapnias's story. In Greece's case, the occupying Nazis attempted to create a local SS-like body of marginalized men disaffected by both the local bourgeoisie and the Left, and living under a permanent cloud of collective disgrace brought on by a previous national humiliation.

His very nickname, Kapnias (his real name was George), originated from the Greek for tobacco (*kapnos*) and for soot (*kapnia*), words whose destructive bitterness Kapnias embraced as signifiers of his image as a bitter, angry man perpetually seeking revenge on a world that never gave him a chance. Until, that is, the Gestapo offered him one; a chance that he grabbed with both hands and which he was savoring to the bitter end, surrounded by his innocent, unsuspecting goats.

In our long conversations, Kapnias appeared intoxicated with the power that his Nazi instructors had lent him. Attuned to his own empowerment from an alliance with the dark side, he reveled in the retreat from decency that was to mark his life thereafter.

"The Germans were above God," he told me. "Unlike the Italians or our own mob, they could use any means to get the job done. Without wincing! With no fear! No passion!" "You had to see them with your own eyes." "They were magnificent" was his last utterance on the matter, his face lit up like a Christmas tree, his heart filled with extra pleasure from noticing that my stomach was turning with every one of his words. And yet I understood where he was coming from.

Being handed that little leather-bound book, which Kapnias did not have the German to read, was like an induction into a European brotherhood: an evil one, undoubtedly, but one that was also vastly more technologically advanced than his own community, giving a marginalized, cowardly man like Kapnias a priceless sense of belonging to some circle of the select. A sense that can elicit a hideous outpouring of violent sentiments, words, acts.

The influence of Kapnias-like misanthropes faded but did not die out after the left-wing partisans were crushed in 1949. Men of his ilk higher up in the state's hierarchy remained central to the postwar state, murdering left-wing parliamentarian Grigoris Lambrakis in 1963,[11] taking power in 1967 with a military coup,[12] and remaining present in various state institutions after that regime's collapse in 1974.

Kapnias died in 2009, as did around that period most of his wartime brethren. However, the serpent's DNA did not perish with them. It remained dormant, awaiting the next crisis to sprout again.

MIGRANT DREAMS, PONZI GROWTH, MOUNTING DISCONTENT

When Greece managed to enter the eurozone in 2001, it was largely due to the influx of migrant labor in the 1990s from across the collapsed Iron Curtain. Spain and Italy also benefitted greatly from foreign undocumented workers who boosted their competitiveness index and helped them put on a display of convergence toward the Maastricht criteria. But while Europe's periphery, from Greece to the Iberian shores and from there to Ireland, was abuzz with the sound of bulldozers and drills funded by stressed bankers like my traveling companion Franz, the gigantic struggle to get these countries into the eurozone had in fact condemned a large segment of their poorer citizens to a slow-burning, unseen recession.

Economic activity was booming but, beneath the surface, good jobs were disappearing: while most investment in the periphery was pumped into building bubbles, traditional manufacturing centers were actually dying out, flattened by a wave of manufactures imported from the more advanced surplus economies.

Bubbles offer great opportunities for spivs but create very little meaningful, sustainable employment, especially when large German, Dutch and French conglomerates rush in to purchase local firms, wind down their manufacturing activities and use them as warehouses to stock goods imported from their own plants.[13] Booming times in Europe's periphery coincided, paradoxically, with falling living standards for the weak. Even when they bought new cars and refrigerators on credit, a sinking feeling consumed them in the knowledge that, one day, the tide of "liquidity" might turn into torrents of liquidations.

True, wages were rising during the eurozone's golden decade, from 1998, when official interest rates were equalized, to 2008. In some cases, such as in Greece, Ireland, France and Spain, we were told that they were rising too fast, making these economies less competitive in relation to Germany, Finland, Holland and others where labor costs per unit of output were either falling or rising more slowly. And yet, discontent among the weak was rising too.

In Germany the reason was obvious: workers worked harder, their companies were showered in unprecedented profit, but wages weren't keeping up and their living standards were stagnant. But why was there even more discontent in countries such as France, Spain and Greece, when official statistics, television presenters, newspaper reports and politicians were telling us that we had never had it so good, that our purchasing power was on the rise, that prosperity was engulfing us?

A close look at the official statistics suffices to dispel the superficial paradox.

Wages were indeed rising in the deficit nations a little faster than the speed with which prices rose on average. So it was true that the average Greek, Irish, Spaniard was indeed doing better. Except that there is no such thing as the "average" Greek, Irish or Spaniard. In fact, the prices of basic goods, such as the things that everyone must buy, however poor, were actually rising much faster than average. Meanwhile, the prices of luxury goods, such as those purchased by the top 10 percent, were falling dramatically.[14] On average, wages were rising, except that the majority of working people were doing far worse than average—and not least because that average was heavily skewed by the huge salaries of the oligarchs' managers and by the rapid drop in prices for goods that only privileged folk could afford.[15]

Alongside this burgeoning division between rich and poor, another insidious fault line was growing: the one between native workers and migrant workers. The latter were more mobile, willing to suffer humiliations that locals would reject and therefore capable of working for less and taking advantage of jobs in places that natives, wedded to immobile families and heavy housing costs, could not reach.

The weak were thus getting weaker, divided, discontented while the strong grew more affluent and cockier than ever. And all this during the largest Ponzi growth scheme in history, during which Spain was inundated with white elephants (e.g., motorways to nowhere), Greece became an endless construction site, spewing highways, metro systems, not to mention the 2004 Olympic sites, and the Celtic Tiger was either building endless rows of apartment blocks in the middle of nowhere or littering Dublin's skyline with commercial "spaces."

Drowned in the cacophony of so much moneymaking, the serpent's egg was incubating nicely. Warmed up by a hidden recession that only the weak felt, unacknowledged by the champagne-popping commentariat, blue-collar workers were increasingly abandoned to the sirens of racist misanthropy. With the Left nursing its wounds from its historic defeat in 1991, when the Soviet empire collapsed, and with social democratic parties terribly keen to jump on financialization's bandwagon, the only political parties that banked on the growing discontent were racist, ultra-nationalist organizations like France's National Front, Italy's Northern League and, of course, Greece's Golden Dawn.

By 2005 the rate at which Wall Street, the City and Frankfurt's banks were minting private money had slowed down a little. That small reduction in the rate of Ponzi growth made it harder for paperless migrant workers to find jobs. To offer an example, as the 2004 Olympics in Athens drew closer, the migrants who had been laboring like the proverbial ants, getting the stadia ready in time for the athletes and dignitaries, suddenly had no jobs. They became more visible and less lucrative. Not only were they "bloody foreigners," but they now had less money to spend too. Similarly in France, and elsewhere throughout Europe, the serpent's hatchlings were ready to break through the egg, blaming the immigrants for a hidden recession afflicting the weaker locals and caused by the eurozone's inherent design faults.

France's electoral map showed a stark shift of votes from left-wing parties traditionally defending the weak to the National Front; socialist president Mitterrand's chickens were coming home to roost. So too in Greece, Italy, Ireland and Spain where center-Left parties, having played a central role in bringing about monetary union, had now lost moral authority and saw many of their votes being lost to the intransigent, nationalist Right.

Around that time, Greece's Nazi elements shifted into high gear, planning a campaign of "cleansing" neighborhoods of foreigners in a manner that brought despair to survivors of the 1930s. Copying the strategy pioneered by the German ultra-rightist National Democratic Party in Eastern Germany in the 1990s, Golden Dawn aimed at "liberating" suburbs in which many of the migrants lived. They called them "brown scum"' and soon set up "citizens' committees" along the lines of supremacist vigilante groups, tolerated (and in many cases aided) by the police.[16]

Before too long, certain areas, like Attiki Square (not far from Athens's city center), became a hunting ground for anyone who dared look different. Migrant-owned shops were targeted Kristallnacht-style on many different nights and the victims learned the hard way that it was meaningless to take the matter to the police. Real estate developers saw in Golden Dawn a nice little earner: buy properties at low prices, have the migrant locals removed forcibly by Golden Dawn and then cash in. Even mainstream television stations gave a platform to the "incensed locals" with their descriptions of migrants as rabies-infected animals that had to be quarantined, if not put down.

Before long, the list of those who had it coming included prostitutes, gays, lesbians, transsexuals and, of course, left-wing migrant-lovers.

Then came the American Minotaur's demise and the subsequent economic tsunami that bankrupted Greece in late 2009 and led to the so-called bailout of May 2010. The steel strings of austerity that accompanied the massive loan agreement demolished Greece's social economy. With Golden Dawn in place and the political center going down the drain along with the country's economy, a Nazi revival was on the cards. The figure of Kapnias suddenly turned from a reminder of a terrible past to a very contemporary presence.

While Greece is an outlier, and the swastika is not being waved by crowds in the rest of Europe, racism and the whiff of evil are spreading throughout the continent. This was made awfully apparent during the summer of 2015, when leaders of supposedly civilized European countries fell over each other as to who would offer sanctuary to the fewest refugees arriving from war-torn Syria. But this should not surprise us.

While the unimpeded movement of goods, money and moneyed executives has always been a sacred cow of globalized finance and the founding principle of free trade zones such as the European Union (or the North American Free Trade Agreement or the Transatlantic Trade and Investment Partnership), the equivalent freedom of movement for people has always been severely circumscribed. No wonder, then, that racism grows in proportion to our free trade zones' economic crises.

NAZIS IN POWER, EVEN THOUGH NOT IN GOVERNMENT

Many will, rightly, point out a great difference between Europe now and the Europe of the 1930s: today, no Nazi party is close to gaining government in Europe. This is, thankfully, true. However, ultra-rightist movements do not need to be in government in order to be in power. Not only has France's National Front legitimized an openly xenophobic, nationalist narrative, but it has heavily influenced the policies of mainstream parties: a large part of France's political spectrum has shifted rightward in a reactive move to prevent the loss of formerly left-leaning working-class votes to them.

Greece's Golden Dawn got its first taste of real power just *before* the election of May 2012, when it would score its first electoral success. It came in the form of a despicable decree issued by the then minister of public order, Mr. Michalis Chrysohoidis, a longtime socialist party minister. Chrysohoidis and his colleague Mr. Andreas Loverdos, the then minister of health, mounted a campaign against the weakest women in Greece. Loverdos even addressed a United Nations conference to inform a flabbergasted audience that Greek "family men" were being put at risk by HIV-infected African prostitutes.[17] The two ministers decreed that the police arrest prostitutes in central Athens (many of them undocumented migrants), forcefully subject them to HIV tests, and have their photographs and names posted on the ministry's website so as to warn their Greek clients.

Over several weeks, police would sweep Athens, arresting, with no warrant, any woman who did not seem to them sufficiently respectable, shove her in a van and take her to the police station where officers would restrain her while nurses extracted blood. And if the HIV test came back positive, they would throw the hapless woman into a police cell, without any counseling whatsoever, charged with endangerment of public health. In one fell swoop, a multitude of a liberal democracy's cherished principles were torn asunder. For what? So that two embattled socialist party politicians could stir up, and profit electorally from, a moral panic based on xenophobic narratives that were grist to the mill of organizations like Golden Dawn.[18]

It is in this sense that Golden Dawn found itself in power even before they entered parliament. Why should its thugs care about governing if their policies were enacted by the legitimate politicians occupying ministries under the command of the troika of Greece's lenders? True ideologues, the Golden Dawn brutes celebrated the conversion of their sinister agenda into Bailoutistan's public policy.

A few weeks later, in June 2012, two consecutive elections delivered a new Greek government, under the leadership of conservative Antonis Samaras. The government lost no time in passing an extraordinary piece of legislation clarifying that Greek citizenship and good grades in college entrance examinations were not sufficient for a young person to enter Greece's police or military academies. What else was needed? Proof of "ithageneia"—that is, of a Greek blood lineage—that naturalized migrants were, naturally, denied. Why? To play to the Golden Dawn voters, who like all fascists have a penchant for blood and land, hoping to entice them back to the fold of the right-wing mainstream.

Thus, for the first time since the Nazi laws of the 1930s, a European country introduced legislation that segregated its citizens (and not just its residents) according to who had the "right blood" and who didn't. A terrifying chill ought to travel fast through our spines at the very thought. And a deep shame ought to fill our hearts that this should be allowed to occur in the world today.

LOTUS EATERS

One hot June afternoon in 1968, a little more than a year after the colonels had come to power and cast a shadow over our lives, my mother and I were walking just outside the ancient stadium where the first modern-era Olympics had been staged in 1896. A newsboy announced, at the top of his voice, that someone called Bobby Kennedy was dead. Suddenly her eyes welled up with tears. I vividly recall her first words after regaining her composure: "He was our last chance."

In my red blanket days, two German-speaking politicians and an American featured as figures of hope. Chancellors of Germany and Austria, Willy Brandt and Bruno Kreisky, were social democrats who had stood up to Greek fascism and created authentic solidarity pockets in which we could take shelter. The American was Democratic senator Bobby Kennedy, the renowned champion of the civil rights movement and, in 1968, a popular candidate for the presidency. For my mother, Bobby Kennedy represented the hope that the United States would regret their support of our neofascist dictators and allow us to return to democratic rule. Her grief at the news of his murder was motivated by a feeling that a powerful defender of the weak had been lost.

With hindsight, Bobby Kennedy represented something else too; he was perhaps the last American who could have kept the spirit of the New Dealers alive in the White House. With his death and with Lyndon Baines Johnson gone from the scene, there was no one to stand in the way of the Nixon Shock that would unleash forces that unhinged Europe irreversibly.

Once upon a time, Europe's social democrats and American New Dealers understood what their role ought to be. They knew that the only chance of civilizing capitalism required the deployment of a portion of the industrialists' profits to fund projects such as hospitals, schools, unemployment insurance and the arts. Bruno Kreisky, Willy Brandt, Swedish social democrat Olof Palme,[19] Britain's Labour Party—they all understood that this was their task. Some were more successful than others but, nevertheless, they all shared that same basic conviction. But when financialization rode into town on the Minotaur's back, sometime after 1980, all this changed.

In the 1980s and 1990s, Europe's social democrats and America's Democrats abandoned the idea that capitalism had to be civilized by driving a hard bargain with captains of industry, supporting organized labor and containing the bankers' natural instincts. They forgot that unregulated labor and financial and real estate markets are profoundly inefficient. They overlooked that inequality is a by-product of that inefficiency. They lost sight of the fact that inequality destabilizes the financial markets and reinforces capitalism's tendency to fall on its face.

What possessed the Clinton administration to dismantle the New Deal's last remaining constraints on Wall Street? After all, it was not Reaganites or neocons but bona fide democrats, like Robert Rubin, Larry Summers and Tim Geithner, who in the 1990s took apart the Glass-Steagall Act and its related legal constraints on finance, thus unleashing Wall Street and turbocharged financialization on an unsuspecting planet. Why did Europe's social democrats abandon the cherished principles of a Bruno Kreisky, a Willy Brandt or an Olof Palme?

The key to an answer lies in the transformation of global economics and finance in the aftermath of the Nixon Shock, under the guidance of men like Paul Volcker.[20] As we have seen, the birth of America's Global Minotaur needed finance to be liberated so that the beast could do its work (supplying German, Japanese, Swedish and, later, Chinese factories with sufficient demand) while also being nourished (by the profits of the German, Japanese, Swedish and, later, Chinese factory owners, who sent them streaming into Wall Street).[21]

With mounting paper profits amassing in the towers of finance, European social democrats and American Democrats in government were lured into a Faustian bargain with Wall Street, the City of London, Frankfurt and Parisian bankers: they would be only too pleased to let reformist politicians take a small cut of their loot—as long as the politicians consented to the complete deregulation of financial markets. Franz and his mates had lending quotas to fulfill and no alternative other than to strike opportunistic bargains with the greatest opportunists among the politicians.[22]

It seemed like the kind of situation that is annoyingly, at least to me, labeled "win-win."[23] Bankers were unshackled and center-Left politicians no longer had to wrestle against the captains of industry for funding of their social programs. Financiers only had to feign displeasure at handing over some crumbs from their substantial table while politicians acquiesced to the logic and the ethic of financialization, suspended their critical attitude to capitalism and learned to believe deeply that the financial sector knows best how to regulate itself.

In Homeric terms, Europe's social democrats became our era's Lotus Eaters.[24] The lotus that made them soft and complicit to the awful practices of runaway finance was the sweet, private money-minting that Wall Street inaugurated and its international copyists scrupulously replicated. Its honeyed juice lulled them into a haze of mythological faith that they could have their cake and eat it, where risk was riskless and where a mystery goose would lay increasing quantities of golden eggs from which the welfare state, which remained the sole surviving connection with their conscience, could be financed.

And so, when in 2008 the vast pyramids of financial capital came crashing down, Europe's social democrats did not have the mental tools, or the moral values, with which to counter the bankers or to subject the collapsing system to critical scrutiny. And unlike their American counterparts, who were back in power after Barack Obama's victory in November 2008, Europe's social democrats did not even have the backing of a functional central bank—given the European Central Bank's straitjacket of a rulebook.

President Obama, from his first day in office, had a Fed willing and able to stand by him every step of the way as his administration attempted to refloat Wall Street and clean up its mess. Undoubtedly the result of these efforts left a great deal to be desired. But imagine how much worse things would have been in the United States, and in the world at large, if the Fed had to labor under the European Central Bank's mandate and with its tools.

Lacking the ethical, intellectual and financial weapons that they and their predecessors had willingly retired, or refused to create, some years before, satisfied instead with a steady supply of financialization's sweet lotus, Europe's social democrats were ready for the fall. Ready to retreat. To bow their heads to the bankers' demands for bailouts to be purchased at the price of self-defeating austerity for the weakest. To shut their eyes to the vicious transfer of the crisis's costs from those responsible for it to a majority of citizens, Germans and Greeks alike, who had been stressed, some suffering, even during the good times: the very people that social democrats were supposed to represent.

Unsurprisingly, European social democracy went to ground, leaving the road open to marching racist ultra-rightist thugs all too happy to act as the protectors of the weak—as long as the latter had the right blood, skin color and prejudices.

METTERNICH'S ECHO

In 1993, with the Maastricht Treaty in full swing, the dominant storyline was that German reunification, following the Berlin Wall's dismantling, was but part of a wider, pan-European unification project that was to begin in the realm of money: the eurozone. Concerns of German dominance, which President de Gaulle, Margaret Thatcher and others had harbored and which remained in the air in France and elsewhere over the years, were dismissed on the basis that East and West Germans wanted to be reunited only while losing themselves in a broader European Union.

Jacques Delors, the former French finance minister and "driver" of the eurozone in his capacity as the president of the Economic Commission, made a big song and dance about the need to limit the influence of large countries through the principle of "subsidiarity": the idea that realms of policy that could be dealt with reasonably competently at the level of the nation-state should be delegated to the national governments to design and implement for themselves. Decentralization was to be the brake on German and French dominance of the union.

At the same time, plenty of commentators, historians and politicians were drawing parallels between European monetary union and the manner in which Germany itself had unified in the first place— not in 1991 but over the course of the nineteenth century. Prior to 1833, what is considered Germany today encompassed a geographical space comprising a multitude of different states, city-states and jurisdictions, each with different standards, time zones and currencies. Trading across these multiple borders was nightmarish and the reason that Germany was so far behind Britain in terms of industrialization, innovation and governance.

German unification began with a customs union known as the Zollverein Treaty of 1833, an agreement between the various territories promoted as a first step toward freer trade and much needed economic integration.

One shrewd observer at the time was deeply concerned with Zollverein. Chancellor Klemens von Metternich of the Austro-Hungarian Empire was the key figure in the so-called Holy Alliance: the league of Austrian, Prussian and Russian monarchies whose common purpose was to impede any political movement, and prevent any change, that might jeopardize the established scheme of things.

Metternich could not fail to notice that the Zollverein Treaty was driven by Prussia, the dominant German kingdom, and excluded the Austro-Hungarian Empire. Just as Beijing today sees as a major threat the American drive to forge a Pacific Basin free-trade zone that excludes China in the form of the Trans-Pacific Partnership (TPP), Metternich too felt that Prussia was up to mischief. In a letter to his emperor he wrote:

Within the great Confederation, a smaller union is being formed, a status in statu in the full sense of the term, which will only too soon accustom itself to achieving its ends by its own machinery and will pay attention to the objectives and machinery of the Confederation only when convenient . . . [O]n every question that comes before the Diet [the Confederation's parliament] (and not only commercial affairs) [it] will act and vote as one according to prior arrangements. Then there will no longer be any useful discussion in the Diet; debates will be replaced by votes agreed in advance and inspired not by the interests of the Confederation but by the exclusive interest of Prussia . . . Even now it is unfortunately easy to determine in advance how these votes will be cast on all the questions where the interest of Prussia conflicts with that of the federal body.[25]

This description could have been written, with very few emendations, to describe my experience of the Eurogroup deliberations as finance minister of a small European nation in 2015. Metternich could be writing about the manner in which matters of crucial importance for various eurozone member-states, especially the ones with large deficits and unbearable debts, were settled on the basis of modern Prussia's "exclusive interest."[26]

In modern times, we imagine that nineteenth-century politicians were primarily using the sword to expand their empires, rather than appealing to the self-interest of prospective subjects. That was not true of the German Confederation. The idea of voluntary accession on the basis of the self-interest of the smaller states was, indeed, central to the Zollverein Treaty. Prussia persuaded the smaller German states to enter into the new arrangements by insisting that they would be better off inside the union, where they would be well positioned to influence matters, than outside, where they would be forced to react passively to decisions the confederation reached.

Even the notion of "subsidiarity," or something close to it, was employed. The promise of decentralized power worked miracles in convincing German states that feared a Prussian-dominated union to enter it. However, some argue that this was a well-laid trap. The German constitutionalist Heinrich Triepel observed that "a looser association of states encourages hegemony more than a tight one . . . the more unitary elements predominate in a federation the more inner firmness there is, and the greater are the obstacles to the creation of a hegemony."[27] Indeed, a surplus state that seeks to dominate a confederacy may achieve this precisely by weakening the confederacy's central institutions: the absence of a political, central surplus recycling mechanism, which is necessary to avert crises and to subdue them when they occur, increases the likelihood of a severe economic downturn; by that stage, with the various member-states now highly integrated, tackling the downturn demands systemic solutions—in other words, centralization. At that point, in the absence of well-defined federal processes for doing so, the centralization proceeds on autopilot and the central institutions are created on the most powerful state's terms.

This is what happened in the German confederacy that began in 1833 with the Zollverein Treaty. It is also what happened more recently in the eurozone after the Maastricht Treaty begat the 2010 euro crisis: every incantation of the merits of "subsidiarity" and decentralization was drowned in waves of authoritarian, unaccountable rule from the center. In the nineteenth century, a swathe of harmonizing legislation emanated from Prussia to establish industrial standards and legislation favorable to Berlin. In the eurozone, all the institutional changes effected since 2010 were done in accordance with the priorities of the Federal Republic.

In 1871 the centralizing process that Metternich had so feared gave rise to the German empire, complete with a central bank (the Reichsbank), a single currency (the Reichsmark) linked to the gold standard and a common parliament (the Bundesrat) dominated by the "Iron Chancellor," Otto von Bismarck. Prussia had only seventeen votes out of fifty-eight in the Bundesrat but, by that stage, enjoyed full control with the assistance of the votes of representatives of smaller states that had fallen, since 1833, within the Prussian zone of influence.[28]

As of this writing, it is highly unlikely that history will repeat itself in precisely the same manner. The eurozone may, indeed, resemble that German confederacy of, say, the 1860s, with a swathe of smaller states competing as to which one will be picked as Germany's best pupil, but the circumstances are quite different. France is important in that, despite its rapid decline after its elites' ill-fated attempt to capture the Bundesbank, it remains difficult to subdue and almost impossible to absorb into a modern-day version of Bismarck's unitary empire.

However, the combination of two impossibilities leaves a huge question mark hanging in midair regarding Europe's future. On the one hand, there is the impossibility of the eurozone continuing with its present terrible architecture, constantly spewing different versions of Greece's tragedy. On the other hand, there is the impossibility of forming a unitary, centralized state with Berlin and Frankfurt at the center and Paris taking its impotence on the chin, accepting vassal status once and for all.

This leaves us with two possibilities: a breakup or a proper federation. The problem is that too much political capital has been invested to allow for a velvet divorce while, at once, the euro crisis is creating so many animosities among European peoples that a proper federation could not be more utopian than at present.

BACK TO THE USA

Few progressive Europeans would argue against a democratic United States of Europe, with a proper government elected on a pan-European ticket and answerable to a proper parliament vested with complete sovereignty over all decisions and matters. But this is pure wishful thinking. The sobering reality is that it is not in the European Union's DNA naturally to evolve into a federation.

The reason why the eurozone is experiencing a never-ending existential crisis that tears Europeans apart is, as we have seen, because of its initial reliance on fair-weather surplus recycling in place of a proper political surplus-recycling mechanism. Even more importantly, its political institutions and the vested interests behind them (in particular, Frankfurt's and Paris's commercial banks) displayed a resilient commitment to not creating such a mechanism even after the crisis had erupted. The big question here is, why?

Why preclude the political surplus recycling that is, as the United States realized in the 1940s, essential to maintaining an asymmetric monetary union?

One reason is that European elites took it for granted that European business could forever freeload on US-directed surplus recycling. They assumed that America would play this stabilizing role perpetually on behalf of Europe. Indeed, this presumption was one of the eurozone's founding principles, laid out in Maastricht, and that I like to refer to as the "principle of perfectly separable debts and banking sectors."

The idea behind it is simple: each euro of debt, whether private or public, stops at the borders of the nation-state. No euro owed should end up being owed by more than one state, whether it is a euro owed by the Greek government to a French bank or an Irish bank's debt to some private creditor. No pooling of debt between European nations, no sharing of the burden of insuring bank depositors, no common fund by which to fight a crisis of the common monetary system.

In an important sense, this hidden principle is a ban on having a political surplus-recycling mechanism. The lack of the latter was, importantly, not due to neglect on the part of the euro's designers; it was intentional. Under this ban, the euro could only function as a stable currency if someone else was stabilizing it. That someone else was the US economy and its Minotaur.

During the era of Bretton Woods, which ended in 1971, and the subsequent era of the Minotaur, Europe's process of integrating markets and bureaucracies, with Brussels as the pivot, proceeded rather smoothly.

As long as the rivers of private, fair-weather liquidity came from the Anglosphere, they allowed Brussels and Frankfurt to maintain the illusion that there was no need to centralize fiscal policies—that fair-weather recycling was all their ramshackle eurozone needed. That there was no need for the European *demos* to keep in check the Brussels-based technocracy and a lawmaking process unconstrained by anything resembling a sovereign parliament.

With national parliaments supposedly exercising democratic control over fiscal policy, the European Union's institutions worked in the interests of an unholy alliance between the original cartel of central European heavy industry, high-output (mainly French) farmers and a burgeoning financial sector.

However, in 2008 the United States lost its capacity to stabilize the global economy through the operation of Wall Street and America's trade and federal government budget deficits. And so the eurozone began to unravel. The more Europe maintained that the events of 2008 could be accommodated within its rules, the greater the crisis afflicting Europeans. The deeper into the crisis Europe descended, the more difficult the Fed and the US Treasury found it to reignite the stalled engine of America's economy.

At that critical juncture, there was no alternative to the centralization of the management of Europe's public debt and, thus, of fiscal policies. But how could fiscal policies be centralized when they remained, in principle, in the remit of national parliaments and governments that were, essentially, bankrupt and in a death embrace with insolvent banking sectors?

The answer Europe opted for was not, even now, to create the federal political union it so badly lacked. Instead it chose centralization of a different sort: by means of large loans to the insolvent nations which, to win the approval of the surplus countries' parliaments, came with punitive strings of austerity attached.

Thus centralization of eurozonal fiscal policy was achieved through the creation of an austerity union that magnified the crisis, caused it almost to dissolve the euro and, finally, when the European Central Bank acted in the summer of 2012 to save the common currency,[29] transferred the crisis from the money markets to the realm of Europe's real economy. Europe's crisis emigrated from the debt (or bond) markets to its industry, shops and benevolent societies while the bureaucrats and the politicians behind the new austerity union celebrated the crisis's resolution.

Throughout, Washington's officials looked on, wondering what, if anything, they could do to help Europe's decision makers get it.

As the fault lines between the surplus and the deficit eurozone member-states deepen, the whole edifice is losing coherence and sliding toward fragmentation. Even the most ardent defenders of the original European design, who tell American officials to mind their own business, now understand this. At last, they have even begun to advocate that, to save the eurozone, there is an urgent need for a political union.

Be that as it may, the rest of us should beware: it is a cardinal error to mistake talk of a political union for a move toward federal democracy.

SCHÄUBLE'S PLAN

"Ideally, Europe would be a political union [. . .] Consider two proposals. Why not have a European budget commissioner with powers to reject national budgets if they do not correspond to the rules we jointly agreed? [. . .] We also favor a "eurozone parliament" comprising the members of European Parliament of eurozone countries to strengthen the democratic legitimacy of decisions affecting the single currency bloc."[30]

The above lines were penned by two influential German politicians who were thought of as true blue federalists in the early 1990s, thanks to their joint articles arguing in favor of political union: Wolf-gang Schäuble, Germany's current finance minister, and Karl Lamers, a member of parliament responsible for foreign affairs policy in Germany's conservative Christian Democratic Union.[31]

In this article Schäuble returned to his favorite theme: a particular form of political union that he favors, offering two examples of how it would work. Superficial readers would think that Germany's powerful finance minister was advocating two proposals that would take Europe toward a federal democracy. He was not.

Currently, the Brussels-based European Commission looks at a member-state's budget and issues recommendations. If the budget goes into a deficit exceeding the Maastricht Treaty maximum of 3 percent, the commission begins to issue warnings that can eventually lead to sanctions. Usually this triggers a long negotiation between the member-state and the commission that becomes the subject of lengthy Eurogroup meetings, leading to some additional austerity for the country in question plus a great deal of creative fiddling with its macro-economic accounting. Schäuble's first radical proposal was for a fiscal overlord to end national sovereignty over budgets. To have the right, and duty, to take a look at, say, France's national budget and either deem it fit to pass—or declare it unacceptable.

This would mark a significant departure from the present practice. Suddenly, a budget that had been approved by a national parliament could be thrown out, at the stroke of a pen, by a Brussels-based Leviathan. Quite naturally, Schäuble's idea provokes sharp reactions, especially in Paris. But we need to grant him this: he is the only German politician to have taken the eurozone's current philosophy and architecture to its "logical" conclusion. Demonstrating remarkable consistency over the years, Dr. Schäuble was repeating, perhaps somewhat more mildly, views that he had outlined twenty years before. For instance, on June 8, 2000, in the *Frankfurter Allgemeine Zeitung,* he took a swipe at the notion of national sovereignty, calling it nonsensical, expressing scorn for the "academic debate over whether Europe is a federation or an alliance of states."[32]

If Dr. Schäuble was right, that there is no noteworthy difference between a federation and an "alliance of states," then the idea that the eurozone could establish a fiscal overlord, with the power to veto national budgets, makes perfect sense. The appointment of such a person to a position of great central power would, indeed, signal closer political union and a move toward federation.

But is there really no difference between a federation and an "alliance of states" or the "Europe of nations"? Of course there is. And it is the difference between democracy and despotism.

NO SOVEREIGNTY, NO DEMOCRACY

One often forgotten fact about liberal democracies is that a constitution's legitimacy is determined by politics, not by its legal niceties. As Tony Benn, the British Labour politician, once suggested, we should constantly ask those who govern us five questions: What power have you got? Where did you get it from? In whose interests do you exercise it? To whom are you accountable? And how can we get rid of you?[33]

Ever since Sophocles's Antigone, we have known that all good women and men have a duty to violate laws lacking political and moral legitimacy. Political authority is the cement that keeps legislation together, and the sovereignty of the body politic that engenders the legislation is its foundation. To claim, as Dr. Schäuble did in 2000, and as he implied again in 2014, that it makes no difference whether the eurozone is an alliance of (independently sovereign) states or a (itself a sovereign) federation of states is to purposely ignore that only a sovereign people can create political authority, whereas an alliance of states cannot.

His alliance of states can, of course, come to mutually beneficial arrangements, such as against a common aggressor (e.g., in the context of a defensive military alliance) or in agreeing to common industry standards or even in the creation of a free trade zone. But such an alliance of sovereign states can never legitimately install an overlord above itself with the right to strike down or overrule a member-state's sovereignty, since there is no collective, alliance-wide sovereignty from which to draw the necessary political authority to do so.

This is why the difference between a federation and an alliance of states matters hugely. For while a federation replaces the sovereignty forfeited at the national or state level with a newfangled sovereignty

at the unitary, federal level, centralizing power within an alliance of
states is, by definition, illegitimate, for there is no body politic that can
legitimize it.

One may retort that the European Union's democratic credentials
are beyond reproach, as the commission is appointed by elected heads
of state who also form the European Council that legislates on behalf
of Dr. Schäuble's alliance of states. Moreover, there is the European
Parliament that has the power to throw out parts of this legislation.
To round off this rejoinder, it is often added that sovereignty is, in any
case, highly overrated and profoundly meaningless in an interdepen-
dent, globalized world. In the global village, the French, the Germans,
all Europeans, even the Greeks, enjoy more sovereignty when they
pool their national sovereignties together into one common European
realm. And if this means that we institute a fiscal Leviathan, with a
remit to keep us all in fiscal awe, and in line with the eurozone's rules,
so be it.

The argument above demonstrates how terribly Western European
appreciation of the founding principles of liberal democracy has been
depleted. The appalling error of such a defense is to confuse political
authority with power. A parliament is sovereign, even if it is not particularly powerful, when it can dismiss the executive for having failed to
fulfill the tasks assigned to it within the constraints of whatever power
the executive, and the parliament, possess. Nothing like this exists in
the eurozone today.

While members of the European Council and the Eurogroup are
elected politicians answerable, theoretically, to national parliaments,
the council and the Eurogroup are themselves not answerable to any
parliament; nor, indeed, to any body politic whatsoever. Moreover, the
Eurogroup, where all the important economic decisions are taken, is
a body that does not even exist in European law, that operates on the
basis that the "strong do as they please while the weak suffer what they
must," that keeps no minutes of its procedures and whose only rule
is that its deliberations are confidential; that is, not to be shared with
Europe's citizenry. Put bluntly, it is a setup designed to preclude any
sovereignty traceable back to the people of Europe.

One may argue that a European country is more powerful within the eurozone than without, but what about its sovereignty? Prussia, as Metternich had predicted, convinced smaller German states that their sovereignty was better protected inside the Zollverein than outside—only to dismantle it in short shrift soon after. This is precisely what is happening in Europe today, except that it is happening faster and with less resistance because it is happening in the midst of crisis. The fact that it will cause Europe's dismantling—as the people of France, Italy and elsewhere will, at some point, say "Enough!"—does not slow down the devastating process.

"Surely, there is no room for small sovereign countries in this globalized world," I was told by another finance minister during a break in a Eurogroup meeting. "Iceland can never truly be sovereign," he concluded, satisfied that he had made his point. Except that his point was hollow. To claim that Iceland's sovereignty is obsolete because it is too small to have much power is like arguing that a poor person with next to no political clout might as well give up her political rights.

To put it slightly differently, small sovereign nations, like Iceland, have choices to make within the broader constraints created for them by nature and by the rest of humanity. However limited these choices might be, Iceland's body politic retains absolute authority to hold their elected officials accountable for the decisions they have reached within the nation's exogenous constraints, and to strike down every piece of legislation that it has decided upon in the past.

In sharp contrast, when the eurozone's finance ministers return home from Brussels, or wherever it is that the Eurogroup and Ecofin has just met, they immediately decry the decisions that they have just signed up to, using the standard excuses: "It was the best we could negotiate" or "I was outvoted." My insistence, as Greece's finance minister, on agreements that I could take back to Athens and defend as consistent with Greece's, and Europe's, interests was attacked as obstinacy, as a form of stubborn unreasonableness. The satisfaction of Europe's powers-that-be at my resignation on July 6, 2015, was owing precisely to my peculiar commitment not to sign any agreement that I could not defend as an economist, a politician, an intellectual and as a Greek. It was considered unacceptable behavior in an institution created to treat sovereignty and accountability as nuisances that impeded the smooth running of Europe's monetary union.

The euro crisis caused this lacuna at the center of Europe to grow hideously larger. Brussels functionaries, German and French officials, representatives of the European Central Bank: they all learned to expect smaller member-state representatives to toe the line, just as representatives of various Soviets were expected to raise their cards during meetings of the Central Committee of the Communist Party of the Soviet Union. And they expect us to return home and tell our national parliaments that, while we disagree with the Eurogroup's or the council's decision, we are too "responsible" to resist.

At the same time, it is not uncommon for representatives of larger, powerful states to blame the others for bad decisions that they consented to, on the basis that they acted under duress, so as not to undermine European solidarity. So even if a majority of Eurogroup members rejected the logic of, say, Greece's bailouts, the Eurogroup adopted it and the troika then took over, ramming the bailout "agreements" through national parliaments too scared of being branded "unreasonable" or "un-European."

No forum or assembly of European citizens (including the so-called European Parliament) could, after that point, strike down these decisions or censure those who had reached them, even after it was clear that they had been atrocious blunders. In this sense, small, powerless Iceland continues to enjoy full sovereignty while the comparatively omnipotent European Union has been stripped of all forms of sovereignty.

Would any of this be ameliorated if Wolfagang Schäuble's second proposal, that of a Euro chamber (exclusively for members of the eurozone) within the European Parliament, were implemented?[34] The European Parliament is, indeed, the only European Union institution that remotely resembles a federal body. Elected directly in pan-European elections, it seems, to the untrained eye, equivalent to the US House of Representatives or to Britain's House of Commons. However, upon closer inspection, the European Parliament is nothing like any parliament consistent with liberal democracy. In the latter, all legislative power is vested in the parliament or congress, with a clear demarcation between executive and legislature. In the European Union, the main legislative organ remains the Council of Ministers, which meets and votes behind closed doors and is composed not of legislators but of members of the member-states' executives. Moreover, the eurozone is ruled by an informal group (the Eurogroup), meeting in secrecy, that never reports to the European Parliament—as it does not, formally, exist.

These revolving doors between legislative power at the center and executive power in the member-states was designed, purposely, in order that laws might be passed without any serious scrutiny by any sovereign parliament vested with the authority of the final arbiter: the people. While the European Parliament has acquired, over the years, new powers alongside the council, it is still not a proper parliament. The fact that it shares legislative power with the European Council and, remarkably, lacks the authority to initiate any legislation means that it lacks the political authority required to legitimize the transfer of sovereignty from the national level to any Euro chamber within the European Parliament. Such a transfer would be the equivalent of transporting water from a local pond to a faraway central reservoir using a sieve.

Wolfgang Schäuble likes the idea of a Euro chamber because he assumes that it would legitimize the actions and authority of his fiscal overlord; that it would provide the "democratic legitimacy of decisions affecting the single currency bloc."[35] However, the only manner in which one can agree with him is by deleting from one's faculties all understanding of what parliaments are meant to be and do.

DEMOCRACY VS. DISCRETIONARY POWER

This section ought to be superfluous. The fact that it is not reflects badly on a world that seems to have forgotten the minimum requirements for a functioning liberal democracy. So here we are, stating what, once upon a time, everyone knew well, namely that the chief purpose of law is to create a level playing field between the weak and the powerful. While a level playing field does not preclude exploitation and serious violations of freedom, it is the very least the rule of law must provide.

To reduce all human interaction to power relations is the opposite of the rule of law and a gateway to despotism. To prevent the reduction of human interaction to power relations, and to keep despotism at bay, the executive's discretionary power must be minimized by a sovereign body politic with the means to minimize it.

From this perspective, Dr. Schäuble's proposals make for bleak reading.

The fiscal overlord he proposes is a type of Leviathan whose remit is binary: to say either yes or no to a budget submitted to her office by a member-state. She will thus have the right to scrap, and "return to sender," government budgets that violate the eurozone's (Maastricht sourced) rules. But how would this work in practice?.

Why will the institution of an official overlord, a fiscal Leviathan, improve the eurozone's governance unless she is vested with discretionary power? Discretionary power to do what?

Let's go back in time a little. To 2009, in Dublin. When Ireland's twin bubbles (of real estate and banking) burst, the government was forced by the European Central Bank to tack onto the state's books private debt, and demand of taxpayers that they borrow mountains of money to repay it.[36]

The result was that the budget deficit, and public debt, skyrocketed, violating the eurozone's rules in the process. Similarly in Spain, whose government was nurturing a pre-crisis debt-to-income ratio lower than Germany's, the 2008 crisis caused the government budget deficit and debt to rise above the Maastricht limits. What would Schäuble's Leviathan have done at that point? Send the Spanish and Irish government's budgets back to Madrid and Dublin? For what purpose?

The fact is that there was no level of austerity that could have driven Dublin's or Madrid's deficit under 3 percent of GDP without demolishing their national economies and leading Ireland and Spain to a hard default on their public debt a year later. Similarly with Italy and France in 2015: there exists no level of austerity that can push their deficits within the rules without, in the process, wrecking the eurozone in the medium term and immediately bringing to power the ultra-Right National Front.

In other words, if the fiscal Leviathan is to play any substantive role, she must be able to say a great deal more than "*nein*." In short, she cannot be binary (i.e., respond with 1 or 0, yes or no). She must be at liberty to propose to national governments alternative budgets that, nonetheless, still break the rules. Of a variety of rule-breaking budgets, some of which are favored by national governments and one by the Leviathan, it must be the Leviathan's that prevails. If not, what is the point of her existence?

But then what happens if the national government resists implementing the Leviathan's preferred budget and turns down her overtures for reasons that the Leviathan deems inappropriate or unconvincing? Surely Wolgang Schäuble must propose that the Leviathan be equipped with the power to steer the final budget in particular ways that cannot flow uniquely and naturally from the existing, agreed upon rules. Massive discretionary power will, therefore, be created at Europe's center *de facto*, even if denied *de jure*.

Returning once again to 2008, suppose Dr. Schäuble's scheme had been in place. Our fiscal Leviathan would have stayed utterly inactive before the euro crisis (at least in the case of the Irish and Spanish budgets that were well within the rules year in, year out) but then would swing furiously into action once the crisis hit, exercising maximal discretionary power across the continent. Would she have displayed the same penchant for interventionism in the case of Ireland as she would have in the case of the German government, which also flouted both the deficit and debt limits prescribed by Maastricht?

Whatever the answer, it is clear that the enactment of the German finance minister's blueprint for improving the eurozone's governance would have, following the events of 2008, propelled the eurozone into the realm of naked power relations between the Leviathan and Europe's crisis-hit societies, violated the rule of law at a European level and denied Europe's weaker citizens and states any constitutional protection from arbitrary, discretionary power.

Granted that any Leviathan would need to have the authority not only to reject but also to fashion member-state government budgets, could a Euro chamber within, or complementary to, the European Parliament provide the missing body politic that protects Europeans from their own executive and maintains the rule of law at the heart of Europe?

The minimal conditions for this protection to be on tap are that the Euro chamber

a) is uniquely empowered to hire or fire the Leviathan;
b) is the source of final authority regarding the contents of each member-state's budget; and
c) has powers that are clearly demarcated by a euro constitution.

It is crystal clear that at least two of these conditions will not be met: neither the German government nor Parisian elites would countenance allowing the Euro chamber to hire or fire the Leviathan. Nor would they dare embark upon the writing of a euro constitution.

It turns out that grafting a federal democracy upon a Brussels-based technocracy is not a simple matter, especially when said technocracy represents a holy alliance between run-of-the-mill apparatchiks, a powerful central European cartel of heavy industry, national politicians who have their own cozy relationship with bankrupt local bankers, and large international banks.

And so it turns out that all talk of gradual moves toward a political union and toward "more Europe" are not first steps toward a European democratic federation but, rather, and ominously, a leap into an iron cage that prolongs the crisis and wrecks any prospect of a genuine federal European democracy in the future.

Throwing the peoples of Europe in that iron cage, and in the name of gradual steps toward a promised United States of Europe, will complete the business of delegitimizing "Europe" in the eyes of Europeans. In a never-ending loop of frightful reinforcement, authoritarianism and economic malaise will continue to feed off each other until Europe is brought to its breaking point.

DECENTRALIZED EUROPEANIZATION.
OR HOW TO REPLACE TINA WITH TATIANA

Iron cages do not evolve naturally into democratic federations. It would be foolhardy to expect a democratic political union to emerge after locking the eurozone's countries together in a system of arbitrary, discretionary power and in the absence of the political surplus recycling necessary to harmonize the union. The dark cloud of permanent austerity-driven, low-investment, high-unemployment equilibrium is the only natural outcome.

None of this augurs well for a democratic federation. Empire builders are impatient with checks and balances on the executive, especially when in a hurry and under duress. Even when their intended actions are good and proper, they are bound to turn nasty in the absence of limits on the executive.

Once the executives' austerity policies pushed Europe into deflation, proposals like those of Wolfgang Schäuble and Karl Lamers reflected the understandable craving for a parliamentary fig leaf by officials seeking even more arbitrary power to achieve their impossible goals. My brief ministerial experience in 2015 allowed me a front seat in meetings in which the German finance minister presented his vision for Europe. What Schäuble had to say was ample confirmation of the preceding assessment: Europe was to salvage its foundering monetary union by means of a disciplinarian political union that was the polar opposite of a democratic federation. And Greece was to be the sacrificial scapegoat that would put the fear of God in France's elites, eliciting their consent to his version of political union.

But enough lamentations about official Europe's natural tendency toward a crisis-fed despotism. Is there a modest, realistic counterproposal? Can we combine deep criticism of the European Union with an appreciation of the tremendous costs that its fragmentation would occasion? Can the existing, terribly imperfect institutions be harnessed to arrest the crisis and create new grounds for reviving democracy in Europe?

Even before the eurozone was officially engulfed in crisis, the above questions preoccupied me. Together with two great friends and fellow economists, Stuart Holland, a former British parliamentarian, and

Jamie Galbraith, the renowned American economist, we set out to create our blueprint for addressing Europe's peculiar crisis.

We were not naïve enough to think that our blueprint would be implemented on the strength of its rationality. No, its purpose was simpler. To be able to counter official Europe's TINA doctrine with our own TATIANA. To respond to Eurocrats insisting that "There is no alternative" (TINA) that respects the treaties and the current rules with the statement "that astonishingly, there is an alternative" (TATIANA).

Our Tatiana, which was entitled "A Modest Proposal for Resolving the eurozone Crisis," is a blueprint for addressing the crisis through Europeanizing its four components (the crises of public debt, banks, underinvestment and the poverty explosion) while decentralizing political power through a reduction of the discretionary power exercised illicitly by the Brussels-Frankfurt-Berlin triangle.

Seen from another, less politically charged perspective, the Modest Proposal's greatest merit is that it offered a way to abandon the eurozone's problematic principle of perfectly separable debts and banking sectors, and to introduce the missing political surplus-recycling mechanism without creating any autocratic, discretionary power at Europe's center and without any immediate need to rewrite the European Union's existing rules and treaties.

How could this seemingly contradictory set of aims be achieved at once? How can we Europeanize the solution to the crisis' components without centralization? Our answer was that the Europeanization of the four subcrises (debt, banks, underinvestment and poverty) can be achieved through redeploying existing European institutions (which is to say, the European Central Bank, the European Stability Mechanism and the European Investment Bank) in a manner that

> keeps the discretionary power of its management at a minimum by stating clear rules that they must follow under their new redesigned roles;
> addresses systematically the eurozone's systemic problems with public debt, banks that are undercapitalized, aggregate

investment that is woefully low and poverty that is on the rampage; and

makes it feasible for national governments to stick to the existing rules of the eurozone.

The reason why no moves toward a political union are necessary under the Modest Proposal, and thus no discretionary power is needed for some new fiscal Leviathan, is that the redeployment we propose

does not require the German, Austrian or Finnish governments to pay for the Greeks' or the Italians' debts or investment needs;

can be effected within existing treaties; and

is to be handled on the basis of fully rule-bound management of existing institutions.

While this is not the place to explain in full our Modest Proposal (which is included instead as an appendix), its intention was to find a way to simulate a federation, a United States of Europe, by means of automated rules that, unlike those of the Maastricht Treaty (and its successors), actually work. Our mission was to devise additional rules that are consistent with the letter of existing rules and which require no new discretionary power for Brussels or Frankfurt. Under them, the four subcrises could be dealt with at the European level—that is, be Europeanized—while real power is returned to national parliaments. Hence my term "Europeanized decentralization."

None of our suggested policies violate the eurozone's existing rules. In fact, they can be implemented fully through the creation of supplementary rules (for the European Central Bank, European Stability Mechanism and European Investment Bank). Rules that, unlike the current ones, throw up no contradictions and, therefore, require no discretionary power for the administrators attempting to implement them. In the process, relieved of major headaches, national governments can respect existing rules more easily and have more room to implement their parliaments' priorities.

ALEXIS DE TOQUEVILLE once wrote that those who praise freedom only for the material benefits it offers have never kept it long.
In today's Europe, those who wax lyrical about the sanctity of the
existing rules are their own worst enemy and the handmaidens of discretionary, autocratic power. Europe's democrats must, for this reason,
beware of those speaking of moves toward political union and "more
Europe" when their real objective is to preserve an unsustainable monetary architecture. Continuing to impose impossible rules opens the
door to the ugly ghosts of our common past.

Given the European Union's history, and the current state of the
eurozone, political union, fiscal union and various other ideas for further centralization are neither viable nor desirable policies. The institutions of the European Union were designed, back in the 1950s and
1960s, in order to bleach politics out of them. And since nothing is as
political nor as toxic as an attempt to depoliticize a political process,
the result was institutions at odds with the concept and practices of a
democracy.

Europeans understand this better now that the euro crisis has
brought to the surface the repercussions of their union's institutional
design. Especially after the crushing in July 2015 of the Greek government in which I served, Europeans are increasingly treating the
Brussels and Frankfurt technocracies as an army of occupation, a little
like the French looked at Vichy administrators. They do not want
Brussels, as it is structured today, to evolve into their central government in response to a crisis of the European Union's own making. And
with good reason.

The German philosopher Jürgen Habermas identified long ago
that capitalism has a tendency to develop a "legitimacy deficit"; that is,
a situation in which citizens, independently of their political beliefs or
ideology, lose confidence in the right of political and administrative authorities to act as they do.[37] As Europeans lose their trust in Europe's
institutions, they are being lured into a dreadful Faustian bargain: accept less democracy now, more centralization tomorrow and, in the
future, you may be getting something akin to a federal state. Alas,
accepting this deal will not bring federation any closer. Instead, it will

bolster the economic crisis and ensure the debt mountains grow
taller, while further suppressing investment into a decent
future;

delegitimize the European Union even more in the eyes of
Europeans;

replace whatever democracy we have left at the national level with
consultative processes that Brussels uses in order to cement a
permanent commitment to deflationary, highly redistributive
policies (in favor, primarily, of banks and, reliably, of the strong
and already powerful);

reduce political debates on economic policy to pseudo-technocratic
discussions among unelected managers whose allegiance
lies with a technocracy created to service the interests of
the ubiquitous central European cartel and an all-devouring
financial sector;

ascribe pretend-accountability to a European parliament, or a
Euro chamber, which, in reality, acts nothing like a parliament
but, rather, uses the semblance of a parliament in order to
conceal the fact that European law is passed in the radical
absence of a genuine parliamentary process; and

entrench in European law the dangerous idea that sovereignty is
passé in the era of globalization.

None of these developments is consistent with a sustainable European Union. At some point, Europeans will shake this monstrosity off their backs and escape from the iron cage under construction around them. Unfortunately, the resulting European disintegration will come at a horrendous socioeconomic cost, today's equivalent of the generalized depression of the 1930s. The trick is to escape the cage without destroying our common home.

The paradox of a continent divided by a common currency must be replaced by another paradox: that of decentralized Europeanization—a rules-based redeployment of key European institutions (the ECB, the ESM and the EIB) with which to attack Europe's four subcrises while reinvigorating Europe's national democracies. Then and only then, once democracy has been revived at the level of the member-states, can we begin the conversation that we must have of what future we want for Europe.

Meanwhile, my firsthand experience of the manner in which Europe is ruled brings to mind, with renewed resonance, the figure of Kapnias, the man whose story I recounted at the beginning of this chapter. His particular form of evil taught me how our loathing of democracy's worst enemies can reinforce their commitment and renew their spirit. It taught me that only steady, unwavering, dispassionate, hate-free resistance can overcome their determination. It taught me that a Greek who had never encountered a Jew, or nowadays a Pakistani, could be programmed to believe that therein lies the cause of all his suffering. It also taught me that the serpent dies hard. That once its DNA is implanted into societies through the humiliation of enforced and unconditional surrender,[38] it lurks for a long, long time, waiting for a systemic crisis to spawn again.

"When I return home tonight, I shall find myself in a parliament in which the third-largest party is a Nazi one," I told Wolfgang Schäuble, in front of the gathered press, in my first visit to the German ministry of finance back in February 2015.[39] It was a plea for joint action. He, and the German press, took it as posturing.

Seven months later, in September 2015, after Dr. Schäuble and the Eurogroup succeeded in overthrowing our government (by asphyxiating us enough for Prime Minister Tsipras to surrender), Golden Dawn increased its share of parliamentary representation,[40] Greece's debt reached greater heights, our society lost its will properly to reform and, most seriously, European democracy was wounded deeply.

The refugee emergency that same summer, with tens of thousands of wretched souls arriving on Greece's shores, and with Europe's and America's leaders bickering on how not to host them, confirmed that Europe's integrity and soul are in disrepair.

New borders, new divisions, greater divergence is the harvest our monetary union has sown in a continent the world had wanted so much to look up to. A dark continent that once produced so much light now exports bleakness and recession to the rest of the world.

It does not have to be this way. Innovative policies can combine the decentralization of power that Europeans crave with the Europeanization of basic, common problems, which they need. But it will take a radical idea to pull this happy paradox off and stop the slithering serpent.

It is a preposterous idea that—you guessed it—also comes from my problematic, insufferable, brilliant neck of the woods: the idea of democracy.

To put the figure of Kapnias to rest once and for all across Europe, Europeans must regain control of their politics and their money from unaccountable technocrats. We need to take a leaf from the Americans' ideological book so as to move from a Europe of "we the governments" and "we the technocrats" to a Europe of "we the European people."

In this process, it would help to extend to our continent's every corner the French triptych of liberty, fraternity and equality, suitably amended to accommodate three fresh principles:

No European nation can be free as long as another's democracy is violated.

No European nation can live in dignity as long as another is denied it.

No European nation can hope for prosperity if another is pushed into permanent insolvency and depression.

Only when these principles are revived throughout Europe will the foul smirk on Kapnias's successors' faces be wiped out.

CHAPTER 8

EUROPE'S CRISIS, AMERICA'S FUTURE

Global finance imploded once in 1929, and again in 2008. In 1929, after Wall Street's banks fell into a black hole of their own making, the common currency of the era began to unravel. It was the gold standard. Soon after, in Europe we ended up with Nazis and assorted fascists in power. In 2008, after Wall Street's banks caved in under the weight of their derivative trades, the common currency of our era began to unravel. It was the euro, a revival of the gold standard in the heart of Europe.

By February 2010 the 2008 blast had reached Europe, bringing to a breaking point its weakest link: Greece. The gold standard–like euro began to buckle, with potentially frightful consequences for Europe's banks, business, people and politics. But instead of fretting over the appalling prospect of a postmodern 1930s, Europe's leaders had different priorities.

Timothy Geithner, the US treasury secretary who had spent the previous twelve months firefighting the crisis on the other side of the Atlantic, could not believe his ears in a meeting with his European counterparts. "We're going to teach the Greeks a lesson," they told him. "[W]e're going to crush them."[1]

Geithner is not known for his humanistic streak. He would have lost very little sleep if it were only a matter of the Greeks being crushed by angry Northern Europeans. Indeed, he told his interlocutors to go ahead if that was their wish: "You can put your foot on the neck of those guys [the Greeks] if that's what you want to do. But you've got to make sure that you send a countervailing signal of reassurance to

Europe and the world that you're going to hold the thing together and not let it go. [That you're] going to protect the rest of the place."[2]

Around the same time, quite independently and in ignorance of Geithner's conversation with Europe's finance ministers, I was voicing my fears of what was about to hit Europe in an article entitled "A New Versailles Haunts Europe."[3] "Turning countries like Greece into sundrenched wastelands," I wrote "and forcing the rest of the eurozone into an even faster debt-deflationary downward spiral, is a most efficient way of undermining Germany's own economy." Surrounded by morally enraged Europeans, Geithner was the only one in the room to have kept his eye on the proverbial ball: the terrible effects that "crushing the Greeks" would have had on the Germans, the French, indeed the Americans.

My fear, and I think Geithner's too, was that history was about to repeat itself. In 1929 all the burden of adjustment was forced upon the weakest debtors. Such a policy cannot succeed since the resulting deflation poisons debt dynamics, and mass joblessness poisons democracy. So it did not succeed. In 2010, once again the greatest burden fell on the weakest of shoulders. Within a few years Europe was losing its integrity and is now at an advanced stage of surrendering its soul.

THE GHOST OF VERSAILLES

Le Figaro's headline in 1992, celebrating the Maastricht Treaty as a new Treaty of Versailles—one that would make Germany pay again for France, and without a single shot being fired—was undoubtedly a dastardly affront to Europe's history.[4] The French conservative newspaper was, clearly, ignorant of the true folly of Versailles. The gist of that sorry treaty was not so much that it crushed Germany economically and caused Germans untold collective pain, but that, in the end, it was an own goal: a terrible deal even for the victors—a self-defeating punitive act that John Maynard Keynes had anticipated early on[5] and the rest of the world came to recognize as such in the 1930s, when it was too late.

While it was offensive for the French conservative newspaper to portray Maastricht as a New Versailles, it is perfectly accurate to draw parallels between Versailles and the eurozone's bailouts, Greece's in particular. In 2010, quoting from Keynes's splendid essay "Dr. Melchior: A Defeated Enemy"[6] but simply changing the names of the protagonists, I wrote[7] of the Greek government's

> insincere acceptance [. . .] of impossible conditions which it was not intended to carry out—an acceptance which made Greece [replacing "Germany"] almost as guilty to accept what she could not fulfil as the troika [replacing "Allies"] to impose what they were not entitled to exact.

Amusing myself further with the extent to which Keynes's severe criticism of the Versailles Treaty applied so fittingly to the Greek drama, I went on to paraphrase from his *The Economic Consequences of the Peace*:[8]

> Moved by insane delusion and reckless self-regard, the Greek ["German"] people overturned the foundations on which we all lived and built. But the spokesmen of the European Union ["Great War's victorious allies"] have run the risk of completing the ruin, which Greece ["Germany"] began, by a bailout agreement ["Versailles Treaty"] which, if it is carried into effect, must impair yet further, when it might have restored, the delicate, complicated organization, already shaken and broken by the 2008 crisis ["The War"], through which alone the European peoples can employ themselves and live.

To many readers it may seem a terrible exaggeration to suggest that the ill-considered Greek bailout posed a threat to Europe and, indeed, to the global economy. But it is not.

The German, French and European central bank officials were wrong to hope that in order to save their banks it would be enough to lend huge, irretrievable sums to Greece and then let my country wallow in permanent depression as a cautionary tale.

This strategy, which was then used as the template for the rest of the European periphery, turning the majority of European states into what I jokingly refer to as Bailoutistan, was always going to backfire on the European economy. Tim Geithner and Jack Lew, his successor in the US Treasury Department, understood this well. They shared the concern that what started in Greece in 2010, with the combination of an absurd bailout and a hideous level of austerity, has put Europe into a position that undermines America's recovery and threatens the prospects of China, Latin America, even India and Africa.

AMERICA'S FUTURE IMPERILED

The United States provided the stabilizers that global capitalism relied upon after the war. Bretton Woods, the broader global plan in which it was embedded, and the brave new post-1971 world of Paul Volcker[9] stood behind capitalism's postwar planetary-scale triumph.

What did America bring to global capitalism with such great profit? Washington's lack of deficit phobia. Deficit phobia goes hand in hand with a penchant for mercantilist surplus fetishism. When deficit-phobic politicians rule the most powerful economies, a 1930s-like beggar-thy-neighbor economic war of all against all eventually rears its ugly head. Countries then compete for the world's reserves and are led, as if by an invisible fist, to a terrible economic equilibrium out of which all sorts of political and moral evil spring.

The world was blessed after 1944 with New Dealers in Washington who understood all this perfectly well and who were committed never to allow the tragedy of the 1930s to revisit the planet. Here is how LBJ's deputy national security advisor Francis Bator described their thinking and their policies in 1968:

> Through most of the postwar period the problem of inconsistency has been masked—and the world spared the damaging effect—because the United States, with the cooperation of the rest of the world, has been prepared not merely to stay out of the competition for reserves, but to play the role of world central bank, pumping out liquidity, letting others satisfy their desires for surpluses and reserves, while at the same time running down its gross reserves and increasing the nation's liquid liabilities. The

system worked precisely because the United States was so long immune to deficit phobia.

Both before and after the Nixon Shock, America was creating a terrain on which the German, Japanese and later Chinese companies and economies could accumulate reserves and surpluses. Washington's readiness to go into the red was, in this important sense, a prerequisite for the rest to succeed. There was no philanthropy in this. Just enlightened self-interest by American officials who understood capitalism's weird ways.

America's capacity to bear the weight of global capitalism on its shoulders diminished perilously in 2008. Wall Street's collapse was contained, by the actions of people like Tim Geithner and Ben Bernanke,[10] but America's global surplus recycling capacities did not recover. From 2009 onward, America's lack of deficit phobia helped draw a line under the Great Recession. The US trade deficit grew again, helping Chinese and German factories somewhat revive their damaged fortunes, and the US federal government's budget deficit continued to offer global investors the safe harbor they craved.[11]

Nevertheless, the US deficits are no longer capable of maintaining the mechanism that kept the global flows of goods and profits balanced at a planetary level prior to 2008. The American Minotaur is badly wounded and incapable of performing the duties that Paul Volcker and others had assigned to it back in the late 1970s. China's government tried valiantly to stabilize its economy and, indeed, the global order, by willfully creating an investment bubble built upon a real estate bubble inflated by regional government land sales.[12] While Beijing's ploy succeeded for a while in keeping Chinese and, to a large extent, German factories churning (by providing them with demand for their products), the bubbles it created are now deflating.

Germany exploited this made-in-China bubble to replace exports that used to go to Europe's deficit countries, such as Spain, Greece and Portugal, whose imports from Germany had collapsed in the meantime. But unlike Berlin, whose deficit phobia prevents it from realizing its duty to help recycle global surpluses, Beijing understood well both its duty and its own limitations. It understood that its capacity to inflate the Chinese economy out of trouble, and in so doing stabilize the surplus European countries, was not going to last long. That unless Europe joined America, Japan and China in helping stabilize the global flows of goods and money, China's bubbles would deflate and the world would sink into deeper trouble.[13]

Washington officials were aware this would happen and have been keeping an anxious eye out for any signs of Europe's return to rationality. Alas, the deficit phobia of Europe's surplus nations, their commitment to what I labeled "the principle of perfectly separable public debts and banking sectors" (see the chapter 7 section "Back to the USA") and their complete subjugation of all other eurozone member-states ensured that Washington, Tokyo and Beijing would be receiving no assistance from an inward-looking, macroeconomically naïve, deficit-phobic eurozone.

Greece, once again, was the litmus test. A test that the Brussels-Frankfurt-Berlin triangle consistently fails. Washington has every reason to be furious with the Europeans for its deficit phobia and its detrimental effects on everyone. Despite the mountains of money that the Fed has printed, by which to stimulate the domestic economy, US-based corporations refuse to invest sufficiently in quality jobs and productive machinery fearing another chill wind blowing from Europe that will, in an infinite feedback loop with China's slowdown, reduce economic activity worldwide. If today the US job market is replete with American workers who would like to work longer hours but cannot, if wages are stuck in a rut, if companies prefer to use spare cash to buy back their own shares (rather than invest), Europe's failings are a large part of the reason.

In short, with America's capacity to stabilize the globe gone, the greatest past beneficiaries of that now-gone capacity, the Europeans, are now abrogating their duties to America and to the rest of the world.

FROM GEITHNER'S APOPLEXY TO LEW'S ANGST

When Tim Geithner encountered the Europeans' gross failure to comprehend the true nature of the eurozone crisis[14] and Greece's symptomatic significance, he was brought to the verge of apoplexy.[15] His successor in the US Treasury Department, Jack Lew, came into the fray when things had calmed down considerably but was still struck by Europe's incomprehension of its negative impact on the global economy.

On October 30, 2013, Lew presented to Congress the Treasury Department's "Report to Congress on Economic and Exchange Rate Policies."[16] With it he took a swipe at Germany, accusing it of exporting economic depression to the rest of eurozone and, indeed, to the global economy. Wolfgang Schäuble's ministry responded the next day with the following statement: "There are no imbalances in Germany that need correction. On the contrary, the innovative German economy contributes significantly to global growth through exports and the import of components for finished products."[17]

There are few occasions in any argument where one side is completely right and the other comprehensively wrong. This is one of them. Jack Lew's Treasury was spot on and the German response utterly ludicrous. The US Treasury Department's underlying analysis was founded on basic macroeconomics that Berlin, and the Eurogroup (as I have personally witnessed), refuses to acknowledge. The rationale is straightforward:

Berlin's plan for eurozone member-states to overcome the crisis relies on a combination of net exports and balanced budgets. Given the great excess of savings over investment in both the surplus and the deficit eurozone member-states, the only way Berlin's plan can work is if the eurozone turns into a mercantilist fiend. What this means, in simple numbers, is that to escape its crisis in this manner the eurozone must reach a current account surplus,[18] in relation to the rest of the world, no less than 9 percent of total European income.

Lest we forget, China was deemed a great destabilizing force on the global order when its trade surplus was at those levels, back in 2008. Since one economy's trade surplus is another's deficit, growing net exports of a large economy (like China's or Europe's) means that it also exports deflation to the rest of the world. A 9 percent eurozone trade surplus would destroy America's, China's, Latin America's, India's, Africa's and South East Asia's hopes for stability and growth.[19] It would mean massive unemployment in the rest of the world, political instability and calls to erect protectionist barriers that would reduce incomes everywhere, including in Germany.

This is why the US Treasury Department looks at Berlin's and Brussels' plans with a mixture of incomprehension and revulsion. Washington understands that if the deficit-phobic policies Berlin has been trying to implement on the rest of the eurozone (beginning with the Greek guinea pig) are to succeed, they will need to destroy whatever balance is left in the global economy. But given that, ultimately, these policies cannot succeed,[20] they are bound to "accomplish" two other tasks at once: further wreck Europe's periphery[21] and deliver a continual deflationary shock to the global economy.

American officials are watching all this from across the Atlantic, fretting at the sight and sound of the forces of deflation that an inane Europe, oblivious to its policies' self-defeating nature, is sending Washington's way. Personal encounters with American officials have led me to the following realization:

> They know America no longer has the power to stabilize the world economy by itself.
> They understand that Europe's policies are detrimental to America's future.
> And they are frustrated that their European interlocutors are not only ignorant of simple macroeconomic laws but, curiously, that they are not even ashamed of their ignorance.

RELIGIOUS RULES RIPENING

When economies founder, religious inventions are never far behind. The eurozone's rules, and their staying power in the face of their abject failures, cannot be understood fully without some grasp of the manner in which religion-sourced thinking gains an upper hand at times of prolonged crisis.

In a debate in September 2015,[22] Emmanuel Macron, France's economy minister, warned that the continuing euro crisis ensnares Europe in a new religious war between Catholics and Calvinists, implying a stand-off between countries east of the Rhine and north of the Alps and the rest. At that point I interjected, in jest, to say that this leaves us Orthodox Greeks out of the picture, possibly as a people forced to implement orthodox economic policies but ending up, due to our failure, catholic in our protestations.

Less humorously, Macron and I were alluding to the lack of serious economic analysis permeating Brussels and Frankfurt and its substitution with a religious commitment to defend the eurozone's original faith. These defenders, I would add, seem to have taken a leaf out of the book of almost every established church, and not just across the Catholic-Calvinist divide. In a sense, they are interdenominational when it comes to manufacturing logically impaired doctrines that politicians then parrot across the continent as unassailable truths.

Economic "analyses" ("dogmas" would be the better name) are endorsed only to the extent that they confirm the European Commission's, or the European Central Bank's, orthodox prophesies. When the facts disagree with them, it is too bad for the facts. Empirical evidence that is damning of Ponzi austerity is, for example, met with a Jesuit-like strategy of arguing at once in favor of the austerity dogma and in favor of the facts that contradict the dogma.

Meanwhile, the bureaucrats' rituals succeed in tightening the Protestant-like circle of true believers to the extent that those excluded (such as those politicians who dare challenge the troika's ritualistic faith) can only be saved through ceaseless repetition of their epiphany and incantations in praise of redemptive austerity.

The American institutionalist Clarence Ayres once wrote about bureaucrats, as if he were referring to the Eurogroup, the European Commission, the European Central Bank, the European Stability Mechanism and the rest, that

> they pay reality the compliment of imputing belief to ceremonial status, but they do so for the purpose of validating status, not for the purpose of achieving efficiency.

In important ways, Europe is being run by a web of Belief that has been separated from Reason and from Evidence. Its ways resemble less the method of Descartes, Hume, Newton or Leibniz made famous and more the network of mythological convictions that anthropologist Evans-Pritchard discovered in the 1930s to be the ideological mechanism supporting the power structures of an African tribe known as the Azande:

> Azande see as well as we that the failure of their oracle to prophesy truly calls for explanation, but so entangled are they in mystical notions that they must make use of them to account for failure. The contradiction between experience and one mystical notion is explained by reference to other mystical notions.[23]

Expediency turns "modern" people too to ritual belief, especially so in the absence of a rational debate in the context of a functioning democracy. In times of crisis and stress, modern societies caught up in ritual beliefs quickly descend into various forms of self-flagellation.

In a 2013 article entitled "We Germans do not want a German Europe,"[24] Wolfgang Schäuble argued that a majority of Europeans support his recipe for ending the eurozone crisis, ignoring most macroeconomists, the US Treasury Department and the rest of the world. "[A] clear majority of people," wrote the German finance minister, "not just in northern Europe, but also in the south—[are] in favor of combating the crisis through reforms, public spending cuts and debt reduction."

This may well be so. But it is beside the point. Bewildered Europeans, caught up in a permanent downward spiral, and devoid of democratic control over those whose decisions determine their lives, turn naturally inward, blaming themselves. Back in the Dark Ages, when the Black Death hit Europe, most Europeans genuinely believed that the plague was caused by sinful living and would be exorcised through self-flagellation. They were, of course, precisely wrong. Something similar is happening today.

Today the dominant text is not the Bible, or its interpretations by those claiming to have a hotline to the divine. Today's governing text in Europe is the rules laid out by the treaties and the bailout agreements: contractual arrangements that those who have entered the "circle of the Euro-faithful" must abide by or else. I know this because I experienced it up close and personally. You have a choice, I was told in no uncertain terms, between the existing terms of your country's bailout agreement (signed by previous governments) and the highway.

Fascinatingly, when I tried to start a conversation on the appropriateness and realism of these terms and the rules they relied upon, the answer was not of the form "the rules are fine, proper and implementable because . . ." but rather "the rules are the rules are the rules . . ."[25]

It was a little like encountering Henry Ford all over again, only this time not in the context of selling his Model T, which a customer could order in any color he liked as long as it was black, but at the level of international economic decision making, where our newly elected government could choose any policy mix it liked as long as it was virtually identical to the calamitous one imposed by the troika on previous Greek governments.[26]

A religious dedication to contradictory rules (that economic forces have no respect for) has brought powerful empires down in the past—the Soviet Union most recently. The European Union seems hell-bent on treading this path to nowhere. The no-bailout rule is a good case in point. It was a heartfelt rule when penned in 1993. But it was impossible to observe in the face of the inevitable euro crisis that hit us in 2010. Tragically, this antinomy guided everything the eurozone did afterward.

Instead of asking "How should we deal with this crisis?" the powers-that-be asked an almost religious question: "How should we bail out Greece, Ireland and the others without seeming to violate the no-bailout dogma?" It takes a second's thinking to realize that, by posing the second question rather than the first, Europe was bound to go astray.

A myriad of sins followed naturally from that wrong turn. While it would have been straightforward, and perfectly legal, to allow Irish banks or the Greek state to default to their private creditors (so as to respect the no-bailout clause), the authorities' guilty desire to bail out the German and French banks (without telling taxpayers that this was what they were doing) led to the need to violate the no-bailout rule by concocting another rule: the no-default rule, which was never part of Europe's original set of rules.

Both the freshly minted no-default rule and the original no-bailout clause were political whims of the strong disguised as legal constraints upon the weak. In reality, the strong break their rules at will and concoct new rules whenever they think it suits them. The most splendid example is Dr. Schäuble's most recent ruling, which is that Greece cannot default within the eurozone but can do so after it is forced to leave the euro. This is a remarkable example because, first, no such rule was ever agreed to and, second, the rules do not permit any member-state to be thrown out of the eurozone.

In brief, it is now clear that Europe's religious dedication to rules is nothing but a veil under which the strong make up the rules as they go along to suit their own political agenda. Perhaps that would be fine if the said agenda was not quick-marching Europe and the global economy into an economic, political and moral morass.

FROM DISSONANCE
TO HARMONY

During the five months in 2015 in which I received an intense crash course at the forefront of Europe's political feuds, I confirmed one thing: a titanic battle is being waged for Europe's integrity and soul, with the forces of reason and humanism losing out, so far, to growing irrationality, authoritarianism and malice.

The rest of the world, America in particular, are concerned but not as much as they ought to be. Europe has twice already in the past hundred years dragged the planet down into appalling quagmires. It can do so again. Europe (as the New Dealers understood in the 1940s) is too important to leave to us Europeans. The whole world has a stake in a victory for rationality, liberty, democracy and humanism in the birthplace of those ideas.

Leonard Schapiro, writing on Stalinism,[1] warned us that "the true object of propaganda is neither to convince nor even to persuade. But to produce a uniform pattern of public utterances in which the first trace of unorthodox thought reveals itself as a jarring dissonance."[2]

During the five months of negotiating at the Eurogroup on behalf of Greece, I bore the brunt precisely of this type of propaganda. My attempts to infuse some rational humanism into the negotiations on my country's fiscal and reform agenda were met with a concerted effort to turn our sensible proposals into a "jarring dissonance." It is quite remarkable, and somewhat disheartening, that an insightful line once written about Stalinism has so much resonance today in the corridors of power in Brussels, Frankfurt and Berlin.

Anyone who dares challenge the official version that "all is well in the best of all possible European Unions" is indeed treated as a jarring dissonance. But dissidents should take heart. False dogmas are condemned eventually to be found out, in Europe as they were in the Soviet Union and elsewhere. What matters now is that, in Europe, they should be found out quickly. For the daily human toll of this crisis is too high and has a capacity to spread its awful wings to reach parts of the planet that do not deserve to have their progress annulled as a result of yet another European debacle.

When Gandhi was asked what he thought of Western civilization, he famously replied that "it would be a very good idea." If asked what we think of the European Union today, we could do worse than re-marking, "What a splendid idea! If only we could pull it off!"

I think we can pull it off. But not without a break from Europe's past and a large democratic stimulus that the fathers of our European Union might have disapproved of.

ACKNOWLEDGMENTS

I began writing *And the Weak Suffer What They Must?* in 2012 after my wife Danae and I moved to Austin, where I had taken up a post at the University of Texas's Lyndon B. Johnson School of Public Affairs. My writing benefited from interaction with students at the LBJ School as well as the great encouragement afforded in Austin by two very special people: Danae and my great friend and colleague Jamie Galbraith.

Soon after I started researching the book, Wendy Strothman threw her lot in as my literary agent, Nation Books agreed to publish it and the book began to take shape. Alas, I failed to finish the first draft before January 2015. It proved a significant failure in view of the unexpected dissolution of Greece's parliament and the sudden calling of the January 25 general election, the result of which was my election to parliament and subsequent appointment as Greece's finance minister. The book's place on the back burner was, thus, immediately guaranteed.

Six months later, I was minister no longer. Indeed, by September 2015, the parliament to which I was elected had also been dissolved. And so, during the summer of 2015, I found the time to return to my manuscript. With my head full of new facts and images from a front-row seat looking out into the heart of Europe's crisis I edited the already written chapters and added new material.

I was careful not to mix into this book my experiences from the negotiations I was involved in during the first half of 2015 and to leave out of my narrative the thriller that led our government to clash with official Europe and with the International Monetary Fund—a clash that ended up in the coup d'état by which our government was effectively brought down, making it possible for me to complete this book.[1] Only insights pertinent to my account of what led to the inevitable euro crisis (in 2010), and to Europe's inability to handle it efficiently ever since (2010–2015), made it into the text. (The thriller will have to wait for another book—to be told, as it deserves to be, from a greater distance.)

Alessandra Bastagli, Will Hammond, among the other good people at Nation Books and Penguin Random House, deserve heartfelt thanks for their splendid editing, as does my brother-in-arms Nicholas Theocarakis for his usual meticulous critical comments. Lastly, I want to thank the countless people who shared ideas, facts, gossip and astute analysis with me, Lord (Norman) Lamont in particular for his gracious guidance regarding the events of 1990–1993 (see chapter 5).

APPENDIX TO CHAPTER 7

Extracts from "A Modest Proposal for Resolving the Eurozone Crisis," by Yanis Varoufakis, Stuart Holland, and J. K. Galbraith, July 2013.

The Eurozone crisis is unfolding on four interrelated domains.

Banking crisis: There is a common global banking crisis, which was sparked off mainly by the catastrophe in American finance. But the Eurozone has proved uniquely unable to cope with it, and this is a problem of structure and governance. The Eurozone features a central bank with no government, and national governments with no supportive central bank, arrayed against a global network of megabanks they cannot possibly supervise. Europe's response has been to propose a full Banking Union—a bold measure in principle which is left permanently in abeyance in practice.

Debt crisis: The credit crunch of 2008 revealed the Eurozone's Principle of Perfectly Separable Public Debts to be unworkable. Forced to create a bailout fund that did not violate the no-bailout clauses of the ECB charter and Lisbon Treaty, Europe created the temporary European Financial Stability Facility (EFSF) and then the permanent European Stability Mechanism (ESM). The creation of these new institutions met the immediate funding needs of several member-states, but retained the flawed principle of separable public debts and so could not contain the crisis. Thus, beginning in the summer of 2012, the ECB came up with another approach: monetizing public debt first through a policy that was announced but was never activated (the Outright Monetary Transactions' Program–OMT) and, in 2014, actual quantitative easing based on the odd principle of buying public debt in proportion to each national economy's size (and not in proportion to its deflationary spiral). While these measures have ameliorated the credit crunch, they have overcome neither the debt crisis nor the deflationary process afflicting the whole of the Eurozone.

Investment crisis: Lack of investment in Europe threatens its living standards and its international competitiveness. As Germany alone ran large surpluses after 2000, the resulting trade imbalances ensured that, when crisis hit in 2008, demand and investment in the deficit regions collapsed. With the burden of adjustment falling on the deficit economies in the deficit zones, which could not bear it, and no mechanism for offsetting by reflation in the surplus nations, the scene was set for disinvestment in the regions that needed investment the most. Thus Europe ended up with both low total investment and an uneven distribution of that investment between its surplus and deficit regions.

Social crisis: Years of harsh austerity have taken their toll on Europe's peoples. From Athens to Dublin and from Lisbon to Eastern Germany, millions of Europeans have lost access to basic goods and dignity. Unemployment is rampant. Homelessness and hunger are rising. Pensions have been cut; taxes on necessities meanwhile continue to rise. For the first time in two generations, Europeans are questioning the European project, while nationalism, and even Nazi parties, are gaining strength.

POLITICAL CONSTRAINTS FOR ANY SOLUTION

Any solution to the crisis must respect realistic constraints on political action. . . . Four constraints facing Europe presently are:

a) The ECB will not be allowed to monetize sovereigns directly in a manner that helps reduce heavy legacy debts in the countries weighed down by them. There will be no ECB purchases of government bonds in the primary market and no ECB leveraging of the EFSF-ESM to buy sovereign debt from either the primary or secondary markets.

b) The ECB's OMT and quantitative easing program does not match stability with growth and, sooner or later, will be found wanting.

c) Surplus countries will not consent to "jointly and severally" guarantee Eurobonds to mutualize debt and deficit countries.

France mainly, will resist the loss of sovereignty that would be demanded of them without a properly functioning federal transfer union which Germany, understandably, rejects.

d) Europe cannot wait for federation. If crisis resolution is made to depend on federation, the Eurozone will fail first. The treaty changes necessary to create a proper European Treasury, with the powers to tax, spend and borrow, cannot, and must not, be held to precede resolution of this crisis.

The next section presents four policies that recognize these constraints.

THE MODEST PROPOSAL—
FOUR CRISES, FOUR POLICIES

The Modest Proposal introduces no new EU institutions and violates no existing treaty. Instead, we propose that existing institutions be used in ways that remain within the letter of European legislation but allow for new functions and policies.

These institutions are:

The European Central Bank—ECB
The European Investment Bank—EIB
The European Investment Fund—EIF
The European Stability Mechanism—ESM

POLICY 1—Case-by-Case Bank Program (CCBP)

For the time being, we propose that banks in need of recapitalization from the ESM be turned over to the ESM directly—instead of having the national government borrow on the bank's behalf. The ESM, and not the national government, would then restructure, recapitalize and resolve the failing banks dedicating the bulk of its funding capacity to this purpose.

The Eurozone must eventually become a single banking area with a single banking authority, a single deposit insurance scheme and a common fiscal backstop. But this final goal has become the enemy of good current policy . . . Our proposal is that a failing bank should be removed from its national jurisdiction and moved to a new, dedicated Eurozone jurisdiction. The ECB appoints a new board of directors with a view to resolving or recapitalizing the bank. In the latter case, the ESM provides the capital and shares equivalent to the needed capital injection will pass to the ESM. Restructuring of the bank may entail a merger, downsizing, even a full resolution of the bank, with the understanding that steps will be taken to avoid, above all, a haircut of deposits. Once the bank has been restructured and recapitalized, the ESM will sell its shares and recoups its costs.

POLICY 2—Limited Debt Conversion Program (LDCP)

The Maastricht Treaty permits each European member-state to issue sovereign debt up to 60 percent of its national income. Since the crisis of 2008, most Eurozone member-states have exceeded this limit. We propose that the ECB offer member-states the opportunity of a debt conversion for their Maastricht Compliant Debt (MCD), while the national shares of the converted debt would continue to be serviced separately by each member-state.

The ECB, faithful to the non-monetization clause in its charter, would not seek to buy or guarantee sovereign MCD debt directly or indirectly. Instead it would act as a go-between, mediating between investors and member-states. In effect, the ECB would orchestrate a conversion servicing loan for the MCD, for the purposes of redeeming those bonds upon maturity.[1]

The conversion loan works as follows. Refinancing of the Maastricht compliant share of the debt, now held in ECB-bonds, would be by member-states but at interest rates set by the ECB just above its (ultra low) own bond yields. The shares of national debt converted to ECB-bonds are to be held by it in debit accounts. These cannot be used as collateral for credit or derivatives creation.[2] Member-states will undertake to redeem bonds in full on maturity, if the holders opt for this rather than to extend them at lower, more secure rates offered by the ECB.

Governments that wish to participate in the scheme can do so on the basis of Enhanced Cooperation, which needs at least nine member-states.[3] Those not opting in can keep their own bonds even for their MCD. To safeguard the credibility of this conversion, and to provide a backstop for the ECB-bonds that requires no ECB monetization, member-states agree to afford their ECB debit accounts super-seniority status, and the ECB's conversion servicing loan mechanism may be insured by the ESM, utilizing only a small portion of the latter's borrowing capacity. If a member-state goes into a disorderly default before an ECB-bond issued on its behalf matures, then that ECB-bond payment will be covered by insurance purchased or provided by the ESM.

POLICY 3—An Investment-led Recovery and Convergence Program (IRCP)

The IRCP we propose is supported by the following facts:

Europe desperately needs growth-inducing, large-scale investment.

Europe is replete with idle cash too scared to be invested into productive activities, fearing lack of aggregate demand once the products roll off the production line.

The ECB wants to buy high quality paper assets in order to stem the deflationary expectations that are the result of the above.

The ECB does not want to have to buy German or Italian or Spanish assets lest it be accused of violating its charter or favoring Germany, Italy, Spain etc.

Here is what the ECB could do to achieve its complex objectives:

The European Investment Bank (EIB) [and its smaller offshoot the European Investment Fund (EIF)] should be given the green light to embark upon a pan-Eurozone Investment-led Recovery Program to the tune of 8 percent of the Eurozone's GDP, with the EIB concentrating on large scale infrastructural projects and the EIF on start-ups, SMEs, technologically innovative firms, green energy research etc.

The EIB/EIF has been issuing bonds for decades to fund investments, covering thus 50 percent of the projects' funding costs. They should now issue bonds to cover the funding of the pan-Eurozone Investment-led Recovery Program in its totality; that is, by waiving the convention that 50 percent of the funds come from national sources.

To ensure that the EIB/EIF bonds do not suffer rising yields, as a result of these large issues, the ECB can be on standby, ready to step into the secondary market to purchase as many of these EIB/EIF bonds as are necessary to keep the EIB/EIF bond yields at their present, low levels. To stay consistent with its current assessment, the level of this type of QE could be set to €1 trillion over the next few years.

In this scenario, the ECB enacts QE by purchasing solid eurobonds; as the bonds issued by the EIB/EIF are issued on behalf of all European Union states (lacking the CDO-like structure of ESM bonds). In this manner, the operational concern about which nation's bonds to buy is alleviated. Moreover, the proposed form of QE backs productive investments directly, as opposed to inflating risky financial instruments, and has no implications in terms of European fiscal rules (as EIB funding need not count against member-states' deficits or debt).

POLICY 4—An Emergency Social Solidarity Program to fight against the rise of poverty (ESSP)

We recommend that Europe embark immediately on an Emergency Social Solidarity Program that will guarantee access to nutrition and to basic energy needs for all Europeans, by means of a European Food Stamp Program modeled on its US equivalent and a European Minimum Energy Program.

These programs would be funded by the European Commission using the interest accumulated within the European system of central banks, from TARGET2 imbalances, profits made from government bond transactions and, in the future, other financial transactions or balance sheet stamp duties that the EU is currently considering.

Rationale

Europe now faces the worst human and social crisis since the late 1940s. In member-states like Greece, Ireland, Portugal, but also elsewhere in the Eurozone, including core countries, basic needs are not being met. This is true especially for the elderly, the unemployed, for young children, for children in schools, for the disabled, and for the homeless. There is a plain moral imperative to act to satisfy these needs. In addition, Europe faces a clear and present danger from extremism, racism, xenophobia and even outright Nazism—notably in countries like Greece that have borne the brunt of the crisis. Never before have so many Europeans held the European Union and its institutions in such low esteem. The human and social crisis is turning quickly into a question of legitimacy for the European Union.

Reason for TARGET2 funding

TARGET2 is a technical name for the system of internal accounting of monetary flows between the central banks that make up the European System of Central Banks. In a well balanced Eurozone, where the trade deficit of a member-state is financed by a net flow of capital to that same member-state, the liabilities of that state's central bank to the central banks of other states would just equal its assets. Such a balanced flow of trade and capital would yield a TARGET2 figure near zero for all member-states. And that was, more or less, the case throughout the Eurozone before the crisis.

However, the crisis caused major imbalances that were soon reflected in huge TARGET2 imbalances. As inflows of capital to the periphery dried up, and capital began to flow in the opposite direction, the central banks of the peripheral countries began to amass large net liabilities and the central banks of the surplus countries equally large net assets.

The Eurozone's designers had attempted to build a disincentive within the intra-Eurosystem real-time payments' system, so as to prevent the build-up of huge liabilities on one side and corresponding assets on the other. This took the form of charging interest on the net liabilities of each national central bank, at an interest rate equal to the ECB's main refinancing level. These payments are distributed to the central banks of the surplus member-states, which then pass them on to their government treasury.

Thus the Eurozone was built on the assumption that TARGET2 imbalances would be isolated, idiosyncratic events, to be corrected by national policy action.

The system did not take account of the possibility that there could be fundamental structural asymmetries and a systemic crisis.

Today, the vast TARGET2 imbalances are the monetary tracks of the crisis. They trace the path of the consequent human and social disaster hitting mainly the deficit regions. The increased TARGET2 interest would never have accrued if the crises had not occurred. They accrue only because, for instance, risk averse Spanish and Greek depositors, reasonably enough, transfer their savings to a Frankfurt bank. As a result, under the rules of the TARGET2 system, the central banks of Spain and of Greece have to pay interest to the Bundesbank—to be passed along to the Federal Government in Berlin. This indirect fiscal boost to the surplus country has no rational or moral basis. Yet the funds are there, and could be used to deflect the social and political danger facing Europe.

There is a strong case to be made that the interest collected from the deficit member-states' central banks should be channelled to an account that would fund our proposed Emergency Social Solidarity Programme (ESSP). Additionally, if the EU introduces a financial transactions' tax, or stamp duty proportional to the size of corporate balance sheets, a similar case can be made as to why these receipts should fund the ESSP. With this proposal, the ESSP is not funded by fiscal transfers nor national taxes.

CONCLUSION: FOUR REALISTIC POLICIES TO REPLACE FIVE FALSE CHOICES

Years of crisis have culminated in a Europe that has lost legitimacy with its own citizens and credibility with the rest of the world. Europe is unnecessarily still on a low-investment, negligible growth path. While the bond markets were placated by the ECB's actions, the Eurozone remains on the road toward disintegration.

While this process eats away at Europe's potential for shared prosperity, European governments are imprisoned by false choices:

between stability and growth
between austerity and stimulus

between the deadly embrace of insolvent banks by insolvent
     governments, and an admirable but undefined and indefinitely
     delayed Banking Union
between the principle of perfectly separable country debts and the
     supposed need to persuade the surplus countries to bankroll
     the rest
between national sovereignty and federalism.

These falsely dyadic choices imprison thinking and immobilize governments. They are responsible for a legitimation crisis for the European project. And they risk a catastrophic human, social and democratic crisis in Europe.

By contrast the Modest Proposal counters that:

The real choice is between beggar-my-neighbour deflation and an investment-led recovery combined with social stabilization. The investment recovery will be funded by global capital, supplied principally by sovereign wealth funds and by pension funds which are seeking long-term investment outlets. Social stabilisation can be funded, initially, through the TARGET2 payments scheme.

Taxpayers in Germany and the other surplus nations do not need to bankroll the 2020 European Economic Recovery Programme, the restructuring of sovereign debt, resolution of the banking crisis, or the emergency humanitarian programme so urgently needed in the European periphery.

Neither an expansionary monetary policy nor a fiscal stimulus in Germany and other surplus countries, though welcome, would be sufficient to bring recovery to Europe.

Treaty changes for a federal union may be aspired by some, but will take too long, are opposed by many, and are not needed to resolve the crisis now.

On this basis the Modest Proposal's four policies are feasible steps by which to deal decisively with Europe's banking crisis, the debt crisis, underinvestment, unemployment as well as the human, social and political emergency.

While broad in scope, the Modest Proposal suggests no new institutions and does not aim at redesigning the Eurozone. It needs no new rules, fiscal compacts, or troikas. It requires no prior agreement to move in a federal direction while allowing for consent through enhanced cooperation rather than imposition of austerity.

It is in this sense that this proposal is, indeed, modest.

NOTES

PREFACE: THE RED BLANKET

1. Glezos, whose political activism began in May 1941 when he climbed, with Apostolos Santas, the walls of the Acropolis to remove, unseen by the German sentries, the swastika flag, has been leading the campaign for German war reparations to Greece and, more poignantly, for the repayment by the German state of an enforced "loan" extracted by German High Command from the Bank of Greece during the occupation.

2. See Karl Marx and Friedrich Engels, *The Manifesto of the Communist Party*.

CHAPTER 1: JETTISONED

1. John Connally's lewd phrase is quoted in Schaller (1996, 1997). So impressed was Nixon with Connally's no-nonsense perspective on what needed to be done with Europe (and, to a lesser extent, Japan) that, according to Kissinger (1979), Ambrose (1989) and Hersh (1983), the president asked his closest confidantes to "figure out how the hell we can get [Vice President] Agnew to resign early" with a view to replacing him with Connally, his "logical successor" as Nixon called him.

2. The "swoop" in question was the delinking of the value of the dollar from gold. Until the Nixon Shock, the US government had promised to deliver $35 to anyone holding one ounce of gold. By severing this link, the dollar was no longer bound to gold. And since all other currencies (as we shall see) were linked, with a fixed exchange rate, to the dollar, Nixon's announcement was tantamount to (a) a declaration that the global monetary system was no longer linked to gold and (b) a foreshadowing of the end of fixed exchange rates between the dollar and other, mainly European, currencies. In effect, Nixon shocked the world by announcing that the monetary system it had taken for granted was being dismantled forthwith. Of course, President Nixon dressed up this awful announcement as a domestic US agenda: "a New Economic Program complete with tax cuts and a 90-day wage and price freeze." See Eichengreen (2011), p. 60.

3. See Silber (2012), chapter 5.

4. For ten months after the Nixon Shock, Washington humored the Europeans with negotiations on how to reestablish the fixed exchange rates

between the dollar and European currencies. An agreement was, indeed, reached (called the Smithsonian Agreement or Accord). Alas, it was too late and in America neither Connally nor Volcker, nor indeed anyone else, truly believed that the "vase," once broken, could be repaired.

5. These were not Connally's exact words (which have not been taken down for posterity), but they do capture quite accurately the spirit of his message to them. Upon exiting these meetings, he diplomatically, and misleadingly, put on a face of "American neediness" when addressing reporters covering his tour of European capitals. His precise words were "We told them that we were here as a nation that had given much of our resources and our material resources and otherwise to the world to the point where frankly we were now running a deficit and have been for twenty years and it had drained our reserves and drained our resources to the point where we could no longer do it and frankly we were in trouble and we were coming to our friends to ask for help as they have so many times in the past come to us to ask for help when they were in trouble. That is in essence what we told them." Transcript of archival material from BBC Radio 4's *Analysis: Dollars and Dominance*, broadcast on Thursday, October 23, at 20:30 BST, 2008.

6. Connally used this precise phrase in November 1971 at a meeting of finance ministers in Rome, in the context of a regular G10 meeting. He was widely reported to have used the same phrase, behind closed doors, during his tour of European capitals in the previous August. See Crawford and Keever (1973).

7. Paul Volcker, who was later to become president of the New York Federal Reserve, before President Carter appointed him chairman of the Federal Reserve in 1978, was instrumental in convincing John Connally to convince President Nixon to jettison Europe. Not everyone in the administration was happy. Indeed, Arthur Burns, who had been appointed, in 1970, chairman of the Federal Reserve by Richard Nixon (and whom Volcker replaced in 1978) had these pointed words to say: "Poor and wretched Volcker—never knowing where he stood on any issue—had succeeded in instilling an irrational fear of gold on his tyrannical master [n.b., he meant John Connally], whom he tried constantly to please by catering to his fear of foreigners (particularly the French) instead of his capacity (not inconsiderable) for straight reasoning." See Ferrell (2010), p. 65.

8. Interestingly, both John Connally and Paul Volcker were lifelong Democrats drafted by Nixon in his Republican administration. This fact put them at odds with a number of Republicans in the same administration

who opposed their combined drive to persuade President Nixon to make his shocking announcement in 1971.

9. See Bator (2001).

10. Francis Bator, who worked closely with President Johnson on what to do with Bretton Woods, published an article in *Foreign Affairs* at the time (see Bator, 1968) outlining in detail the administration's plans to effect a gradual transformation of Bretton Woods. The idea was to introduce far greater flexibility into the system, without, however, destroying it, as its sudden disintegration would cause enormous social damage both within and without the United States.

11. This characterization of Volcker is Richard Nixon's. He called him that when he heard that Volcker might have been responsible for a story leaked to the *Wall Street Journal*, to the effect that America was facing a "tremendous crisis on the international monetary front." Nixon feared that Volcker had leaked the story to put pressure on Connally to do that which, in the end, Nixon himself did on August 15, 1971: end the Bretton Woods system.

12. A full account of both the underlying economic forces undermining the postwar US-designed global financial order and the Europeans' strategic errors follows.

13. White had earned his economics PhD at Harvard and had served in the US Treasury Department as assistant to Secretary Henry Morgenthau Jr. A convinced internationalist, he not only helped create the International Monetary Fund (IMF) (which, like the World Bank, had been designed in Bretton Woods as the system's twin institutional pillars), but also became the IMF's first managing director. In 1947 he resigned abruptly under a cloud of innuendo that he had acted as a Soviet spy. He died the following year of a heart attack.

14. War undoubtedly makes for odd bedfellows. In 1925 John Maynard Keynes had authored a pamphlet, entitled "The Economic Consequences of Mr. Churchill," lambasting Churchill (who would in 1943 send him to Bretton Woods to represent his government) for having dragged Britain back into the gold standard. In that pamphlet, Keynes argued that the pound had been fixed at too high a value *vis-à-vis gold* and prognosticated, accurately, that the gold standard would prove a ball and chain for the British economy, causing an unnecessary, never-ending recession. Keynes's pamphlet can be credited for having depleted support for the gold standard, among opinion makers, to an extent that, following the crash of 1929, Britain was among the

first countries to exit the gold standard; which it did in 1931 to ameliorate for the Great Depression, two years before President Roosevelt pulled the United States out too. Perhaps it is worth noting also that the aforementioned pamphlet's title was a wordplay on the earlier book that had made Keynes famous: *The Economic Consequences of the Peace*, published in 1919, which presciently warned that the harsh reparations imposed by the Versailles Treaty upon a defeated Germany would inflict as much pain on the vengeful victors as it would on Germany.

15. As a young man, who had observed the Versailles Treaty proceedings, Keynes authored *The Economic Consequences of the Peace*; a pamphlet presciently predicting how the harsh treatment of defeated Germany, after the First World War, would bring about an almighty midwar economic slump throughout Europe (see Keynes, 1920). In 1936 Keynes's views on capitalism were captured in his tour de force, *The General Theory of Employment, Interest, and Money* (see Keynes, 1936). By September 1941 Keynes had instilled these thoughts in a "plan" for the future of global capitalism that he presented at Bretton Woods in 1944 (see Keynes, 1980). His take on the task he and his fellow negotiators had undertaken at the Bretton Woods conference is summed up in this sentence: "We have had to perform at one and the same time the tasks appropriate to the economist, to the financier, to the politician, to the journalist, to the propagandist, to the lawyer, to the statesman—even, I think, to the prophet and to the soothsayer." See Keynes (1980), p. 101.

16. Thucydides, *The History of the Peloponnesian War,* Book 5, s. 89: "δυνατα δε οι προυχοντες πρασσουσι και οι ασθενεις ξυγχωπουσιν."

17. Thucydides, *The History of the Peloponnesian War,* Book 5, s. 90, my translation.

18. Keynes's warning came in the form of a famous pamphlet entitled "The Economic Consequences of the Peace." See Keynes (1920).

19. The decoupling of the dollar from the yen, the franc and the deutsche mark caused European and Japanese manufacturers to lose much of their advantage vis-à-vis American multinationals (as the dollar plummeted). Meanwhile, the dollar price of oil skyrocketed, jeopardizing further German and Japanese manufacturers whose exposure to foreign oil imports was always greater to that of American producers.

20. Perhaps the most stunning epitaph of Keynes's proposal came in 2011, in the midst of the euro crisis. Here is how I described it in the epilogue to my book *The Global Minotaur: America, Europe and the Future of the World Economy* (see Varoufakis, 2013):

I was ever so surprised, the other day, listening to a radio interview by Dominique Strauss Kahn, the IMF's managing director, responding to a journalist's question about how the global economy ought to be reconfigured in the aftermath of the 2008 Crisis. His astonishing answer was, "Never in the past has an institution like the IMF been as necessary as it has been today . . . Keynes, sixty years ago, already foresaw what was needed; but it was too early. *Now is the time to do it. And I think we are ready to do it!*" (emphasis added) The date was 21 January 2011. Four months later, Strauss Kahn was forced to resign his stewardship of the IMF, following his arrest in a New York hotel on sexual assault charges that were, subsequently, dropped.

21. See George Krimpas's "The Recycling Problem in a Currency Union," which appears as an addendum to chapter 12 of Varoufakis et al. (2011).

22. See Keynes (1932).

23. In Keynes's 1941 words, under fixed exchange rates "the burden of adjustment [will be thrown] on the country which is in the *debtor* position on the international balance of payments; that is on the country which is (in this context) by hypothesis the *weaker* and above all the *smaller* in comparison with the other side of the scales which (for this purpose) is the rest of the world." Keynes (1980), p. 27; italics in the original.

24. The Federal Insurance Deposit Corporation.

25. When President Roosevelt suggested that the only thing Americans had "to fear is fear itself," he was alluding to the self-fulfilling terror that prevents private surplus funds from being invested when most needed, and to the need for political intervention that overcomes this fear through directing investments to states and regions where the greatest debts, unemployment and deficits are concentrated. Roosevelt's vision was to be later reinforced, after Pearl Harbor, by his administration's eye-opening experience of running the war economy, gathering decisive evidence, if any was needed, that there is nothing natural about high unemployment and that depression is a failure of policy, not an act of God that we ought to submit to.

26. It is worthwhile comparing Nevada's fate with that of Ireland, a member-state of that "other" currency union, the eurozone. Just like Nevada, in 2008 Ireland faced a massive collapse of its real estate and banking sectors. But unlike Nevada, Ireland had to fend for itself when it came to propping up its banks and paying its unemployment benefits. Lacking a printing press, it had to go cap in hand to the money markets to borrow huge quantities of money that, in Nevada's case, had been paid for at the federal level. Naturally, the money markets, caught up in their credit crunch mentality, would

not cough up the money at anything below usurious interest rates. Thus, Ireland ended up accepting a massive loan from European governments, the European Central Bank and the International Monetary Fund, which rendered the Irish state insolvent and pushed its society into long-term negative equity. Nevada, in the meantime, exited the crisis quickly and with very little debt in comparison.

27. Similarly with America's military budget that, from the early phase of the Second World War, was mobilized not only in order to win the war against Japan and Germany but also the war against the scourge of unemployment and the bane of poverty that persisted in the wake of the Great Depression. To this day, when Boeing or Lockheed are awarded defense contracts, these come with conditions forcing contractors to build production facilities in deficit states like Tennessee or Missouri. Such surplus recycling, ushered in for the first time by the New Dealers in the 1930s and 1940s, allowed the "dollar zone," also known as the United States of America, a degree of protection from recessions that began in the deficit regions and spread out like menacing bushfires into the surplus states.

28. Besides the IMF, which is still with us (performing, post-1971, a very different role to that envisaged for it at Bretton Woods), a second institution was designed at the 1944 conference. It was the International Bank for Reconstruction and Development (IBRD), today known simply as the World Bank. Whereas the IMF was proposed by Keynes as the world's central bank, to issue and manage the world currency, the IBRD's purpose was to mobilize idle savings and turn them into productive investments in relatively underdeveloped, deficit nations. And just as the IMF ended up functioning very differently, so did the World Bank. Nevertheless, of these two Bretton Woods institutions, it is the World Bank that remains more faithful to Keynes's initial intentions for it.

29. In this context, the IMF had an additional role: it would provide short-term loans to nations that needed to defend their exchange rates due to some unexpected trade deficit or while the IMF was in the process of approving a devaluation.

30. If we add to this the speculator's cost of borrowing from the French banks, which they would now have to fork out themselves, it is easy to see why the Bundesbank's intervention was a scary prospect for the speculators.

31. German surpluses are only recycled to the rest of Europe by means of what I earlier referred to as fair-weather recycling; that is, the kind of recycling effected by Frankfurt's commercial banks. This type of recycling, as

explained above, inflated bubbles during the good times and did nothing to aid recovery once the bubbles burst. In contrast, American surpluses, during the Bretton Woods era, were directed by means of a political recycling mechanism that smoothed out credit shortages in the deficit countries at times of crisis and prevented the buildup of bubbles during periods of growth.

32. A development partly due to the increased productivity and improved technology of German and Japanese industries; improvements unlikely to have materialized without the consistent support of American policy makers.

33. Computed at the Bretton Woods fixed rate of $35 per ounce.

34. Prior to the Nixon Shock, there were two markets for gold: the official market, in which large banks and governments traded their stock of gold at $35 per ounce, and the unofficial or shadow market, for example, the informal transactions between jewelers and private individuals who traded gold at a smaller scale but at prices considerably higher than the official $35 per ounce. By the late 1960s, the unofficial price had risen to $55 per ounce, revealing the Bretton Woods' system high stress levels. However, for the speculators to make big profits from their bets (that gold would rise further), it was essential that the big players (e.g., the banks and governments) were also unleashed from the official $35 per ounce price.

35. Exactly as the French authorities relied on the Bundesbank to keep the deutsche mark price of the French franc stable.

36. In 1968 a desperate situation called for a desperate measure. Central banks agreed to stick to the $35 per ounce gold price when trading the gleaming metal among themselves but allowed the commercial price of gold to rise at will, even when it came to large scale trades between banks.. This twin price—one official, one unofficial—was a major defeat for global capitalism. The West could no longer berate the Soviets for lying about the true value of the ruble, quoting an official exchange rate that bore no relation to the ruble's black market value. Now, the dollar also had two values, in terms of gold: one official, one unofficial. Furthermore, this "solution" did not solve anything much really. The greater the divergence of the unofficial price of gold from its official $35 value the greater the confidence of speculators that they would, in the end, force Washington to devalue the dollar relative to gold and to other currencies.

37. The "special relationship" that Britain was proclaiming with the United States, as a replacement of its imperial reach, was interpreted by de Gaulle as evidence that, if Britain were to be admitted to the European Union, it would act as Washington's Trojan horse.

38. In 1965 President de Gaulle ordered the removal of 25,900 bars of gold, weighing more than 350 tons, from the basement under the New York Federal Reserve and their transportation to Paris. It was a logistical nightmare whose symbolism was made more poignant because it involved the French navy's unfriendly return to the shores of the United States. (See the *New York Times*, March 2, 1965, p. 45). The trigger, however, for the Nixon Shock was the British government's demand that $3 billion held by the Bank of England be swapped for American-held gold, at the official $35 per ounce (which was trailing the unofficial price by at least $18). That announcement was made on Wednesday, August 11, 1971. It was the straw that John Connally and Paul Volcker ensured would break Bretton Woods' back. And this is what they convinced President Nixon to do on the following weekend, in their Camp David meetings.

39. See Stephey (2008).

40. After the Nixon Shock, the French government changed its tune instantly. From open hostility to the idea of a dollar-backed global financial system (see chapter 3), President Pompidou began demanding that the United States reconstitute Bretton Woods, even if that meant a lower dollar value (in relation to gold and other currencies). When Washington rebuffed the French president's "demands," Pompidou began to plead. President Nixon indulged him in December 1971 with an agreement at the Smithsonian Institution in Washington, in the context of a G10 meeting. The idea was to give Bretton Woods another chance, with new, more "realistic" exchange rates. Except that it was too late. The genie was out of the bottle and it refused to get back in. Within eighteen months, major currencies were floating "freely" and Europe was in deep trouble. But more on this in the following chapter.

CHAPTER 2: AN INDECENT PROPOSAL

1. Kurt Schmücker was not atypical of the Christian Democrats that ruled West Germany uninterruptedly from 1949 until 1969. At the tender age of eighteen, in 1937, he joined the Nazi party and, three years later, went to war, serving in the Wehrmacht till the bitter end. A year after the war had ended, he joined the Christian Democrats and became the party's youngest member of federal parliament in the 1949 elections. In 1963, after Ludwig Erhard (an accomplished economist who had been minister of finance since 1949 and had overseen Germany's most impressive economic reconstruction, 1949–1963) became Germany's chancellor, Schmücker took over the Ministry of the Economy. Having only completed a typography course, Schmücker nursed much

anxiety about his capacity to take over Erhard's role. As it turned out, both men (Erhard and Schmücker) were booted out of government in 1966, as a result of Germany's first postwar recession, which was, arguably, engineered for political purposes by the nation's central bank: the fierce Bundesbank.

2. The EEC was renamed European Union in the Treaty of Maastricht, November, 1, 1993, at the same time that the rules governing the common currency, the euro, were agreed to. In this book I shall be referring to the EEC as the European Union, for purposes of continuity.

3. Their conversation began with Schmücker addressing Giscard's concerns that free trade within the European Union would create trade imbalances that would destabilize the exchange rate between the franc and the deutsche mark. He suggested that EU (or EEC as it was then called) members should sign a formal contract and abide by agreed rules of contact regarding government fiscal and monetary policies so that the system could be stable. Giscard had other thoughts (the dialogue below is quoted in Schoenborn, 2014):

> GISCARD: This is too little! We have not yet talked about it in the government, but de Gaulle has told me that dangerous developments as we are now experiencing cannot be avoided or overcome without a common currency of the EEC countries. *We need a single currency for the EEC!* [n.b., emphasis added]
>
> SCHMÜCKER: In order to achieve the same effect, the currencies can also be maintained nominally while the monetary policies of the individual Member States are put under strict discipline through contractual rules.
>
> GISCARD: Why choose this system, which works only as long as everybody goes along?
>
> SCHMÜCKER: I am just looking for a successful method without obliging France to renounce her sovereignty. A single EEC currency would be a supranational matter. So far France has been speaking out against any kind of supranational arrangement.
>
> GISCARD: de Gaulle has told me explicitly that he deems a single EEC currency necessary. He takes the view that no other way remains. If one state repeatedly pushes another into inflation, the only ones to benefit are the Socialists.
>
> SCHMÜCKER: What do we do, if the other four will not join in? The creation of a monetary union is a decisive political step forward. Once the monetary union is accomplished, further political consequences will automatically ensue. Erhard's attempts to advance the political union have not produced the desired response from all governments. Hence

we can expect that the proposal will be skeptically received. Or do you imagine that France and Germany should forge ahead?

GISCARD: An agreement between France and Germany should be considered only if the others do not participate. In this case the agreement must be drafted in such a way that others will have the option, both legally and practically, to join in at any time.

4. See Gray (2007).

5. "Planification" refers to the penchant French administrators have had since the time of Napoleon for grand, large-scale planning. Examples of "planification" span urban development, energy policy (especially the plan that resulted in the extraordinary production of more than 95 percent of electricity by state-owned and -designed nuclear power stations), the creation of an advanced military-industrial complex, the superfast railways crisscrossing France and spilling into Britain and Belgium, even projects like the supersonic Concorde and the Airbus industries—the successful competitor to Boeing.

6. A full account of de Gaulle's "designs" that Erhard frustrated, and thus became Germany's chancellor follows.

7. See Schoenborn (2014).

8. Giscard was a committed Keynesian who had little time for de Gaulle's conservative views on how an economy should be managed. In particular, he harbored considerable contempt for Jacques Rueff, an economist who believed strongly in the gold standard and whom de Gaulle considered his economic guru. As a result, Giscard's time as finance minister in de Gaulle's cabinet was a precarious tenure.

9. To give one such example, in 1962 General Motors fired French autoworkers without consulting with the French government. A year later, in 1963, it purchased French automaker Simca and immediately proceeded to fire a segment of its workforce. Meanwhile, General Electric was eyeing a number of plants that Paris viewed as of strategic importance for France.

10. The phrase "exorbitant privilege" is frequently, and mistakenly, attributed to de Gaulle. Its rightful procreator was Giscard. Here is how Jacques Rueff, the French economist whose economic theories Giscard rejected (but with whom he had to work, since de Gaulle considered Rueff to be his favorite economic intellect), explained what Giscard had meant by "exorbitant privilege":

[W]hen a country with a key currency runs a balance-of-payment deficit—that is to say, the United States, for example—it pays the creditor country dollars, which end up with the latter's central bank. But the dollars are of no use in Bonn or in

Tokyo or in Paris. The very same day, they are re-loaned to the New York money market, so that they return to the place of origin. Thus the debtor country does not lose what the creditor country has gained. So the key-currency country never feels the effect of a deficit in its balance of payments. And the main consequence is that there is no reason whatever for the deficit to disappear, because it does not appear. (Rueff, 1971, p. 78)

11. See Ball (1982), p. 271.

12. Konrad Adenauer made his mark in German politics well before the Second World War, serving as Cologne's mayor from 1917 to 1933. A devout Catholic and a committed opponent of Prussia's dominance of Germany, he used his office to argue for a new Rhinish state, within the Weimar Republic, liberated from Berlin's iron rule. When his efforts led nowhere, he initiated talks with French officials with a view to establishing an autonomous Rhineland within the context of a grand Central European design that would bring forth German-French reconciliation. While he was later acquiescent to the rising Nazi party, which he tried to accommodate within city hall, the Nazis considered Adenauer an "unsafe" patriot (for having come so close to the French in the 1920s). At war's end, a bombed out Cologne found itself in the British zone and Adenauer was asked to serve again as the city's mayor. He agreed but then, in December 1945, suffered the humiliation of being dismissed by a British army general for "incompetence," when, in reality, his dismissal was due to his public statements condemning his city's unrestrained wartime bombing by the RAF. Adenauer never forgave the British for this humiliation.

13. John Wills Tuthill, at the time US ambassador to the European Economic Community.

14. In 1953 the United States famously convened a conference in London that was to "cajole" Germany's creditors to accept a huge reduction of the defeated country's debt to them.

15. See Schoenborn (2014).

16. See NSC Meeting Memo, February 5, 1963, 4.30 p.m., FRUS, 1961–1963, vol. 13, 175–79; Memorandum of Conversation, Carstens and Rusk, February 5, 1963, 6 p.m., ibid., 186; NSC Meeting, January 31, 1963, ibid., 162, Kennedy Library.

17. The preamble emphasized "the supreme importance of transatlantic cooperation" and was first thought of as a "solution" of the Elysée Treaty "problem" by American officials, who lost no time in letting Erhard's office know that it should be considered. The preamble, in essence, annulled the treaty's spirit of creating a Franco-German alliance independently of the

United States. According to Erhard's presentation of the preamble to Bonn parliamentarians, the preamble was essential in order "to liberate the Elysée Treaty from any wrong interpretation of German policy."

18. See Schoenborn (2014).

19. From 1945 to 1958.

20. So fierce was de Gaulle's opposition to the idea of an American-designed European economic community (that emerged formally in 1950 as the European Coal and Steel Community) that he went into the political wilderness until 1958, when the Fourth Republic's collapse gave him an opportunity to refashion the French constitution, and France's politics, in his image.

21. American readers ought to take note that de Gaulle's sharp criticism of the US postwar global plan was one that significant American policy makers shared. For example, George F. Kennan (a diplomat whose Long Telegram from Moscow begat the logic of "containing" the USSR) and Robert Taft (the Senate Republican leader who opposed President's Roosevelt's New Deal) also deplored the prospect of a world divided into an American and a Soviet sphere, in opposition to each other. Their difference from de Gaulle was that the French president had the means and the determination to make the American "bloc" unmanageable.

22. See Connolly (1995), p. 7.

23. Their thinking was simple: if the French state forfeited the right to print money (either by reverting to the gold standard or by adopting the deutsche mark), prices would stop rising and the trade unions would lose all bargaining power over employers; with the government unable to boost overall demand, especially during a slump, the trade unions would have a choice between accepting high unemployment (which would destroy their power base) and accepting low wages. In short, by forfeiting the printing presses the French state would ensure that organized labor became less militant, more "German." And if this also meant a greater propensity to recession, it was considered a small price to pay. Today, with France in permanent stagnation under the euro, France's elites are simultaneously unapologetic regarding that choice of theirs, and concerned about the rising tide of discontent and anti-European, racist ultranationalism.

24. "By war!" See Connolly (1995), p. 7.

25. Erhard's rebellion against Adenauer should be placed in the context of many Germans' fear of an American withdrawal. Paul Volcker is quoted by his official biographer as saying that he "recalled JFK's threat . . . to cut off military aid to Europe unless Europeans promised not to attack the dollar as the world's currency." See Silber (2012), p. 55.

26. Recall the previous chapter.

27. In a fascinating, and exceedingly rare, coincidence of opinions both the *Wall Street Journal* and *Pravda* (the Soviet Communist Party's official newspaper) hailed de Gaulle's call for a return to the gold standard as "inspired." The *Wall Street Journal* did so because it never had liked the New Dealers, following the way the Roosevelt administration dealt with Wall Street, while the Soviets, as one of the planet's primary gold producers, had every reason to see demand for gold rise.

28. Quoted in Laughland (1997), p. 231.

29. Jacques Rueff was an influential economist whom de Gaulle had known for years before turning to him, in 1958, to disinflate the French economy at the time the general was making his political comeback (that saw him found the Fifth Republic before becoming its first president). De Gaulle was nursing painful memories of how he had lost power shortly after the war ended because of runaway inflation. So when Rueff succeeded in killing inflation off in 1958 (which involved erasing a number of zeros from the currency, tying the franc's new value firmly onto the dollar, and keeping state outlays under strict control), de Gaulle was impressed. Rueff was a "goldbug," a believer in tying the quantity of paper money to the quantity of gold in the state's possession, in a bid to prevent politicians from messing with the currency's value. This helps explain why de Gaulle, in his attempt to discredit America's dollar-backed global financial system, turned to the gold standard as an alternative. However, it is this author's considered opinion that de Gaulle was an opportunistic adopter of the gold fetish, unlike Rueff, who was a true believer. Perhaps it is important also to note that Rueff was a member of the libertarian Mont Pelerin Society, alongside economists like Friedrich von Hayek and Milton Friedman. For the significance of this society see Mirowski and Plehwe (2009). De Gaulle, who was wedded to the French tradition of a state-planned economy, tolerated Rueff's libertarian economic views only because, unlike Hayek, Rueff accepted the state's leading ethical, cultural and social role in society.

30. According to Allin (2011), de Gaulle felt that just as the USSR was overstretched logistically and militarily across Eurasia, the United States was overstretched financially across the breadth and width of the Bretton Woods system.

31. See Dallek (1995). Germany's return to a pastoral economy was the express intention of the Morgenthau Plan, named after Henry Morgenthau Jr., US treasury secretary, co-signed by the United States and Britain on September 16, 1944. In the spring of 1945, after Germany had surrendered to

the Allies, General Eisenhower issued a directive to US commanders in Germany, coded JCS1067, ordering them to desist from " taking steps toward the rehabilitation of Germany [or] designed to maintain or strengthen the German economy." JCS1067 clearly stated that deindustrialization and a reduction of German living standards were the intention. On August 1, 1945, at the Potsdam Conference, the United States, the USSR and Britain agreed on the "reduction or destruction of all civilian heavy-industry with war potential" and on "restructuring the German economy toward agriculture and light industry." In 1946 the Allies reduced Germany's steel production to less than six million tons annually; that is, around 75 percent of Germany's prewar steel output. As for car production, it was decided that output should dwindle to around 10 percent of what it was before Germany invaded Poland.

32. See Dallek (1995).

33. See Reinert (2004), p. 158.

34. For a longer exposition of the historical events in this section, see Varoufakis (2013), chapter 3.

35. Even though, it must be said, the United States had a track record on this: after the Versailles Treaty, of 1919, which imposed intolerable reparations upon Germany after the Great War, America was unique among the victors in having supported the German economy with credit and bilateral deals that lessened the unbearable burden the treaty had placed upon the defeated country.

36. Secretary of defense and previously secretary of the navy.

37. James Byrnes's successor as secretary of state, and deliverer of the infamous Marshall Plan.

38. George Marshall's successor in the State Department.

39. Recall chapter 2.

40. Heavy industry centers are typified by large, networked, powerful corporations. To cover their overheads they must produce large output and contain their labor costs. This means that local people (mostly wage earners) cannot consume all that the factories are producing. This is why powerhouse economies require a surrounding hinterland that will generate the necessary demand for these surplus goods. If the exchange rate between the powerhouse economy and the hinterland is fixed, the hinterland will remain in a permanent trade deficit in relation to the powerhouse economy. To keep financing these permanent deficits, surplus recycling is necessary. In good times banks play that role, which chapter 1 described as fair-weather recycling.

41. De Gaulle briefly came out of retirement in 1954 to shoot down, in the French national assembly, the idea of a European defense community,

confirming his firm rejection of a German-French alliance under the Pax Americana umbrella. Then, in 1958, when France was deeply embroiled in the hideous Algerian colonial war, he was summoned as prime minister to sort out the mess. Only he, as the nation's war hero, had the authority to pull French troops out of France's own Vietnam. After that, and with Jacques Rueff's successful monetary reforms that killed inflation off, the road was clear for the general to rewrite the constitution (thus creating the so-called Fifth Republic) and move into the presidency. It was at that stage that he, very reluctantly, accepted the notion of a united Europe, revolving on the Franco-German axis, in which France would play the dominant administrative roles.

42. Kennan was working in the US embassy in Moscow from where, in February 1946, he sent the Long Telegram analyzing the reasons why the United States ought to consider the task of containing the USSR its top priority. At that same time, Greek left-wing partisans, who had led a glorious resistance against the Nazis, were being persecuted by the British-backed government and Nazi sympathizers. In March 1946, a regiment of these partisans declared hostilities against the government and thus Greece's second, and most lethal, civil war began. The Truman Doctrine was America's declaration that what begins in Greece ends up as a major confrontation with the USSR. Kennan's Long Telegram and the Greek civil war inaugurated the Cold War.

43. The Truman Doctrine committed funds and resources to supporting the Greek national army against the partisans, who received next to no support from a Soviet Union bound by its Yalta Agreement commitments to concede to Greece remaining in Britain's sphere of influence. And when Britain withdrew from the Greek civil war, exhausted by its own economic crisis in 1946, it passed the baton to President Truman. Thus the Cold War began officially.

44. Harry Truman had moved into the White House after President Roosevelt's passing in 1945. He declared his doctrine on March 12, 1947.

45. Who was to make a comeback in 1957 as chairman of Deutsche Bank; a post that he kept until 1967.

46. See Becker (2013).

47. On October 28, 1940, as the German armed forces were wiping the floor with Allied forces, Mussolini gave the Greek government an ultimatum: surrender or be invaded. Greece rejected it, Italy invaded from already occupied Albania and a ramshackle Greek army defeated the invaders, scoring the first allied victory of the Second World War. Hitler was forced to delay

his invasion of the Soviet Union and divert his forces to the Balkans in order to subdue the "annoying" Greeks. This five-month delay helped the Soviets immensely as the German troops, by the time they reached Russia's steppes, had to reckon with . . . General Winter. Moreover, from 1942 to 1944, Greek partisans constantly engaged the Nazi occupiers, causing considerable damage and confining them to the urban centers. The price the Greek population suffered was immense, in terms of murders, persecution, destruction of the country's infrastructure and famine.

48. Naumann, F. (1915, 2012).

49. See Coudenhove-Kalergi (1923).

50. His words in a letter dated September 7, 1914, quoted in Laughland (1997), p.115.

51. During the first year of the Marshall Plan, the total sum involved was in the order of $5.3 billion, a little more than 2 percent of the United States' GDP. By December 31, 1951, when the Marshall Plan came to an end, $12.5 billion had been expended. The end result was a sharp rise in European industrial output (about 35 percent) and, more importantly, political stabilization and the creation of sustainable demand for manufacturing products, both European and American.

52. See Rosamond (2000), pp. 20–21.

53. Technically speaking, the European Union was formed in 1993, with the Maastricht Treaty. Before that it was known as the European Economic Community, or European Common Market—the "natural" evolution of the original European Coal and Steel Community. For simplicity, throughout this book I use the term "European Union" to refer to the continuum of institutions and treaties which began in 1950 and, in the process, yielded today's European Union.

54. See the *New York Times*, March 2, 1965, p. 45

55. Lyndon B. Johnson had to restrain his own administration officials from lashing out at the French. Prompted by them to respond belligerently, he turned them down flat, saying that "when someone asks us to leave their house, we leave." See Bator (2001).

56. As explained previously, no politician likes headlines announcing "devaluation." Equally, politicians of surplus countries, whose exchange rate needs to go up, know that such a revaluation will anger exporters (whose goods and services will now cost foreigners more and thus suffer a fall in sales).

57. Recall that, under the Bretton Woods arrangements, finance ministers met regularly at the IMF's Washington's offices to discuss any necessary

changes in the official exchange rate between their currencies. In those meetings, and while the dollar and the franc were under pressure from speculators, American officials were routinely telling their German counterparts
something simple: "Either your Central Bank—the Bundesbank—must print
more deutsche marks, or you must agree to an increase in the value of the
deutsche mark here and now." German politicians were in a difficult position.
They could not fully control what the Bundesbank did. Moreover, when they
agreed to increasing the value of the deutsche mark, they risked incurring the
wrath of the Bundesbank and of German exporters: a supremely powerful alliance that shared an interest in low German inflation (the Bundesbank's main
concern, and the reason it was reluctant to print more and more deutsche
marks) and a stable (nonrising) exchange rate consistent with export growth.

58. See Connolly (1995), p. 7.

59. Willy Brandt, the Social Democrats' progressive leader, was vice chancellor. He emerged from that role with his reputation and image strengthened
to the extent that, by the 1969 general election, he succeeded in winning
sufficient votes to form the first social democratic administration (in alliance
with the small Free Democratic Party), pushing the Christian Democrats in
opposition for the first time. Karl Schicker, from the Social Democrats, and
Franz Josef Strauss, leader of the ultraconservative Bavarian Christian Social
Union, shared the economic ministries during the years of that grand coalition. (Strauss was minister of finance and Schiller minister of the economy.
Later, in 1971, Schiller moved to the Ministry of Finance.)

60. Cut to 1997. Europe was preparing for its common currency and
Germany was dictating to the rest of Europe its terms for abandoning its
cherished deutsche mark and turning the Bundesbank into a franchise of the
jointly "owned" European Central Bank. One of these conditions was that
the whole of Europe submit to a *Stability and Growth Pact* brimming with the
philosophy of 1967.

61. Monetary tightening usually involves boosting interest rates. By increasing the cost of borrowing francs, or equivalently increasing the interest
paid to those who save francs, Paris aimed to attract more money to French
bank accounts from abroad. If investors indeed responded by converting
their dollars and deutsche marks to francs, in order to take advantage of the
higher franc bank account interest rates, the international demand for francs
would increase, thus boosting the French currency's value—as de Gaulle had
intended. The downside, of course, of an interest rate rise was that the cost of
investing in France rose and, all other things being equal, economic activity
and jobs would suffer. Which is precisely what happened on this occasion.

62. He was, of course, referring to France's nuclear bomb, using the effeminate diminutive term for it. See Stuermer (2011).

63. See Gray (2007).

64. See Gray (2007).

65. These were the events and developments that take us, full circle, to the beginning of chapter 1 and John Connally's (the Nixon treasury secretary) brash invocation to his president to "screw the foreigners."

66. The Maastricht Treaty was the legal foundation of the euro, the new common currency.

67. I owe this quotation to Klaus Kastner.

68. Four years after *Le Figaro*'s outrageous article, Lucas Delattre was writing in the pro-European *Le Monde*: "At bottom, Chancellor Kohl has succeeded in obtaining peacefully what others have attempted to obtain by conquest since Bismarck: a zone of peace and of prosperity all around Germany" (January 1, 1996). What changed? How did we go from the euro operating like another Versailles Treaty that made Germany "pay" to a German triumph that Bismarck would applaud? The answer is that, in 1993, the Bundesbank ensured that France's monetary ambitions were crushed. The fact that millions of Europeans suffered unemployment and hardship in the process was nothing more than collateral damage. But more of this in later chapters.

CHAPTER 3: TROUBLED PILGRIMS

1. The European Monetary System was meant as a European version of Bretton Woods, following the latter's unraveling after the 1971 Nixon Shock; see chapter 2. See Ludlow (1982).

2. *Corriere Della Sera*, September 16, 1978, mentioned in Ludlow (1982), p. 182.

3. Schmidt was also a former finance minister (1972–1974) who replaced the popular Chancellor Willy Brandt in 1974 after a spy scandal implicating a Brandt aide forced the latter's resignation. Like Brandt, Schmidt ruled in coalition with the small Free Democratic Party (FDP). But in 1982 the FDP swapped sides, voted Schmidt out of office, and went into a new coalition with the Christian Democrats under Chancellor Helmut Kohl—the man who would, together with Giscard's successor, President François Mitterrand, inaugurate the euro in 1992 (signing the so-called Maastricht Treaty that replaced the EMS with the common currency known as the euro).

4. See, for instance, Connolly (1995).

5. Marshall (2012) reports that Giscard and Schmidt later suggested that

the idea for a European central bank "came" to them in the Aachen Cathedral when paying their respects to Charlemagne.

6. Recall the explanation in chapter 1 of why a common currency, or fixed exchange rates, squeeze the deficit nations into the ground in times of crisis in the absence of political surplus recycling, which the gold standard certainly lacked. See section "Political Surplus Recycling, or Barbarism."

7. Which, under finance minister and head of the Reichsbank (as the German central bank was known during and before the war) Hjalmar Schacht, was unrestrained by the gold standard and free to adjust the quantity of money in a manner that enabled the Nazi regime to boost output and employment from 1933 to 1938.

8. See chapter 2 for a reminder of how the president of the Bundesbank admitted to having taken "strong action" to topple Erhard's government.

9. Countries that were meant to join the European Union the following year. In the end only Britain, Ireland and Denmark joined in 1973, Norway refusing to do so to this day.

10. The constraints were even tighter than in Bretton Woods. Whereas under Bretton Woods currencies were allowed to fluctuate by plus or minus 1 percent in relation to the dollar, in Europe's "snake" the permitted oscillations were limited to plus or minus 0.75 percent in relation to the deutsche mark. This meant that, for instance, the Belgian franc was meant to stay within the extremely tight range of 19.85 BFs and 20.15 BFs to 1 deutsche mark. To confine the Belgian franc to such an extremely "low tunnel," Belgium's and Germany's central banks would have to intervene constantly, with the former using up its stock in marks and dollars to buy Belgian francs, and the latter printing deutsche marks also to buy Belgian francs.

11. "[O]nce the sequence of bankruptcies has begun, incomes are destined to fall while the private and public debts to the foreign banks remain the same. The price of a fixed exchange rate is a bankrupt state in a death embrace with impecunious citizens and an insolvent private sector." See chapter 1, section entitled "Political Surplus Recycling, or Barbarism."

12. For example, the European Exchange Rate Mechanism (ERM) in the early 1990s. See chapter 4, section entitled "Frankfurt's Long Shadow."

13. On February 28, 1978, to be precise.

14. See Gilbert (2003), p. 143. Schmidt's preference for a right-wing victory in France is less puzzling than it seems at first. Even though he was on the center left, he feared that a center-Left French government would go into a spending spree that the Bundesbank would see as casus belli, making

it impossible for Schmidt to convince Germany's elites to accept monetary union with France.

15. Recall chapter 2.

16. Recall the detailed account in chapter 2.

17. Located in Coventry, England.

18. See Volcker (1978–1979).

19. It is also full of clues as to Chancellor Schmidt's thinking regarding the necessity of the European Monetary System. But more on this later.

20. "Unearned income" refers to rents, income from the ownership of paper assets (e.g., bonds and stocks), property rights over a piece of land that happens to contain gas or oil, etc. In contrast, "earned income" refers to wages for labor services provided and profit from entrepreneurial activity.

21. During the Great Depression, paradoxically, real wages did not fall. Indeed, they increased a little. Of course money wages, that is wages measured in dollars, fell steeply. But prices fell even faster, ensuring that those with jobs saw their purchasing power rise. Of course the problem, which made that depression "great," was that very few workers managed to keep their jobs so as to benefit from the increased real wages.

22. This is a common theme in all serious studies of inequality. See Galbraith (2012), Stiglitz (2013) and Piketty (2014).

23. In the first two decades of the twentieth century, financialization occurred in conjunction with the creation of the first networked corporations. As the construction of electricity power stations and grids required massive capital investment, smaller banks combined forces to forge megabanks which then financed the new megacorps (such as Edison, General Electric, Ford, etc.). The rise of the megabanks created a surge of newly minted private money (as the bankers had the capacity to lend much larger sums), which boosted the stock exchange, creating the "roaring" 1920s—which, of course, crashed and burned in 1929.

24. Recall the exchange in Thucydides's *Peloponnesian War* between the Athenian generals and the Melians whom they enslaved, after having razed their city to the ground. See chapter 1, "And the Weak Suffer What They Must . . ."

25. See Marquis de Condorcet (1795).

26. Recall the opening lines of chapter 1.

27. That the Soviet sphere of influence was also to be severely damaged added considerable impetus to his project.

28. The same attitude resurfaced in Berlin in the early 2000s, when US-sourced private money minting was making it possible for the rest of Europe to boost its purchases of German exports while the German state was keeping a lid on German wages and state expenditure.

29. Recall the explanation in chapter 1 of why capitalism faces a stark choice between political surplus recycling and fair-weather recycling, which leads, eventually, to barbarism.

30. I first used the allegory of a Global Minotaur, by which to describe the second postwar phase of American economic dominance, in an article jointly authored with Joseph Halevi; see Halevi and Varoufakis (2003). Later it became the title of my book on the global crisis; see Varoufakis (2011).

31. See *Le Monde*, November 16, 2011. "La décision de faire participer la Grèce à la monnaie unique était une grave erreur." Interview by Jérôme Gautheret.

32. See *Les Echos*, February, 18, 2015. Valéry Giscard d'Estaing: "La Grèce doit sortir de l'euro." Interview by Nicolas Barré.

33. "Eurexit" is my neologism for the expulsion of Europe from the dollar zone, following the 1971 Nixon Shock. Regarding Grexit, Giscard is not the only eurozone pioneer to contemplate it seriously. Germany's finance minister, Wolfgang Schäuble, is another one.

34. This dialogue, between Mitterrand and Delors, was related to me by former British parliamentarian and economics professor Stuart Holland, a colleague and a friend of mine who worked at that time, in the early 1990s, as Delors's advisor. Stuart was privy to these conversations and his account will be appearing in his biography, when it is finished.

35. Recall the previous chapter's account of how the European Union was constructed as the political administration of a Central European heavy industry cartel, unlike the United States that was always a political mechanism by which to mediate between belligerent social classes and antagonistic vested interests.

36. See below. The Werner Report was written between 1969 and 1970 and was submitted to the European Commission in 1970, foreshadowing Europe's monetary union.

37. See the article that appeared in the *New Statesman* on March 12, 1971, entitled "The Dynamic Effects of the Common Market." Also reprinted in Kaldor (1980).

38. See previous note.

CHAPTER 4: TROJAN HORSE

1. Readers can watch this speech online. Just visit YouTube and type into the search box "Margaret Thatcher's last speech as prime minister" or "in Parliament."

2. The Eurogroup is, in effect, the body that makes all the important decisions concerning the running of the eurozone, one of the world's largest economies. It consists of the finance ministers of the eurozone member-states, the president of the European Central Bank, the economics and finance commissioner of the European Commission and, interestingly, a representative from the International Monetary Fund (usually the head of the IMF's European desk but on occasion the managing director herself). Remarkably, the Eurogroup is an informal body. While its power is immense, it does not exist in European law and is accountable to no properly instituted body (e.g., it is not answerable to the European Parliament). Europe's democratic deficit is nowhere as pronounced as in the Eurogroup.

3. See previous note.

4. Quoted in Connolly (1995), p. 121.

5. Recall chapter 3.

6. When the financial crisis hit the United States in 2008, the state of Nevada did not have to borrow from international investors in order to bail out the banks operating in Nevada or to pay the unemployment benefits of the laid-off construction workers. The federal government did that through the FDIC (Federal Deposit Insurance Corporation) and its federal social security and unemployment insurance funds. This is why Nevada bounced back, instead of falling into a black hole of state insolvency that would have led to huge austerity which, in turn, would have shrunk further the Nevadan economy. Federal institutions capable of stabilizing both banks and state governments were, clearly, what the eurozone needed; for example, a proper banking union that would include FDIC-like powers to resolve and recapitalize at the level of the union.

7. Such examples included the European Financial Stability Facility, its successor (the European Stability Mechanism) and the so-called Banking Union, instituted in 2014, which sounds very much like a US-like federal system for supervising and dealing with bank failures (the FDIC-Fed) but which, in reality, is a pseudo-union confirmed in the breach of federal principles rather than in their observance. See chapter 5.

8. European Union law was traditionally initiated, debated and passed at the European Council comprising heads of European governments (as well

as the councils of ministers representing member-states on particular issues). European legislation is determined at an intergovernmental level, with national parliaments signing off after the event and without any opportunity to introduce amendments to the laws that heads of governments agreed upon earlier. This process of European law-making preceded the creation of the European Parliament. Courtesy of its late arrival on the European political landscape, the European Parliament always played second fiddle to the European Council. Even today, after decades of struggling to acquire more legislative powers for itself, the European Parliament has no right or capacity to initiate legislation but is confined to a rubber-stamping role.

9. Which is, of course, the claim of the Scottish National Party and its campaign for Scottish national independence.

10. Under the pretext of the "emergency" their monetary union had amplified.

11. Recall Volcker's University of Warwick speech (see section entitled "That Goddamn Volcker, Again" in chapter 3) in which he advocated a "controlled disintegration in the world economy" as "a legitimate objective for the 1980s."

12. Once again, enounter the awful dilemma of a deficit country's government: it must either abandon its ambition to keep its currency pegged to that of a surplus country or introduce policies that reduce the nation's deficits (trade and government budget deficits) by means of austerity that diminishes incomes, destroys jobs and lowers the state's capacity to come to the aid of its weaker citizens.

13. A German carmaker who manufactures gearboxes in Portugal, engines in Slovakia and car electronics in Germany, and who plans to sell these cars in Europe, rests in peace when these countries use the same currency. Prior to the euro, the expectation of exchange rate fluctuations between Portugal's escudo and the deutsche mark introduced a despised element of uncertainty. Oligopolists prefer to worry about the fluctuation of demand for their wares (e.g., cars), which they can handle through discounts or intra-European trading, than to have their cost accounting all messed up by the vagaries of the foreign exchange markets.

14. Schmidt proved instrumental in organizing the failure, and eventual overthrow, of the radical leftist government that took over in Portugal after the 1975 revolution that ended a long right-wing dictatorship. He also played a key role in preventing the left from making gains during the transition of Spain from Franco's fascist regime to parliamentary democracy.

15. Greek pensions had already declined by approximately 40 percent between 2011 to 2014. The majority of Greece's poor were low-pension over-sixty-year-olds for whom life had become nasty, brutish and increasingly short (i.e., life expectancy began to fall for the first time in seventy years). Against that background, Greece's creditors were demanding of me acquiescence to a further cut in pensions amounting to more than 1 percent of national income; they also proposed the elimination of a small sum (around 100 euros monthly) that was being paid to those ridiculously low pensions (e.g., on 200 euros per month).

16. A deficit country (e.g., France) operating within a monetary union with a surplus country (like Germany) cannot avoid a capital flight the moment the monetary union is hit by a crisis. At the slightest hint that the monetary union may dissolve, and that the two countries will re-create their national currencies, anticipating a devaluation of the deficit country's money, savers prefer to take their cash out of the banks of the deficit country and transfer it to some bank in the surplus country. Thus money emigrates en masse from the deficit to the surplus country, economic activity in the deficit country wanes and, as a result, the deficit country's tax revenues fall and its national budget goes increasingly into the red. This is the reason why the euro crisis put France's national budget under increasing strain.

17. As the crisis of the monetary union builds up, the capital flight from the deficit countries into the surplus country benefits not only the surplus country's banks but also its government. The reason Germany's government budget benefitted from the euro crisis ("moving into the black") was that much of the foreign money coming into Germany was used to buy government bonds (i.e., German public debt). As demand for these bonds increased, the German government could issue new bonds offering lower interest rates (think of these interest rates as the price Germany had to pay to borrow: the greater the demand for its debt, the lower the price Berlin had to pay). Indeed, the flow of money from the deficit countries to Germany's public debt helped Germany's government save more than 80 billion euros (between 2011 and 2014) in the form of much reduced cost of debt servicing.

18. A sequence of such U-turns was to follow over the years. The Greek socialist party (PASOK) government in 2010 was a case in point, followed a few months later by the Spanish and Portuguese socialist parties, and the Irish Labour Party (which participated in a full-on austerity government following the collapse of Ireland's banks). President François Holland, of France, also underwent such a transformation immediately after his election in 2012. However, the most spectacular conversion of an anti-austerity European

government to one pursuing an austerity agenda was that of our own Syriza government in Greece—an intense stand-off between us and the Eurogroup led, in July 2015, to utter capitulation (and, of course, to my resignation from the Ministry of Finance). The exact process by which our government was defeated is another story that cannot be covered here.

19. Trichet would inherit the presidency of the European Central Bank in 2003. Perhaps the most lamentable central banker ever, he increased interest rates a couple of months before the world of finance imploded in the fall of 2008. If that were not enough, a year after the euro crisis commenced, in 2011, he did it again: he increased interest rates once more just as Europe's monetary union was falling of a cliff.

20. See Connolly (1995), p. 97.

21. As always, any increase in the Bundesbank's interest rates made it that much harder for the franc to keep up with the deutsche mark's value, forcing the French authorities into even more austerity (and the political and social costs that this entailed) in order to maintain the semblance of a strong franc.

22. In the end, the process took three years longer (the euro was inaugurated in 2000) but, more importantly, the process was nothing as smooth as planned.

23. Quoted from a report by Daniel Gros and Nils Thygesen (see Gros and Thygesen [1992])), who sat on the Jacques Delors–led commission whose job was to design the euro, entitled One Market, One Money. Years later, I came across Daniel Gros, while serving as Greece's finance minister, in various fora in Brussels. He had the same faith in the superior logic of the monetary union's design and, remarkably, the perpetual clash between that faith and reality dented neither his belief nor his professional standing.

24. Total public debt could not exceed 60 percent of national income and government budget deficits had to stay below 3 percent of national income. Puzzlingly, no limits were placed on private debts and deficits, the result being Ireland's and Spain's crises in 2009–2011.

25. See Connolly (1995), p. 121.

26. The "no" vote was unexpected because all the mainstream parties had recommended a "yes" verdict. This was not the only such phenomenon. In Ireland and in France, "no" votes to similar questions did exceedingly well despite the mainstream parties' campaigning in favor of the Brussels line.

CHAPTER 5: THE ONE THAT GOT AWAY

1. Recall from the previous chapter how Margaret Thatcher's downfall was triggered by her intransigent opposition to Europe's monetary union.

Tony Benn (1925–2014) was a doyen of Britain's Left. A member of Parliament for almost fifty years, and cabinet minister in Harold Wilson's government, Benn was an exemplar of Britain's democratic socialist tradition. In the 1975 referendum that brought the United Kingdom into the European Union, Benn opposed entry on the grounds that the European Union was undemocratic and would dilute the power of Britain's Parliament. His position resonated powerfully with that of British conservatives who also feared the diminution of Parliament's authority, albeit for different reasons; namely, the imperative to hold to the principle of one nation–one Parliament–one currency (see chapter 4's section entitled "Not in Its Nature"). Today, a new Labour leader, Jeremy Corbyn, who has been influenced greatly by Tony Benn, is trying to work out his strategy over the European Union while the current Tory prime minister, David Cameron, is preparing Britain for an in-or-out referendum that will decide whether Britain leaves the European Union altogether or stays to continue whining from within, confined to the increasingly lonely space reserved for countries that are in the Union but not in the eurozone.

2. Except, of course, the case where one nation-state imposes upon all the rest its own standards, rules and regulations, as the United States has been attempting to do with the Trans-Atlantic and Trans-Pacific trade deals (known as TTP and TTIP).

3. All developments spearheaded by the shift toward financialization that came after the Nixon Shock and Paul Volcker's Minotaur-related exploits. See chapter 3 (especially the section entitled "A Timeless Beast") and Varoufakis (2011, 2013).

4. Take for example the housing market. When prospective buyers have more money, in aggregate, to spend on a fixed number of houses, more money is chasing after each house, thus pushing house prices up—a typical case of inflation in the housing market.

5. That is, increasing interest rates every time the Bank of England estimated that the total amount of money (a measure called M3, which included banknotes and liquid deposits; e.g., current account deposits) was rising at a faster rate than the quantity of goods and services produced.

6. The European Monetary System–European Exchange Rate Mechanism that was inaugurated in 1978 (recall chapter 3).

7. As the pound-mark exchange rate weakened, and each pound bought fewer deutsche marks, the (sterling or domestic) price of German imports into Britain rose. At a time when the dollar was also rising vis-à-vis the pound (pushing transport and energy costs up), and Britain's post-1983 growth

sucked into the UK more imports, prices rose across the board. The weaker the pound the higher the rate of inflation. This is why, by 1990, German inflation was so much lower than Britain's.

8. In practical terms that meant setting a target exchange rate between the deutsche mark and pound sterling of 2.95 to 1 with a plus or minus 6 percent margin of fluctuation. This meant that, if the pound fell below 2.775 deutsche marks, Britain's authorities were committed to intervening (by buying deutsche marks or pushing British interest rates up) in order to keep the pound within the agreed-to band.

9. In a private communication, he told me, "We needed to lower our inflation rate urgently and actually the ERM did achieve that spectacularly. The effect was felt via inflationary expectations for a long time afterwards and that helped created the boom that benefitted Blair and Brown. I don't think we would have got inflation down so far so quickly without being in the ERM. The mistake was in not withdrawing from the ERM as I urged Major in summer 1992 when inflation had fallen and was in a further downward trajectory."

10. The pound always rises when the Labour Party loses an election, especially when opinion polls are pointing to a Labour victory. Nothing enthuses the money markets more than an unanticipated Tory victory.

11. The Bundesbank was ultra-worried that the federal government's largesse toward East Germans would boost inflation. To contain it, it increased interest rates.

12. See Connolly (1995), p. 142.

13. See Connolly (1995), p. 148.

14. Lamont's relief was motivated by true blue Tory instincts. EMS-ERM membership translated into terribly tight money. Monetarists, like Lamont, believe that reducing the quantity of money during recessionary times makes any recession much worse. So the EMS-ERM forced Lamont to borrow and spend more as a fiscal counterbalance to tight money. But this went against Lamont's ideological repulsion toward deficit spending. By exiting EMS-ERM, Lamont was able to let interest rates slide, increase the money supply and thus unhook himself from the necessity to follow what he considered to be a Keynesian fiscal policy.

15. Lamont's own account, as he related it to me, follows: "What happened was that I was in Washington on September 18 and I was asked by a reporter why I was so cheerful. I replied, 'It's a beautiful sunny day. But it's funny you say that, as my wife said she heard me singing in the bath this

morning.' So the story is not quite as the myth has become. But the press rightly perceived that I did not regard our exit from the ERM as an unmitigated disaster. My view is that the ERM performed a task as an anti-inflation tool and that it disintegrated in my hands when it had fulfilled its usefulness. We benefitted from being in and we benefitted from getting out."

16. After the Labour Party won government in 1997, the new prime minister, Tony Blair, was keen to join the political project that was the euro. Just as in the case of John Major, Blair's chancellor, Gordon Brown, slammed the brakes on entry into the eurozone long enough to give the euro a chance to demonstrate its unsuitability. Lamont and Brown, whatever their failures, proved pivotal in keeping Britain out of the eurozone, the result being that economic errors committed during their reign had rather mild effects on their economy, when compared to the calamity unfolding in continental Europe. The reason of course was that the British finance ministry, the treasury, benefitted from the constant support of a Bank of England willing and able immediately to counter recession with looser money. This capacity was, sadly, designed out of the European Central Bank at the behest of a Bundesbank whose condition for not strangling the euro at birth was precisely that: the ECB should not have either the capacity or the institutional tendency to come to the aid of recessionary economies under its purview.

17. Sweden and Finland experienced a large influx of foreign money while the EMS-ERM illusion lasted. Speculators were attracted to high profit rates and, once they believed that their currency value (when measured in deutsche marks) was stable, licked their lips in anticipation of high returns from sending their money to Stockholm and Helsinki. Swedish and Finnish banks lent the inflowing capital as if there was no tomorrow, helping create bubbles in various sectors. When the EMS-ERM broke down, and the Nordic currencies devalued, a mountain of debt in foreign currency became unpayable, the debtors went bust, and so did Sweden's and Finland's banks. In 1992 the governments of Sweden and Finland were forced to step in, bail out the banks, nationalize them, and sell them back to the private sector after they had been cleansed of bad loans. While the resulting recession was sharp, the manner in which the banking disaster was dealt with should go down in history as a success story. If only the eurozone had dealt with its 2008–2012 banking crisis in a similar manner.

18. France has a unique constitution that allows for the "cohabitation" of a socialist president and a conservative prime minister, if the latter secures a majority in parliament in midterm elections.

19. The "yes" vote won with 50.8 percent, with just below 540,000 votes separating the "yes" from the "no," out of 26,381,000 votes cast.

20. By "looser money" economists refer to a readiness to set lower interest rates. Lower interest rates in Germany was always good news in deficit countries like Britain and France, as they lessened the flow of capital from them to Germany.

21. The first one being that Berlin wanted a single currency for political reasons and for liberating German exporters from the fear of constant devaluations of their foreign clients' currencies.

22. That loss had to wait for the euro crisis to hit in 2010, setting off a chain reaction that led to Paris losing control of . . . Paris.

23. Allowing a British trade unionist, who had opposed the privatization of Britain's electricity industry, to tell me once, triumphantly, that the sector was renationalized—except by the "wrong" nation!

24. The friend shall remain anonymous as he is currently in a European Union post that might be jeopardized by such a revelation.

25. Recall the section entitled "France's Slow-Motion Defeat," chapter 4.

26. Recall the section entitled "Aspirational Riffraff," chapter 4.

27. On the day the European Central Bank was inaugurated in Frankfurt, a number of officials likened its establishment to the coronation of Charlemagne and the creation of a Christian European empire. It may not be too indelicate at this point to add a further footnote: that it took the hideous murder of thousands of Muslim men in Srebrenica a year later, in 1995, and the spectacular failure of European United Nations' peacekeepers to protect them, before Europe discovered that there was such a thing as home-grown Muslim European citizens for whom a revival of Charlemagne's legacy offered no solace.

28. A political surplus recycling mechanism steps in when the fair-weather recyclers, the banks, exit in a hurry, leaving behind them ruins and unpayable debts. A political mechanism of investing into these regions, during their Great Depression, is the only way the fixed exchange rate can be maintained without emptying the deficit country of people and turning it into a giant golf course for visiting bankers. Recall chapter 1's section entitled "Political Surplus Recycling, or Barbarism."

29. A shorter version of this was told to me by Lord (Norman) Lamont as we were preparing for a head-to-head debate; I believe it was in Melbourne. Our friendship began more or less at that point.

30. *Le Figaro*, September 18, 1992.

31. Italy and Spain should, in this context, suffer greater recession by keeping the lira and the peseta higher than was optimal for their labor markets, while Germany should revalue its currency, at the expense of its exporters, to accommodate the "franc fort" fantasy.

32. Connolly (1995), p. 170, quotes Keynes (1924) thus: "Each time the franc loses value, the Minister of Finance is convinced that the fact arises from everything but economic causes. He attributes it to the presence of foreigners in the corridors of the Bourse, to unwholesome and malign forces of speculation. The attitude is rather close to that of the witch doctor who attributes the illness of cattle to the 'evil eye,' and the storm to an insufficient quantity of sacrifices made before some idol."

33. This being the only way that the depressed country's exports could become competitive without further reductions in wages and domestically produced prices.

34. I did not believe that the second option, the threat of enforced exit, was credible. It is mainly for this reason that I resigned when my prime minister told me he was about to capitulate to Greece's lenders, fearing that their threat was credible. I shall have much more to say on this in a full account dedicated to the Athens Spring and its crushing.

CHAPTER 6: THE REVERSE ALCHEMISTS

1. This is banker-speak for securing an interest rate somewhat above the bank's own borrowing rate and, hopefully, above interest rates charged to the bank's average client.

2. After the 2008 financial sector implosion, the banks with the most risk managers ended up in the deepest of black holes. The Royal Bank of Scotland, to give one example, employed *four thousand* risk managers and ended up needing a 50 billion pound bailout from the British taxpayer.

3. During 1998–2007, interest rates were falling everywhere as credit was being turbocharged by the shenanigans of the West's financiers. However, Germany's increasing trade surplus (in relation to Europe's south) and the resulting flow of money from South Europe to Germany meant that the price of money (the rate of interest) in Germany was always lower than in the South.

4. The greater the supply of loans to a debtor like the Greek state, the lower the interest rate the bank had to charge to convince the debtor to take on even more loans. Thus the difference, or "spread," between the interest rates paid by the Greek and the German governments shrunk, giving an even greater boost to the banker's commitment to lend even more money to such debtors.

5. One way to help a "stressed" debtor is to reduce the interest rate charged or, equivalently, to prolong the repayment period without charging additional interest. Such interest rate relief, naturally, reduces the value that the creditor will recoup.

6. An IOU (I owe you) is a piece of paper on which I write: "I, Yanis Varoufakis, confirm that I shall pay the bearer of this piece of paper a sum of X euros by such-and-such a date. This piece of paper is freely transferable." To the extent that I am considered creditworthy, such an IOU has market value and could be sold by a bearer who prefers a sum less than X now than to wait until the specified date to collect X euros.

7. And when these IOUs expired, the whole process was repeated, with the banks issuing new IOUs that the government guaranteed again so they could be swapped with the IOUs about to expire.

8. The only difference between us was that I was not sufficiently motivated to keep quiet about it. But that's another story.

9. Peter Hartz, who designed these reforms, was Volkswagen's personnel director. There is a nice irony here in view of Volkswagen's implication in the major emissions scandal, which cast a long shadow over German manufacturing.

10. Mini-jobs restricted workers to sixteen hours per week, at a standard monthly salary of 400 to 450 euros.

11. Poorer Greeks' money wages and pensions were rising by something like 3.5 percent, a large rise by European standards of the time. The official inflation rate, they were told, was only 3 percent. So their purchasing power must have been rising too. But it was not. The reason is that the inflation rate for poorer Greeks was much higher, at around 9 percent, but the inflation rate for richer Greeks was . . . negative. Negative? Yes. If you owned a mansion in Athens's northern suburbs that you had paid for by means of a mortgage, the large drop in interest rates effected by the practices of my fellow traveler Franz and his colleagues meant that your living costs fell! So, during the first few years of the euro, during the "good times," the Greek grasshoppers were prospering while the ants struggled. By 2010 the grasshoppers had taken their loot out of the country, without paying taxes due, and it was the ants that were called upon to bail out the bankrupt state and the bankrupt banks through pension cuts, wage cuts, cuts in their health services, etc.

12. Unnecessarily. A recession that Europeans did not have to have. Allowing Greece to default and restoring German and French banks to health the way that the Swedes and the Finns had done in 1992 would have avoided this recession. See chapter 7 (section entitled "Decentralized Europeanization.

Or how to replace Tina with Tatiana" for examples of alternative policies to mindless austerity).

13. Data made available by the Bank of International Settlements.

14. The IMF had already developed the reputation of a global, ruthless bailiff, following the Third World debt crisis, the Latin American crisis and the Southeast Asian crisis. Ironically, at a time, in 2010, when its managing director, the infamous Dominique Strauss-Kahn, was trying to soften the IMF's image, Chancellor Merkel insisted it should be part of the troika. She needed it to come in order to convince her own members of parliament that the bailout's austerity conditions would be brutally imposed. Thus the IMF's makeover failed as it became embroiled in another sequence of "rescues" that forced the weak to suffer that which they did not deserve.

15. Which was of course necessary given that the first bailout was always going to fail, being nothing more than the original Ponzi austerity scheme.

16. In the end Syriza did not win that election but came in a strong second. Its victory eventually came on January 25, 2015, in an election that I contested successfully and which resulted in my becoming Greece's minister of finance.

17. Seeing that the ECB was buying Greek bonds, the theory went, investors might have been encouraged to do so too.

18. This ploy might have worked except that Mr. Trichet, in a move of baffling folly, preannounced the amount the ECB would spend on these purchases to counter the speculators. It was an open invitation to speculators to make money, as long as they could spend more money than the ECB was willing to. In Wild West terms, it was the equivalent of Clint Eastwood rolling up to the site of the showdown announcing to his opponent how many bullets he had left in his revolver. As long as the opponent had one more, his fate was sealed. Then again, there is a simpler explanation as to why Mr. Trichet and the ECB did this: they only cared about making the French and German banks whole (by buying for them at full price the Greek government bonds whose value had crashed), with the story about striving to keep Greece in the money markets being only a poor excuse.

19. In the first Greek bailout, of May 2010, Europe's ridiculously hard line toward Greece was no to a haircut, no to debt relief, yes to a huge loan (worth 110 billion euros) with high interest rates. The only beneficiaries were, of course, the beneficiaries that the bailout had been designed to benefit: French and German banks. Once their losses were averted, Brussels and Frankfurt began to plan for the inevitable haircut that would hit small, Greek bondholders and, tragically, the Greek pension funds whose charter obliged

them to hold their capital in Greek government bonds. So a second bailout, which included a haircut for the weak, was ratified fully by the spring of 2012. To contain the skyrocketing debt, bonds held in private hands were haircut substantially, twice—once in the spring of 2012 and once again in December 2012 (that time under the guise of a "debt buyback"). In short, in 2012 Greece's private debt was cut, in real value terms, by 85 percent. Except that the bankers and the ECB (which, under Trichet, had purchased more than 50 billion of Greece's public debt) were fully protected. The Greek state borrowed another 130 billion euros from which to infuse 50 billion into Greek banks and up to another 50 billion to pay back the ECB, which behaved like a hedge fund holdout. The only victims of the haircut were the smallholders of Greek debt and pensioners, whose pension funds were effectively robbed of their capital base.

20. The first countries to violate the Maastricht Treaty rules were Germany and France, almost immediately after the euro was established. In particular, following the 2001 dot-com recession, Berlin had a choice between breaking the 3 percent budget deficit limit, which was part of the Maastricht rules, or imposing harsh austerity upon the German economy. It opted for the former. Similarly with France a few months later.

21. Which were already issuing their own worthless IOUs with guarantees from the insolvent Greek state.

22. Through the so called Emergency Liquidity Assistance (ELA) program of the ECB.

23. Between 2008 and 2010, when the banks' immediate needs were taken care of by the ever-so-generous taxpayers, the eurozone's debt to income ratio rose from 66.2 percent to 80 percent. Then, between 2010 and 2014, austerity pushed the euro area's debt above 91 percent of GDP. However, in the countries where the greatest austerity was imposed, debt exploded. The following table tells the sad tale of Ponzi austerity:

Year	Eurozone	Greece	Ireland	Portugal	Spain	Italy
2008	66.2%	105.4%	25%	68.3%	36.1%	103.6%
2010	80%	129.7%	64.4%	83.7%	54%	116.4%
2014	91%	175%	123%	129.7%	92.1%	130%

24. This is the "moral hazard" argument, according to which the possibility of common debt would give each an incentive to indulge in loose living.

25. So Germany would bear around a quarter of the liability as its national income was a quarter of the eurozone's.

26. See Geithner (2014). In addition to his account of this incident in his book, Geithner had a lot more to say in a recorded interview with the *Financial Times*'s Peter Spiegel (published on Spiegel's blog here: http://blogs.ft.com/brusselsblog/2014/11/11/draghis-ecb-management-the-leaked-geithner-files/). The former US treasury secretary is quoted as saying this, referring to said meeting: "They turn to me in their meeting, they ask me for my views, my normal views which you'll find boringly familiar at this point, and a bunch of their ministers go walk out afterwards and say: 'Who's Geithner to tell us what to do?' . . . That wasn't so great."

27. Central banks do not, literally, print money on such occasions. This is what they do instead. Every commercial bank has an account with its central bank (e.g., the Bank of America has such an account at the Federal Reserve, Deutsche Bank an account at the European Central Bank). Instead of printing cash and handing it over to them, the central bank allows the commercial bank to draw money from its accounts with the central that the commercial bank never deposited there—something akin to an overdraft facility. In exchange, the commercial bank hands over to the central bank, as collateral, some asset (e.g., a stack of mortgages or personal loans that the central bank can collect money from in case the commercial bank defaults or goes bankrupt). The central bank's hope is that the commercial bank will then lend this money to its own customers (e.g., companies and families wishing to buy a house or a car) with the desired effect of stimulating the real economy.

28. Monti had an impressive record both as an economics professor and, especially, as the European Commission's commissioner for competition policy. In that role he famously clashed with behemoths like Microsoft and was acknowledged as a skilled and honest operator. However, his image was tainted once he came to be seen as Mrs. Merkel's "appointee" to Italy's highest office despite the fact that, once in office, he acted in the interests of Italy and put up a major struggle at the European Council to bring on a proper banking union (see below, section entitled "Monti's Mutiny"). (On a personal note, Mario Monti and I have since discovered a great deal of common ground and a mutual appreciation of our perspectives on what Europe must do to overcome its crisis).

29. Ireland was felled by its banks and the real estate developers. The tsunami of capital from Germany's banks was flowing straight into Ireland's commercial banks, which were then lending it on to real estate developers. White elephants in Dublin's financial district, row upon row of new blocks of flats in the middle of nowhere, and second and third mortgages were the

outcome. With prices racing ahead creating a semblance of homeowner wealth, credit card use multiplied and a generalized consumer spending spree occurred. When the credit crunch spread from Wall Street and London, land prices collapsed, construction workers were laid off, mountainous debts went bad and the banks themselves, the Anglo-Irish Bank in particular, imploded. In a move that will remain in Irish annals as a stigma comparable to the potato famine, the Dublin government succumbed to ECB blackmail: make the German creditors of Ireland's commercial banks whole, even a bank that was closed down and thus no longer systemically important for Ireland's financial sector, or else.

30. See *The Threepenny Novel*, Brecht (1989), in which the following exchange appears between two characters named McHeath and Peachum. McHeath says, "Brute force is out of date—Why send out murderers when one can employ bailiffs?" To which Peachum replies, "Admittedly, murder is a last resort, the very last—but it is still useful."

31. The differences between Greece and Ireland, and the cause of their debt crises, are instructive. Ireland had a tiny debt before 2008. Greece had a large one. The reason is simple: capital flow from the surplus countries was directed into the Greek state, which, in turn, passed it on to developers (e.g., those who built highways, 2004 Olympic sites, etc.). In Ireland, the same capital flow went directly into the banks, which then passed it on to the developers, bypassing the state. Thus, Irish public debt was tiny while private debt was gargantuan—the opposite case to that of Greece. But when the crisis hit, the result was the same: the Irish state took on the burden of private debt and collapsed. The Greek state just collapsed.

32. Of course, a few months later, on the last day of June 2015, the ECB shut down our entire banking system to force our government into accepting the troika's bailout logic. It was the price we had to pay for refusing to let our central bank be blackmailed.

33. By purchasing its treasury bills and bonds.

34. Imagine, dear reader, what would have happened in 2008 in the United States if it were structured along the lines of the eurozone. The Nevadan banks would have to be recapitalized by the state government of Nevada, without help from the Fed, and at a time the state government would also be borrowing to fund increased unemployment and Social Security payments. The state government would immediately lose access to money markets, become insolvent and, thus, cause the world's banking "community" to cut off all banks domiciled in Nevada from international markets. State and banks

would be in free fall. If, further, the state was forced by Washington, DC, to accept a huge bailout loan from the federal government on condition of extreme austerity that would shrink Nevadans' incomes significantly, there would be two outcomes: Nevada would be well and truly finished and Missouri or Mississippi or New Mexico would be the next states to fall under the contagion that would begin in Nevada, as jittery investors would think twice before lending to other weak state governments. This is precisely what happened to the eurozone, beginning of course with Greece.

35. In contrast to institutions like the EFSF that (as we saw above) amplified financial shocks, rather than absorbed them.

36. Which was later beefed up in an article entitled "Banking union must be built on firm foundations," *Financial Times*, May 12, 2013.

37. The banking union agreed to in the end specified that, when a bank needs capital injections, the first thing that happens is that the national government provides the capital needed to raise the bank's minimum capital ratio (T1) to 4.5 percent of its assets. After that, a series of haircuts must follow. First to have their hair cut are the shareholders and bondholders, followed by the depositors with more than 100,000 euros in the bank. Only if these haircuts are not enough to render the bank solvent does the European Stability Mechanism chip in with 80 percent of the remaining funds needed (with the national government picking up the remaining 20 percent of the tab).

38. As happened in Cyprus in 2013.

39. Noyer's point was simple: the ECB had lost control of interest rates. A profitable, creditworthy Italian or Spanish business had to borrow at huge interest rates reflecting the Italian or Spanish state's woes. It was an admission that Europe's central bank had lost control of Europe's money and that Italian and Spanish business were facing an uphill struggle. See "Verbindung zwischen Banken und Staaten muss durchtrennt warden," *Handelsblatt,* July 18, 2012, http://www.handelsblatt.com/politik/konjunktur/christian-noyer-im -interview-verbindung-zwischen-banken-und-staaten-muss-durchtrennt -werden/6886472.html.

40. Speech by Mario Draghi, president of the European Central Bank, at the Global Investment Conference in London, July 26, 2012. See https://www .ecb.europa.eu/press/key/date/2012/html/sp120726.en.html.

41. Additionally, to placate Berlin, Mario Draghi made a pledge that OMT would not be activated for countries that had not submitted themselvesf to the "strictures" of the . . . troika. This was a more draconian stipulation than it seems at first. No Italian or Spanish government would survive long if it

surrendered to the invasive troika. Which meant that OMT would only be activated if Italy or Spain were so far down the black hole of insolvency that their governing parties acquiesced to their loss of power.

42. As the interest rates of government bonds (i.e., the rates at which a government borrows) fall, commercial banks make less money from lending to the government. So, at least in theory, they have a greater incentive to lend to business instead. As commercial banks redirect money from lending to government to lending to business, the supply of money to the private sector increases, the price of that money falls (i.e., commercial interest rates decline) and, hey presto, business enjoys lower interest rates.

43. That is, the creation of central bank money to be lent indirectly to member-state governments—the absolution of what the Maastricht Treaty deemed the greatest of sins.

44. The fact that a few weeks earlier Syriza, Greece's upcoming left-wing party, had just been defeated in Greece's general election, allowing for another coalition government (that would remain in the troika's pocket) to be formed, gave further cause for optimism around Frankfurt and Brussels that the worst was over.

45. In the case of the Irish banks, the private bonds that they had purchased were uninsured. In the case of Greek state bonds, their buyers also knew that these were Greek law contracts, meaning that they could be given a haircut (written down) by a future stressed Greek government. This is precisely why the interest rates were higher than in Germany. Higher risk, higher rewards. As long as the gamble was paying off, the German bankers reaped benefits that they shared with no one. But when the gambles turned bad, as Irish banks and the Greek state failed, they demanded that the taxpayers of Greece and Ireland pay up, as if they had bought insurance from them.

46. Naturally, the government tore up, or "retired," the promissory notes once it took them back from the central bank.

47. As were, of course, the Greek pension funds, except that no one really ever cared about the pensioners.

48. Note that there is strong suspicion that Greek bankers lent the 10 percent to one another, to pretend they had raised that capital according to the law.

49. See Germany's financial daily *Handelsblatt*, http://www.handelsblatt .com/downloads/8124832/1/stellungnahme-bundesbank_handelsblatt-online .pdf.

50. OMT constituted an open invitation to bond dealers to test the ECB's resolve at a time of their choosing. It was a temporary fix bound to stop working when circumstances emboldened the bond dealers.

51. From an economic viewpoint, the very low interest rates are only partly due to the OMT announcement and Mr. Draghi's "whatever it takes" statement. The latter pushed the interest rates on Italy's and Spain's debt down. But it was the generalized austerity and the very low level of investment that pushed profit and growth rates down. An economy featuring low investment and no growth also results in low average profit rates. Recession, low profits and low returns to money (i.e., low interest rates) go together. So while OMT "worked" to subdue the cost of servicing Italy's and Spain's public debt, it worked too well in an austerian environment—in that it caused a generalized deflation that kept the eurozone permanently stuck in recession.

52. See Keynes (1936), p. 183.

53. Except when QE pushed the yen or the dollar down, thus helping Japanese and American exporters mop up foreign demand, adding a beggar-thy-neighbor dimension to its effects.

54. This is why in its never enacted OMT program Mr. Draghi had to introduce, as a condition, that the country whose bonds the ECB purchases must first be put into the straitjacket of a troika program.

55. Directed and produced by Carol Reed, based on a Graham Greene novel, *The Third Man* was released in 1949.

56. "But to my mind, though I am native here / And to the manner born, it is a custom / More honour'd in the breach than the observance." *Hamlet*, by William Shakespeare, 1602.

CHAPTER 7: BACK TO THE FUTURE

1. The Golden Dawn Party, whose deputies sat in Greece's parliament immediately opposite the ministerial box, is often referred to as a neo-Nazi party. This is wrong. There is arguably nothing "neo" in their Nazi ideology. They worship Hitler, their symbol is a variant of the swastika, they dress like Nazis, they salute like Nazis. In short, they are fully fledged Nazis bereft of any pretense to a makeover for the twenty-first centrury.

2. Georgia Xenou was the great-grandmother of my daughter, my first wife Margarita's grandmother.

3. By 1947, under the Truman Doctrine, the persecution of the civil war from the West's perspective had been passed on from Britain to the United States. British troops were withdrawn and replaced by US military advisers.

The scene of the injured Xenos's torture and murder is described in an eyewitness account published in Greek in two volumes. The book is entitled *The Dead Brigade* and its author was Constantine Papakonstantinou, whose nom de guerre was Captain Belas. See pp. 623–24 of volume 1 (1986, third edition 2002).

4. As mentioned in chapter 1, I made that point to the gathered journalists in the press conference at the Federal Ministry of Finance in Berlin, in February 2015, as part of a plea to the German finance minister and the German public to support the new Greek government's efforts to stem recession and root out the emergent Greek Nazi party.

5. After the end of the Great War, Eleftherios Venizelos, the pro-British anti-royalist republican, secured on behalf of Greece the right to administer the Asia Minor coastal city of Smyrna (today's Ismir). However, soon after the Greek army took control of Smyrna, Venizelos's government collapsed and the new royalist government ordered the Greek army to march on Ankara. This is what gave Kemal a great emotional advantage. Countless incensed Turks joined his army and, eventually, Kemal managed to push the Greek army into the sea and proceed to ethnically cleanse from the region millions of ethnic Greeks who had been living in Asia Minor since the time of Homer. In Greece, that defeat, circa 1922, is to this day known as the Catastrophe.

6. My references to Nazism as "the serpent" are due to the impression left upon a younger version of me by Ingmar Bergman's 1977 film *The Serpent's Egg*, a story highlighting the distorted pseudo-scientific imperatives behind the Nazi experiment. The title itself was borrowed from a line of Brutus's in Shakespeare's *Julius Caesar*: "And therefore think him as a serpent's egg / Which hatch'd, would, as his kind grow mischievous / And kill him in the shell" (act 2, scene 1).

7. By the time the Red Army had entered Berlin's outskirts, only seven hundred men of the Charlemagne SS brigade had survived, fighting tooth and nail in defense of Hitler. In the last two days no more than thirty were standing in Berlin's city center.

8. Try your luck with the rest of the quotes quiz here:

> a. "The solution to economic problems . . . with the eventual object of a European customs union and a free European market, a European clearing system and stable exchange rates in Europe, looking towards a European currency union."
>
> b. "The results of excessive nationalism and territorial dismemberment are within the experience of all. There is only hope for peace by means of a

process which on the one hand respects the inalienable fundamental patri-
mony of every nation but, on the other, moderates these and subordinates
them to a continental policy . . . A European Union could not be subject to
the variations of internal policy that are characteristic of liberal regimes."

c. "A new Europe: that is the point, and that is the task before us. It does not
mean that Italians and Germans and all other nations of the European
family are to change their spots and become unrecognizable to themselves
or to one another, from one day or one year to the next. It will be a new
Europe because of the new inspiration and determining principle that will
spring up among all these peoples . . . The problem of the hierarchy of
states will no longer arise. At least in its usual form, once we have cut off
the dragon's head; that is, the notion of state sovereignty. Moreover, this
does not have to be done outright, but can be achieved indirectly, e.g., by
creating interstate European bodies to look after certain common interests
(exchange rates, communications, foreign trade, etc.)."

d. A following quote comes from a well-received, at the time, policy docu-
ment that recommended the need to "put forward a European con-federal
solution based on free cooperation among independent nations [culminat-
ing into uniting Europe] on a federal basis. [To see this federation process through], all that is required of European states is that they be loyal,
pro-European members of the community and cooperate willingly in its
tasks . . . The object of European cooperation being to promote peace,
security and welfare for all its peoples."

e. "We must create a Europe that does not squander its blood and strength
on internecine conflict, but forms a compact unity. In this way it will become richer, stronger and more civilized, and will recover its old place in the
world. . . . National tensions and petty jealousies will lose their meaning in a
Europe freely organized on a federal basis. World political development consists inevitably in the formation of larger political and economic spheres."

f. "It is not very intelligent to imagine that in such a crowded house like that
of Europe, a community of peoples can maintain different legal systems
and different concepts of law for long."

g. "In my view a nation's conception of its own freedom must be harmonized
with present-day facts and simple questions of efficiency and purpose . . .
Our only requirement of European states is that they be sincere and enthusiastic members of Europe."

The authors are:

a. From a report submitted by Hans Frohwein in June 1943 to the Foreign
Ministry's "Europe Committee," entitled "Basic Elements of a Plan for a

New Europe," with section subtitle "The Economic Organization of Europe." Reprinted in Lipgens, pp. 122–123.

b. Alberto De Stefani, Mussolini's first finance minister. De Stefani was dismissed two years after his appointment but remained a full member of the Grand Council of Fascism until the regime's collapse. This statement comes from 1941.

c. Camillo Pellizzi, editor of *Civiltà Fascista,* in an article entitled "The Idea of Europe"and in a letter to Ugoberto Alfassio-Grimaldi, September 4, 1943, in Lipgens, *Documents on the Hitory of Europena Integration,* vol. 1. Pellizzi was an academic who propagandized fascism and was elected to university chairs in the dubious fields of history and doctrine of fascism (University of Messina, 1938) and doctrines of the state (University of Florence, 1939). He survived the war's end to live the drab life of an academic sociologist.

d. Cécile von Renthe-Fink, Nazi diplomat holding the rank of minister of state. In 1943 (when the above quoted statement was issued), together with Joachim von Ribbentrop (Hitler's foreign minister 1938–1945), Renthe-Fink proposed the creation of a European Confederacy. Under this scheme, Europe would feature a single currency that would be managed by a European central bank based in Berlin. The proposed European economic and monetary union would be subject to common legislation on labor market policies and a free trade agreement. Interestingly, the greatest supporter of the von Ribbentrop–Renthe-Fink idea was Frenchman Pierre Laval. Laval was "prime minister" of Vichy, the Nazi vassal French "state" that Hitler had created in parts of France that he did not care to occupy. Pierre Laval was so keen to see France as part of a single-currency union with Germany that, in a letter to Hitler, he proposed to include in it France's colonies so as to bring about an "atmosphere of confidence" to the new, uniting Europe.

e. Vidkun Quisling, the notorious Norwegian Nazi collaborator, "prime minister" of occupied Norway, whose name has become synonymous with "collaborator." After the war, a Norwegian court convicted him for treason, war crimes and embezzlement. He was executed by firing squad in Oslo on October 24, 1945. He made this particular pro-European Union statement in 1942.

f. Adolph Hitler, addressing the Reichstag, 1936.

g. Joseph Goebbels, 1940.

9. See Lipgens (1984), p. 72.

10. Ibid., p. 73.

11. That murder was the theme of Costa Gavras's film *Z.*

12. Leading to the red blanket of my childhood; see chapter 1.

13. The reason for purchasing local manufacturers, shutting down local production and turning the firms into warehouses from which to sell imported wares is simple: eliminate local competitors to the imported goods, using their distribution network in the process.

14. The official rate of inflation reflects the average price increases of the "representative" citizen's goods and services "basket." Except that the "representative" citizen does not exist. Put differently, she is a figment of the statistician's imagination—a creature consuming parts of each good or service in proportion to the total expenditure on these goods or services in the economy. In other words, the rich get richer, and the more they spend the more the official rate of inflation reflects the price inflation of the rich. For example, in an economy of falling interest rates and increasing rents, with the rich occupying increasingly opulent houses, housing costs appear to be falling in the official statistics. The pain poorer families face from increasing rents is bleached out of the statistics as the falling mortgage repayments of the rich grossly outweigh the rising rents of the poor.

15. The standard joke that "when Bill Gates walks into a pub everyone becomes a millionaire *on average*" suffices to make the point that there is no such thing as the average or representative person and, moreover, when the average increases this may very well mean nothing good for the majority.

16. See Varoufakis (2013), "The Serpent's Greek Lair" in the *Witte de Wit Review*, November, http://wdwreview.org/desks/the-serpents-greek-lair/.

17. The race card was thus added to the misogyny: the vast majority of prostitutes in Greece were either native Greek or migrants from Eastern Europe.

18. In the end, most of the women apprehended, tested and put on display were native Greek, mostly drug dependent. See *RUINS*, a splendid documentary available, with English subtitles, here: https://www.youtube.com/watch?v=9zyEegBtC1Q.

19. Sweden's social democratic prime minister, in office between 1969 and 1976.

20. See the chapter 3 section entitled "That Goddamn Volcker, Again."

21. See the chapter 3 section entitled "A Timeless Beast" and, for a longer treatise, Varoufakis (2011).

22. See the chapter 6 section entitled "Frenzy."

23. Whatever happened to "mutual advantage"? I suppose the same people who diminished industry and devalued labor, through their financialization exploits, felt an urgent need to diminish the English language too.

24. In Homer's *Odyssey* (Book IX), the lotus was one of the many impediments that vengeful gods put in Odysseus's path to prevent him and his men from returning home to Ithaca. It was, together with the Sirens' song, perhaps the most dastardly. Unlike the Cyclops or the menacing seas, enemies that brought out the best in them, the lotus fruit made them soft and happy, unwilling to bother with the business of going back to sea to struggle for their eventual homecoming. Odysseus had to resort to brute force to make his men return to the boats. He had to "force them to be free" (anticipating a famous expression by Jean-Jacques Rousseau).

25. See Klinkowstroem (1880).

26. On an aside, Metternich has an important Greek connection, one that resonates with various themes in this book. He was the greatest opponent of Greece's national liberation struggle that began in 1821 and ended up with the establishment of the modern Greek nation-state. His concern was that the creation of a Greek state would undermine the Ottoman Empire (which it did!) thus disturbing the balance of power between the Ottoman, Russian, Austro-Hungarian and British empires. To prevent the success of the Greek revolutionaries, Metternich cajoled the Russian tsar not to support the Greeks and even promised the British full repayment of Austrian debts if London were to support his policy of strangling the Greek revolution at birth. Lord Byron and other philhellenes targeted many of their slings and arrows at Metternich. One wonders what Europe would be like today if Britain, Russia and France had not, in the end, altered their position by coming to the Greeks' aid in the decisive Navarino naval battle of 1827.

27. See Triepel (1906), as quoted in Laughland (1997).

28. Henry Kissinger once wrote this about the effect of the way Germany was unified on its world outlook: "The reason German statesmen were obsessed with naked power was that, in contrast to other nation-states, Germany did not possess any integrating philosophical framework. Bismarck's Reich was not a nation-state, it was an artifice, being foremost a greater Prussia whose principal purpose was to increase its own power . . . It was as if Germany had expended so much energy achieving nationhood that it had not had the time to develop a concept of its own national interest . . . The Kaiser wanted to conduct Weltpolitik without even defining the term or its relationship to the German national interest" (Kissinger, 1994, p. 137).

29. See chapter 6's section entitled "Whatever It Takes?"

30. See "More integration is still the right goal for Europe," by Karl Lamers and Wolfgang Schäuble, *Financial Times,* August 31, 2014. Note that the

German finance minister chose to publish this piece as the debate on the eurozone's failure to shake off the euro crisis was flaring up again following a speech delivered at Jackson Hole by Mario Draghi, the ECB's president, in which Mr. Draghi acknowledged the deflationary pressures upon Europe's common currency area and the role of universal austerity in fomenting them.

31. The Christian Democratic Union is the party of Chancellor Angela Merkel, previously led by Helmut Kohl, the pro-European leader that led Germany's reunification and forged an alliance with President Mitterrand along the lines of creating the single currency: the euro.

32. See also another highly influential 1994 joint paper (again with Karl Lamers) entitled "Überlegungen zur europäischen Politik"; visit https://www .cducsu.de/upload/schaeublelamers94.pdf.

33. Speech to the House of Commons, November 16, 1998 (Hansard, vol. 319, col. 685, from 7:20 p.m., debate topic: European Parliamentary Elections Bill).

34. Drs. Schäuble and Lamers, in their previously quoted 2014 *Financial Times* article, suggest a Euro congress or chamber comprising members of European Parliament from the eurozone member-states (i.e., excluding British, Swedish, Hungarian members whose countries do not share the euro). Other proponents of "more Europe" have suggested that the Euro chamber should consist of members of national parliaments in proportion to their country's population size, so as to extend the existing sovereignty of national parliaments over fiscal matters and, ultimately, to legitimize the eurozone's fiscal overlord.

35. This is also the view of the so-called Glienicker Gruppe of German economists comprising Armin von Bogdandy, Christian Calliess, Henrik Enderlein, Marcel Fratzscher, Clemens Fuest, Franz C. Mayer, Daniela Schwarzer, Maximilian Steinbeis, Constanze Stelzenmüller, Jakob von Weizsäcker and Guntram Wolff. Another group, this time comprising French economists, also holds similar views. They are known as the Piketty Group, consisting of Thomas Piketty, Florence Autret, Antoine Bozio, Julia Cagé, Daniel Cohen, Anne-Laure Delatte, Brigitte Dormont, Guillaume Duval, Philippe Frémeaux, Bruno Palier, Thierry Pech, Jean Quatremer, Pierre Rosanvallon, Xavier Timbeau and Laurence Tubiana. For a critical comparative account of these two groups' views, see Galbraith and Varoufakis (2014).

36. Recall chapter 6's section entitled "Despotism."

37. See Habermas (1975).

38. As Germany was in 1919 with the Versailles Treaty, France, Greece and many others after 1939, or Europe's periphery currently under the troika's watchful eyes.

39. Recall the preface.

40. Golden Dawn increased its seats from seventeen to eighteen (in the three-hundred-member chamber), retained its status of the third-largest party in parliament and, tragically, became the largest party to oppose the troika's failed economic program, thus putting a bid in as the leading opponent of a program that 80 percent of Greeks disdain.

CHAPTER 8: EUROPE'S CRISIS, AMERICA'S FUTURE

1. Tim Geithner is now on the public record (see the transcripts of the Geithner tapes released by Peter Spiegel in his *Financial Times* blog, http://blogs.ft.com/brusselsblog/author/peterspiegel/). These are his exact words on what Europe's leaders told him: "'We're going to teach the Greeks a lesson. They are really terrible. They lied to us. They suck and they were profligate and took advantage of the whole basic thing and we're going to crush them.' [That] was their basic attitude, all of them." See also Geithner (2015).

2. From the "Geithner" tapes released by Peter Spiegel; see previous note.

3. Which can be now be found on my blog, yanisvaroufakis.eu or at the URL http://yanisvaroufakis.eu/2010/11/21/a-new-versailles-treaty-haunts-europe-and-this-time-it-is-not-just-me-thinking-so/.

4. See chapter 5's section entitled "Europhilia, Germanophobia and the French Elites."

5. See Keynes (1920).

6. See Keynes (1949).

7. See note 26.

8. See Keynes (1920).

9. A period that I have labeled, for better or for worse, the era of the Global Minotaur (1971–2008); see chapter 4 as well as Varoufakis (2011).

10. Interventions that were despicable in many ways, the manner in which they rewarded Wall Street bankers in particular. Nonetheless, they were interventions that succeeded in arresting the global free fall. See Varoufakis (2011) as well as the last chapter of the later editions (2013 and 2015).

11. When the crisis hit America in 2008, investors found themselves in the paradoxical position of rushing to buy US treasury bills in large numbers. The economy that caused the crash benefitted from the investors' rush to buy bonds issued by the country that also issues the world's reserve currency. A

reminder of what Giscard d'Estaing described as America's exorbitant privilege; see chapter 3.

12. For the complete argument, see Varoufakis (2011); see chapter 9 of either the 2013 or 2015 edition.

13. Indeed, this process began in August 2015, as Chinese share and land prices lost a large portion of their value.

14. Recall too chapter 6, the section entitled "Ignorance."

15. Geithner's apoplexy is writ large in his taped discussion published in Peter Spiegel's *Financial Times* blog; see http://blogs.ft.com/brusselsblog/2014/11/11/draghis-ecb-management-the-leaked-geithner-files/.

16. See http://www.treasury.gov/resource-center/international/exchange-rate-policies/Documents/2013-10-30_FULL FX REPORT_FINAL.pdf.

17. See http://www.ft.com/intl/cms/s/0/821fbcba-41b1-11e3-b064-00144feabdco.html?siteedition=uk&siteedition=intl#axzz2j5g4LpZX.

18. Defined as the difference between total receipts from exporting goods and services and total expenditure on imported goods and services.

19. Recall that the eurozone's national income is much greater than China's was in 2008. So a 9 percent eurozone current account now would be three times as great as China's was in 2008. Looking at actual percentages, China's and the eurozone's current account surpluses are, today, about the same, at 2.1 percent of national income. In contrast, in 2008, China sported a 10 percent surplus whereas the eurozone registered a small deficit.

20. For example, success in pushing Europe's current account surplus to such heights will also boost the euro's exchange rate, causing exports to diminish to lower levels.

21. The reader will, I hope, appreciate my appreciation of American pragmatism on these matters. US officials and commentators have the capacity to agree with "lefties" like this author when the issues boil down to simple matters of logic. In recent times I noticed that Democrats and Republicans alike agree with me on these issues without much hesitation. So far I have been quoting in this book New Dealers and Democrats, like Geithner and Lew. Here is what Professor Martin Feldstein, a Republican, had to say about the construction of the eurozone back in 1992: "If a country or region has no power to devalue, and if it is not the beneficiary of a system of fiscal equalization, then there is nothing to stop it suffering a process of cumulative and terminal decline leading, in the end, to emigration as the only alternative to poverty or starvation." Quoted in Godley (1992).

22. Addresses at the 41st Forum of The European House-Ambrosetti, September 5, 2015, Lake Como.

23. See Evans-Pritchard (1937).

24. *The Guardian,* July 19, 2013; see http://www.theguardian.com/comment isfree/2013/jul/19/we-germans-dont-want-german-europe?INTCMP= SRCH.

25. John Maynard Keynes argued that such a blind commitment to "rules" and "contracts" is the real parent of revolution. In his *Tract on Monetary Reform* (p. 68) he had this to say: "When . . . we enter the realm of State action, *everything* is to be considered and weighed on its merits. Changes in Death Duties, Income Tax, Land Tenure, Licensing, Slavery, and so on through all ages, have received the same denunciations from the absolutists of contract—who are the real parents of Revolution."

26. Without the slightest exaggeration, I was told that the basic parameters of the "program" were nonnegotiable but that we could implement them with "maximum flexibility." Which sounded almost okay, until one realized that "maximum flexibility" boiled down to a choice between cutting child benefits and reducing the minimum pension. Or having enough leeway to regulate how much yogurt goes into an ounce of tzatziki.

AFTERWORD: FROM DISSONANCE TO HARMONY

1. Leonard Schapiro (1900–1983) was an eminent student of Soviet communism and professor at the London School of Economics.

2. Quoted in Connolly (1995), p. xvi.

ACKNOWLEDGMENTS

1. Strictly speaking, the Syriza government survived, with Prime Minister Tsipras and the majority of ministers still in place. However, our government was forced to overthrow itself; that is, to abandon its most cherished principles as the price its members had to pay to stay in office. It was a price I was not prepared to pay.

APPENDIX TO CHAPTER 7

1. For a member-state whose debt to GDP ratio is 90% of GDP, the ratio of its debt that qualifies as MCD is 2/3. Thus, when a bond with face value of say €1 billion matures, two thirds of this (€667 million) will be paid (redeemed) by the ECB with monies raised (by the ECB itself) from money markets through the issue of ECB bonds.

2. Any more than a personal debit card can be used for credit.

3. Article 20 (TEU) and Articles 326-334 (TFEU) provide that: "Enhanced cooperation should aim to further the objectives of the Union, protect its interests and reinforce its integration process. Such cooperation should be open at any time to all Member States. The decision authorizing enhanced cooperation should be adopted by the Council as a last resort, when it has established that the objectives of such cooperation cannot be attained within a reasonable period by the Union as a whole, and provided that at least nine Member States participate in it."

The Council approval of an enhanced cooperation procedure may be unanimous or by qualified majority.

REFERENCES

Allin, D. (2011). "De Gaulle and American Power," in *Charles de Gaulle's Legacy of Ideas*, B. M. Rowland (ed.), New York: Lexington Books.

Ambrose, S. E. (1989). *Nixon, Vol. 2: The Triumph of a Politician 1962–1972*, New York: Simon and Schuster.

Ball, G. (1982). *The Past Has Another Pattern*, New York: Norton.

Bator, F. (2001). "Lyndon Johnson and Foreign Policy: The Case of Western Europe and the Soviet Union," in *Presidential Judgment: Foreign Policy Decision Making in the White House*, A. Lobel (ed.), Washington: Hollis, 2001.

Bator, F. (1968). "The Political Economics of International Money," *Foreign Affairs*, 47(1).

Becker, A. (2013). "German Economic Miracle: Thanks to Debt Relief," *Deutsche Welle* website, http://www.dw.de/german-economic-miracle-thanks-to-debt-relief/a-16630511, last accessed December 20, 2014.

Brecht, B. (1989). *The Threepenny*, trans. C. I Isherwood and D. I. Vessey, London: Penguin.

Condorcet, M. de (1795). "Outlines of an historical view of the progress of the human mind: being a posthumous work of the late M. de Condorcet," London: Johnson.

Connolly, B. (1995). *The Rotten Heart of Europe*, London and Boston: Faber & Faber.

Coudenhove-Kalergi, R. N. (Graf non) (1923), *Pan-Europa*, Vienna: A. A. Knopf, second edition 1926.

Crawford, A. F. and J. Keever (1973). *John B. Connally: Portrait in Power*, Austin: Jenkins.

Dallek, R. (1995). *Franklin D. Roosevelt and American Foreign Policy: 1932–1945*, Oxford: Oxford University Press.

Eichengreen, B. (2011). *Exorbitant Privilege: The Rise and Fall of the Dollar*, Oxford: Oxford University Press.

Evans-Pritchard, E. E. (1937, 1976). *Witchcraft, Oracles and Magic among the Azande*, Oxford: Clarendon.

Ferrell, R. H. (ed.) (2010). *Inside the Nixon Administration: The Secret Diary of Arthur Burns, 1969–1979*, Lawrence: University Press of Kansas.

Funk, W. (1942). "Das wirtschaftliche Gesicht des neuen Europa" in *Europäische Wirtschaftsgemeinschaft*, Berlin: Verein Berliner Kaufleute und Industrieller & Wirtschafts-Hochschule Berlin.

Galbraith, J. K. (2012). *Inequality and Instability: A Study of the World Economy Just Before the Great Crisis,* Oxford: Oxford University Press.

Galbraith, J. K. and Y. Varoufakis (2014). "Wither Europe? The Modest Camp versus the Federalist Austerians," openDemocracy.org, June 11, 2014, https://opendemocracy.net/can-europe-make-it/james-galbraith-yanis -varoufakis/whither-europe-modest-camp-vs-federalist-austeri.

Geithner, T. (2014). *Stress Test: Reflections on Financial Crises,* New York: Broadway Books.

Gilbert, M. (2003). *Surpassing Realism: The Politics of European Integration Since 1945,* Oxford: Rowman and Littelfield.

Godley, W. (1992). "Maastricht and All That," *London Review of Books,* 4(19), October 8, 1992, 3–4,

Gray, W. G. (2007), "Floating the System: Germany, the United States, and the Breakdown of Bretton Woods, 1969–1973," *Diplomatic History,* 31(2), 295–323.

Gros, D. and N. Thygesen (1992). *European Monetary Integration: from the European Monetary System to the European Monetary Union,* London: Longman.

Habermas, J. (1975). *Legitimation Crisis,* T. McCarthy (trans.), Boston: Beacon Press, German original published in 1973.

Halevi, J. and Y. Varoufakis (2003). "The Global Minotaur," *Monthly Review,* 55 (July–August), 56–74.

Hersh, S. (1983). *The Price of Power: Kissinger in the Nixon White House,* New York: Simon and Schuster.

Kaldor, N. (1980). *Collected Economic Essays of Nicholas Kaldor,* London: Wiley, published on behalf of the Royal Economic Society; see chapter 12 entitled "Further Essays on Applied Economics," 187–220.

Keynes, J. M. (1980). "Closing Speech, Bretton Woods Conferences, July 22, 1944," in D. E. Moggridge (ed.), *Collected Writings of John Maynard Keynes,* Vol. XXVI, Activities 1941–1946; *Shaping the Post-War World, Bretton Woods and Reparations,* London: Macmillan, for the Royal Economic Society.

Keynes, J. M. (1925). *The Economic Consequences of Mr. Churchill,* London: Hogarth Press.

Keynes, J. M. (1920). *The Economic Consequences of the Peace,* New York: Harcourt Brace.

Keynes, J. M. (1936). *The General Theory of Employment, Interest and Money,* London: McMillan.

Keynes, J. M. (1924). *A Tract on Monetary Reform*, London: Macmillan.

Keynes, J. M. (1932). "The World's Economic Outlook," *Atlantic Monthly* 149 (May), pp. 521–526.

Keynes, J.M. (1949). *Two Memoirs: Dr. Melchior—a Defeated Enemy and My Early Beliefs*, New York: A. M. Kelley.

Kissinger H. (1994). *Diplomacy*, New York: Simon and Schuster.

Kissinger, H. (1979). *The White House Years*, New York: Simon and Schuster.

Klinkowstroem, A. de (1880). *Mémoires, documents et écrits divers laissés par la prince de Metternich chancelier de cour et d'état*, Paris: Plon.

Krotz, U. and J. Schild (2012). *Shaping Europe: France, Germany and Embedded Bilateralism from the Elysée Treaty to 21st Century Politics*, Oxford: Oxford University Press.

Laughland, J. (1997). *The Tainted Source*, London: Little Brown.

Lipgens, W. (ed) (1984). *Documents on the History of European Integration, Vol. 1: Continental Plans for European Union 1939–1945*, New York: Walter de Gruyter.

Lipgens, W. and W. Loth (eds) (1988). *Documents on the History of European Integration, Vol. 3: The Struggle for European Union by Political Parties and Pressure Groups in Western European Countries 1945–1950*, New York: Walter de Gruyter.

Ludlow, P. (1982). *The Making of the European Monetary System*, London: Butterworth.

Marshall, M. (2012). *The Bank: Birth of Europe's Central Bank and Rebirth of Europe's Power*, New York: Random House Business.

Mirowski, P. and D. Plehwe (2009). *The Road from Mont Pelerin: The Making of the Neoliberal Thought Collective*, Cambridge: Harvard University Press.

Mitchell, B. (2015). *Eurozone Dystopia: Groupthink and Denial on a Grand Scale*, Cheltenham: Edward Elgar.

Naumann, F. (1915, 2012). *Mitteleuropa*, trans. by C. M. Meredith from the original classic edition, London: Forgotten Books.

Piketty, T. (2014). *Capital in the Twenty-First Century*, Cambridge, MA: Belknap Press.

Reinert, E. S. (2004). *Globalization, Economic Development, and Inequality: An Alternative Perspective*. Aldershot: Edward Elgar.

Rosamond, B. (2000). *Theories of European Integration*, Basingstoke: Palgrave Macmillan.

Rowland, B. M. (ed.) (2011). *Charles de Gaulle's Legacy of Ideas*, New York: Lexington Books.

Rueff, J. (1971). *The Monetary Sin of the West*, New York: MacMillan.

Schaller, M. (1997). *Altered States: The United States-Japan Relations since the Occupation,* New York: Oxford University Press.

Schaller, M. (1996). "The Nixon 'Shocks' and the United States–Japan Strategic Relations," Woodrow Wilson Center, Washington, DC.

Schoenborn, B. (2014). "Chancellor Erhard's Silent Rejection of de Gaulle's Plans: The Example of Monetary Union," *Cold War History,* 14(3), 377–402.

Silber, W. L. (2012). *Volcker,* New York: Bloomsbury Press.

Stephey, M. J. (2008). "A Brief History of the Bretton Woods System," *Time,* October 21; see http://content.time.com/time/business/article/0,8599,1852 254,00.html, last accessed on December 9, 2014.

Stiglitz, J. (2013). *The Price of Inequality: How Today's Divided Society Endangers Our Future,* New York: W.W. Norton.

Stuermer, M. (2011). "The General and the Germans," in *Charles de Gaulle's Legacy of Ideas,* B. M. Rowland (ed.), New York: Lexington Books.

Triepel, H. (1906). *Unitarismus und Föderalismus im Deutschen Reich,* Tübingen: J. C. B. Mohr (Paul Siebeck).

Varoufakis, Y. (2015). "Dr. Schäuble's Plan for Europe: Do Europeans Approve?" *Die Zeit* (29), July 15, 2015. English version available at http://www .zeit.de/2015/29/schuldenkrise-europa-wolfgang-schaeuble-yanis-varou fakis.

Varoufakis, Y. (2011). *The Global Minotaur: America, Europe and the Future of the World Economy,* London: Zed Books; second edition 2013, third edition 2015.

Varoufakis, Y., J. Halevi and N. Theocarakis (2011). *Modern Political Economics: Making Sense of the Post-2008 World,* London and New York: Routledge.

Varoufakis, Y., S. Holland and J. K. Galbraith (2013). "A Modest Proposal for Resolving the Eurozone Crisis," https://varoufakis.files.wordpress.com/ 2013/07/a-modest-proposal-for-resolving-the-eurozone-crisis-version-4-0 -final1.pdf. Available in book form in German (published by Kunstman) and in French (published by the Veblen Institute), with a foreword from former French prime minister Michel Rocard.

Volcker, P. A. (1978–1979). "The Political Economy of the Dollar," *FRBNY Quarterly Review,* (Winter) 1–12 (Fred Hirsch lecture at Warwick University, Coventry, England, November 9, 1978).

INDEX

ABOUT THE AUTHOR

Yanis Varoufakis is the former finance minister of Greece. A professor of economic theory at the University of Athens and a former member of parliament for Athens' largest constituency, he is the author of the book *The Global Minotaur: America, the True Causes of the Financial Crisis and the Future of the World Economy,* among others.

 # The Nation Institute

NATION
BOOKS

Founded in 2000, **Nation Books** has become a leading voice in American independent publishing. The inspiration for the imprint came from the *Nation* magazine, the oldest independent and continuously published weekly magazine of politics and culture in the United States.

The imprint's mission is to produce authoritative books that break new ground and shed light on current social and political issues. We publish established authors who are leaders in their area of expertise, and endeavor to cultivate a new generation of emerging and talented writers. With each of our books we aim to positively affect cultural and political discourse.

Nation Books is a project of The Nation Institute, a nonprofit media center dedicated to strengthening the independent press and advancing social justice and civil rights. The Nation Institute is home to a dynamic range of programs: the award-winning Investigative Fund, which supports ground-breaking investigative journalism; the widely read and syndicated website TomDispatch; the Victor S. Navasky Internship Program in conjunction with the *Nation* magazine; and Journalism Fellowships that support up to 25 high-profile reporters every year.

For more information on Nation Books, The Nation Institute, and the *Nation* magazine, please visit:

www.nationbooks.org

www.nationinstitute.org

www.thenation.com

www.facebook.com/nationbooks.ny

Twitter: @nationbooks